# Ecological Borderlands

NATIONAL WOMEN'S STUDIES ASSOCIATION /
UNIVERSITY OF ILLINOIS FIRST BOOK PRIZE

*A list of books in the series appears at the end of this book.*

# Ecological Borderlands

## Body, Nature, and Spirit
## in Chicana Feminism

CHRISTINA HOLMES

**UNIVERSITY OF
ILLINOIS PRESS**
Urbana, Chicago, and Springfield

Library of Congress Cataloging-in-Publication Data
Names: Holmes, Christina, 1979– author.
Title: Ecological borderlands: body, nature, and spirit in
    Chicana feminism / Christina Holmes.
Description: Urbana : University of Illinois Press,
    [2016] | Series: NWSA/UIP first book prize | Includes
    bibliographical references and index.
Identifiers: LCCN 2016017322 (print) | LCCN 2016029803
    (ebook) | ISBN 9780252040542 (hardback) | ISBN
    9780252082016 (paper) | ISBN 9780252098987 (ebook)
Subjects: LCSH: Ecofeminism—Mexican-American
    Border Region. | Mexican American women. |
    Women—Mexican-American Border Region. |
    Women and the environment—Mexican-American
    Border Region. | Environmental justice—Mexican-
    American Border Region. | Feminism. | Mexican
    Americans—Study and teaching. | BISAC: SOCIAL
    SCIENCE / Feminism & Feminist Theory. | SOCIAL
    SCIENCE / Ethnic Studies / Hispanic American
    Studies. | SOCIAL SCIENCE / Gender Studies.
Classification: LCC HQ1194 .H65 2016 (print) | LCC
    HQ1194 (ebook) | DDC 305.48/86872073—dc23
LC record available at https://lccn.loc.gov/2016017322

*To all who practice loving connection*

# Contents

# List of Illustrations

# Acknowledgments

This book evolved over several years and I am thankful for all the varied kinds of support it received. Its earliest supporters include my dissertation adviser Cathy Rakowski, as well as Jill Bystydzienski, Cricket Keating, and Guisela Latorre in the Department of Women's, Gender, and Sexuality Studies at the Ohio State University; they mentored me as I developed the project and completed graduate studies. They gave me space to pursue the topic despite the fact that ecofeminism had a tarnished reputation in feminist studies at that time and they shared expertise and emotional support along the way. The project also grew stronger from the input of religious studies scholars working with questions of gender and sexuality, including Tanya Erzen and Hugh Urban. This project is indebted to Mary Carter and the women at the Women's Intercultural Center in Anthony, New Mexico, who invited me into their lives over the years. Their work is an inspiration and I hope others learn from it. I am also inspired by the artists featured here and the critics who have begun the conversations on which my own work builds—they are creating beautiful worlds and motivating social, political, and economic transformation. I am especially humbled that Juana Alicia and Amalia Mesa-Bains shared images of their art with my readers.

Thank you to the National Women's Studies Association and the University of Illinois Press; sponsorship of the First Book Prize provided a pathway for this book's publication and it continues to open doors for other aspiring feminist scholars. It has been a true pleasure to work with Dawn Durante and the team at the University of Illinois Press—I treasure their support and guidance. This work was also made possible by the Ohio State University, through its mentors and dissertation funding; DePauw University, my new home that granted time and funding to conduct additional research while giving me a wonderful group of colleagues from which to draw social and intellectual sustenance; and the University of Sydney, where I was welcomed as a visiting scholar and offered work space, a tremendous library, and good conversation with eco-minded colleagues while completing book revisions. To my careful readers, including Meryl Altman, Magdalena Nijander-Brock, Molly Uline-Olmstead, and anonymous reviewers: your feedback strengthened this book and made publication possible; review work can be a tedious task and your responses were as generous as they were sharp. Special thanks to Ryan Puskas for being on call at all times for critical technology support and for listening to me talk about this book for too many years. And thanks to my family—including my broadly defined chosen and furry family—for being cheerleaders throughout the journey. This book is yours, too, and I look forward to the next collaboration!

# Ecological Borderlands

1. Ana Tierra, *Tree of Life*, watercolor painting donated to Women's Intercultural Center.

# INTRODUCTION

## Ecological Borderlands

### Connecting Movements, Theories, Selves

> With awe and wonder, you look around,
> recognizing the preciousness of the earth, the
> sanctity of every human being on the planet,
> the ultimate unity and interdependence of all
> beings—somos todos un país. Love swells in
> your body and shoots out of your heart chakra,
> linking you to everyone/everything. . . . This
> conocimiento motivates you to work actively
> to see that no harm comes to people, animals,
> ocean—to take up spiritual activism and the
> work of healing. Te entregas a tu promesa
> to help your various cultures create new
> paradigms, new narratives.
>
> —Gloria Anzaldúa, "now let us shift . . ."

The image that opens this book (figure 1) beautifully illustrates relationships and practices that knit human, nature, and spirit bodies together. The image is of a watercolor donated to a women's center that serves Mexican American women in the U.S. Southwest, Gloria Anzaldúa's borderlands (1999). It encapsulates the kind of ecological consciousness and expansion of self that is at the heart of the Chicana feminist and Mexican American art activism and scholarship featured in this study.[1] In light of recent chemical and oil spills, protests about fracking, and devastating climate-related storms across North America, the popular response toward embracing "green culture" has been an individuating one, particularly through the consumption of greenwashed products that include everything from hybrid cars to household cleansers. As popular and scholarly anxiety over environmental catastrophe grows, ecofeminism, the branch of feminist theory that is perhaps best poised to intervene, remains marginal among feminists and other academics. This is the case even as interest in new materialist and Anthropocene feminism ascends following the publication of volumes such as Stacy Alaimo and Susan Hekman's *Material Feminisms* (2008) and Diana Coole and Samantha Frost's *New Materialisms* (2010). Ecofeminist philosophy has fallen out of favor with feminists writing through the poststructural turn because of the perception that some scholars have simplified and essentialized the concepts of *woman* and *nature*. The too-easy dismissal of ecofeminist work forecloses important questions that ecofeminism raises regarding women's environmental activism and the gendered effects of environmental degradation. We need to consider how our relationships with each other and with the environment shape efforts toward justice or risk being left out of the conversation even as we challenge some of the shortcomings of ecofeminist theory production. A survey of the strategies employed by Chicana feminists and Mexican American writers, artists, and activists living and working in the border bioregions has much to offer ecofeminism and feminist theory. One of the aims of this book is to revitalize ecofeminist theory by investigating its intersections with other theoretical traditions, including Chicana and new materialist feminisms. To that end, *Ecological Borderlands* asks: What are the key debates in ecofeminism that need to be revisited in order for feminists to pay more serious attention to the ecological facets of justice? What characterizes the environmentalism that grows out of the conditions that shape Mexican American women's lives in the U.S. Southwest? How does this environmentalism challenge or rework the dominant characterization of ecofeminism?

In centering works by Chicana feminists and Mexican American activists—some who do and do not identify as *Chicanas*—I do not mean to ascribe a unifying identity or presuppose any "natural" characteristics that bring together this particular group of women. Instead, I focus on Chicana studies as an emerging field with its roots in the political activism of the 1960s, including debates about identity, nationalism, and resistance that have evolved during six decades of scholarship and activism. From its inception, questions about just relationships among humans and between humans and the land took center stage; they were forged out of forced displacements and efforts to reconceptualize a politics of belonging in an era that continues to be marked by colonialism's legacy. The border region, including the diverse bioregions it encompasses, is a site of ecological activity and subject production; I borrow Anzaldúa's notion of the borderlands for this book's title precisely because this region creates an *ecological borderlands*—one marked by translocal and transnational flows of people, flora, and fauna, as well as by a multiplicity of economic, political, and cultural paradigms. Bioregions follow their own rules; because ecosystems may be shared across a national border yet differ within a single state, for example, activists have had to develop creative strategies and  alliances (*conocimiento*, as Anzaldúa names it) that are not often recognized within other frameworks of environmentalism.

## Ecological Genealogies and Status Quo Stories

> How might feminist theory generate a proliferation of stories about its recent past that more accurately reflect the diversity of perspectives within (or outside) its orbit? How might we reform the relationship between feminism's constituent parts to allow what are currently phantom presences to take shape? Can we do feminist theory differently?
>
> —Clare Hemmings, "Telling Feminist Stories"

In the United States, the term *ecofeminism* describes many things, including how the domination of women may be linked to the domination of nature, examination of women's environmental activism, and exploration of the spiritual ties between women and the natural world. Ecofeminist theories criticize the historically negative image of women and nature that exists in patriarchal cultures that measure nature by its market value, marking both women and nature as other and thus exploitable (Merchant 1990; Mies and Shiva 1993; Salleh 1997; Hawthorne 2002). Intersectional ecofeminism provides an analysis of how women of color are animalized more heavily and in different ways than white women, for example (Adams 1993; Harper 2011). However, some ecofeminists also positively identify women with nature. They have pointed to women's greater contact with the environment due to farming and conservation work, their reproductive capabilities and care work, or their sense of a spiritual connection with Mother Nature in order to describe the origin of a woman-nature identification and to argue that women are well-positioned to protect the environment (Shiva 1997).[2] Ecofeminists from all over the world have created a diverse body of work that explores ways to think about the historical, material, symbolic, and theoretical links between feminism and environmentalism and/or between women and nature (as well as the ways in which "link" thinking fails in certain contexts). Catriona Sandilands offers one of the most complete genealogies of ecofeminism in *The Good-Natured Feminist* (1999), which will help those unfamiliar with ecofeminism to get oriented within the field.[3] I provide a condensed overview of the genealogy here and comment on the limitations of ecofeminism *and* feminist critiques of the field to show where works from Chicana feminists and Mexican American artists, activists, and scholars intervene in and collaborate to push feminist environmentalisms into new directions.

From the genesis of the concept *ecofeminism* onward, Sandilands traces a problematic and resilient thread of identity politics that stems from the radical cultural feminist debates on the "nature question" of the 1970s and '80s (1999, 5–6). French feminist Françoise d'Eaubonne celebrated a woman-nature connection and is credited with coining the term *ecofeminism* in the early 1970s. In contrast to d'Eaubonne, Sherry Ortner's 1974 essay "Is Female to Male as Nature Is to Culture?" links women's cultural devaluation to their association with nature and thus argues that women need to participate in more social and creative projects to shift their alignment *from* nature *to* culture. Importantly, Sandilands figures these two poles as the grounds on which ecofeminist debates regarding women's difference from men and their difference from or similarity to "nature" were waged. This is consequential because the way these debates are framed links ecofeminism more closely to the radical Western feminist search for the origins of patriarchal control and women's difference from men than to anything else. In other words, we are not linking ecofeminism to questions of land sovereignty and decolonization that were also prominent in the 1960s and '70s, for example.

Sandilands's genealogy continues to chart the course of radical feminist debates from Shulamith Firestone's (1970) claim that patriarchy is rooted in women's reproductive differences, a theory that advocated reproductive technologies to free women from their association with the natural world and the biological processes that constrain their lives. Again, framing the debate in terms of poles, Sandilands contrasts Firestone's text with Mary Daly's *Gyn/Ecology* (1978), which argued that women's reproductive capabilities were devalued along with the natural world—women's difference from men, far from being seen as a failure or lack, should be celebrated as a source of strength. Daly, Sandilands argued, represents the larger trend in the 1970s to reject liberal or equal rights approaches to ending women's oppression (1999, 9). The alternative and more radical aim was to revalue women's inherent difference from men and to create separate spaces where women could discover their full potential. Sandilands surmises that "new relations to nature were an integral part of this culture; women's 'special' knowledges of reproduction and their experiences of mediating between nature and culture were part of their difference from men and thus needed to be discovered and freed" (1999, 10). Feminist discourses on religion and woman-centered spiritualities also shaped ecofeminist thought at the time. Some spiritualist accounts turned

4

away from a search for the origins of patriarchy toward an alternative story of prepatriarchal bliss in a nature-centered, matrifocal society (Starhawk 1997).[4] Sandilands claims that the identification between women, particularly their purported special knowledge rooted in their biological and spiritual connec-  ⊻ tions with nature, provided grounds on which to root an identity politics and give political weight and legitimacy to women's arguments. This identitarian woman-nature connection, she suggests, permeates all the explicitly and self-identified ecofeminist literature that followed those cultural feminist debates regarding the "nature question."

Despite the growing theoretical complexity of radical feminist texts, Carolyn Merchant's *The Death of Nature* ([1980] 1990) broadened the argument regarding the patriarchal roots of nature-woman oppression by showing that capitalism and development also play a role. Merchant traces a shift in thought that saw nature no longer as organic and mysterious, but as instrumental; here, the dual control of women and nature through technology and circulation through a capitalist system links women and nature in a devalued relationship. For Merchant, Bina Agarwal (1997), and others who identify with socialist ecofeminism, Sandilands argues that, although they shift away from a biological association of women with nature, in emphasizing the sexual division as socially organized yet central to women's relation to the environment, they ⊻ continue to link women and the natural world as having a relationship of identity based on a privileged epistemological standpoint (Sandilands 1999, 61). It is assumed that women, by virtue of socialization and reproduction, have a *essentialist* closer, better understanding of the natural environment and are better able to *POV?* protect it. Within this genealogy, a radical cultural ecofeminism responds to limiting earlier trends in Western liberal feminism and socialist critics respond to what they see as the shortcomings of radical cultural feminists.

Scholarly trends shifted again as social ecofeminists developed critiques against reductionist tendencies in both radical and socialist approaches. Among the oft-cited social ecofeminists, Sandilands discusses Ynestra King's "The Eco-Feminist Imperative" (1983), Val Plumwood's "Ecofeminism: An Overview and Discussion of Positions and Arguments" (1986), and Judith Plant's "Ecofeminism" (1991). Each offers a theory of interconnectivity or intersubjectivity while critiquing hierarchical dualisms in Western culture. This approach is nicely summarized by Karen Warren's "logic of domination," ⊻ which points out a tradition of dualist and hierarchical thinking in Western philosophy (including Western feminist theory). Under this logic, binaries such as man/woman, mind/body, culture/nature, and a host of others are subject to a logic such that the first term in a binary pair is culturally privileged and seen as superior to the second term, justifying its domination (Warren 1990, 123). This logic permeates institutions in which it manifests materially and systematically in the lives of individuals.

Given their understanding of binaries and dualist thought, social ecofeminists recognize problems in cultural feminist philosophies that simply maintain patriarchal dualism by reversing the valuation of gender binary terms (woman/man, nature/culture—woman and nature are connected and the characteristics and values shared by each, such as nurturance and reproductive potential, are superior). Similarly, they find socialist strategies overly rationalist and culture centered, propping up reason/emotion, culture/nature binaries that maintain masculinist values. Despite social ecofeminists' efforts to transcend binaries through embracing a position of radical otherness (e.g., pointing to the rational, social, and economic functions of reproduction and mothering as seen in King 1989), Sandilands finds a problematic deployment of standpoint theory and resultant identity politics embedded in all three positions. This is a problem, she writes, not just for the vague and idealized conceptualization of "woman," but for that of "nature" as well:

> In accounts that emphasized dualistic conceptual frameworks, such as that in which what is "not masculine" became the truth of essential femininity, so too did that which is "not culture" become the natural state from which we came and toward which we must aspire. . . . The particular social creation of nature that many ecofeminists wanted to promote and politicize was misrecognized as a nature given *in* nature. (1999, 68–69)

Even among antidualist positions, theorizing begins with human injustices, identities, and agency rather than a more complex understanding of an agential nonhuman world that is not transparently knowable to human subjects. Thus, for Sandilands, a posthumanist destabilization of both human and nature identity and subjectivity is required. I agree that ecofeminism is well served by a posthumanist agenda; new materialist feminisms have begun to address this with a greater emphasis on the agency of the nonhuman world and I hope to add to this discussion in the following chapters; however, counter to assessments in *The Good-Natured Feminist*, I do not believe postidentitarian strategies are optimal given the historical and political landscape of particular regions and communities.[5] Deployments of identity can be compatible with a posthumanist agenda. Indeed, some Chicana studies scholars theorize an open and relational identity that is historicized with respect to gender, race, class, ethnicity, sexuality, and regionality. A politics of identity can be coalitional, strategic, and temporary; as I will discuss in more detail, the in-betweenness of Anzaldúa's *nepantlera* or new mestiza is a clear example of this (1999, 2002).

We need to consider *how* feminist stories are told (Hemmings 2005); I am concerned with the limits on thought that are imposed by useful, even compelling, but overdetermining conceptual frameworks such as the liberal versus radical/cultural versus socialist conceptions of Western feminist theory that dominate this and other ecofeminist genealogies.[6] Briefly, I shift the focus away from what must be fit into a Western feminist theory paradigm toward Karen Warren's analysis of the manifold ways in which ecofeminist theorists and activists describe the woman-nature connection across the varieties of ecofeminism. Warren offers a pluralistic taxonomy of the interconnections between "human-Others" and "nature-Others" based on "historical and causal, conceptual, empirical, socioeconomic, linguistic, symbolic and literary, spiritual and religious, epistemological, ethical and political interconnections" (2000, xv). This taxonomy can help us think outside the schools of Western feminist thought, decentering the hegemonic Western origin story and imposed interpretive framework. We can see how Vandana Shiva's work on the Chipko movement in India—employing symbolic, religious, and economic frameworks—may be understood as part of the ecofeminist movement. Wangari Maathai's Green Belt movement to plant trees in Kenya could belong to ecofeminism. Both movements began and grew to prominence in the 1970s, during the time when Western feminists are credited for linking nature and gender oppression and activism together. As Noël Sturgeon's (2003) study of the Women's Environment and Development Organization (WEDO) caucuses at the U.N. Fourth World Conference on Women confirms, environmental feminism has been more transnational and multicentered than some genealogies would suggest. Questioning the field's supposed Western centrism and what belongs to ecofeminism are important tasks throughout this book.

The resurgence of ecological awareness in feminist theory need not necessarily be rooted in ecofeminist philosophy; material and Anthropocene feminisms contribute to conversations on the relationship between social and ecological justice (although, as Greta Gaard attests, such works may be ecofeminist outgrowths by another name; 2011). In revisiting ecofeminism, I also note that while there are useful ideas that can be reclaimed and reworked, ecofeminist theory maintains its own exclusions; Chicana and Mexican American activists and scholars are among those who are absent from the canon. In fact, several Chicana/o and Latina/o studies scholars have concerns about the relationship between ecofeminism and their work. In interviews with Chicana environmental justice advocates, Malia Davis (1998) found resonances with the activists' beliefs about connections between the oppression of women and nature, but they did not identify with the movement or its perceived woman-centered approach that fails to recognize how men in their lives were also impacted by environmental degradation. Gwyn Kirk (1998) and Ellen O'Loughlin (1993) also warn of the dangers of co-opting Chicana/ Latina organizing under the umbrella of ecofeminism—a field that, as many genealogies show, is dominated by white and middle-class women of European descent.[7] Borderlands environmentalism has its own origin and history that other theories and movements have failed to account. Although chapter 1 delves deeper into this history, here I will note that environmental activism and theories of just human-nature relationships stem from a unique history of Spanish and American imperialism from the colonial period to the present day. This borderlands environmentalism derives from multiple sources, including action for land grants; water access; culturally significant uses of the land (e.g., animal grazing, keeping a garden for *curandera* work); displacement as a result of the sitings of freeways, prisons, and incinerators; workplace dangers such as pesticides and chemicals used in factory work; food insecurity; and health-care access. In each case, organizing tactics differ, impacts on men and women in the community differ, and activists' understanding of their identity and relationship to the environment differs. Even when issues are shared across different communities (such as pesticide use in farming), positionality shapes how environmental harms are experienced. O'Loughlin's work on the coalition between farmworkers and consumers during the United Farm Workers (UFW) grape boycotts shows this clearly: "My position when choosing whether or not to eat a grape at my friend's house is not the same as that of the worker who picked that grape. But our positions are connected, and in more than one way" (150). The immediacy of the danger and the greater cumulative effect on farmworkers' bodies leads to a different relationship to the land and to an urgent need for justice. Similarly, the pregnant female farmworker stands in a very different place than both the men she works alongside and the middle-class mother-consumer at the grocery store targeted by the boycott.

Much of the environmental scholarship in Chicana/o studies is situated within an environmental justice framework that uses a social science orientation to document and respond to ecological injustices, yet silences remain around the ecological themes in cultural production. Andrea Parra argues that, "like mainstream feminism, perhaps ecocriticism has been constituted as primarily an Anglo domain" (1999, 1100). María Herrera Sobek (1998) began to trace environmental themes in the work of Chicanas from the 1970s onward, yet ecocritical analyses—even of widely read authors like Gloria Anzaldúa and Cherríe Moraga—are only beginning to emerge (Steele 2008; Ybarra 2004, 2009). In bridging social sciences approaches to the study of movements and humanities-based approaches to the study of cultural production, we can see

a more complete picture of the ways Chicana and Mexican American women ✗
have worked for justice. I consider themes that are not obviously environmental, but in highlighting relationships between women and nature, they reveal
themselves as ecological; this includes exploring the potential for women to
become appropriate subjects to their own landscapes, a feat that is particularly
important within the work of Chicana and Mexican American women considering the urgency of reclaiming a postcolonial landscape from an imperialist
and patriarchal presence.[8]

There is a strong tradition of reclaiming geographic and discursive space
within Chicana studies that has roots in the early days of the Chicano movement's reclamation of Aztlán, the Aztec homeland of the U.S. Southwest. However, as is evident in these works, becoming appropriate in the land is no easy ✗
task and requires a radical revisioning of "home."[9] Works such as Lourdes Portillo's documentary *Señorita Extraviada* (2001) and Sandra Cisneros's novel
*The House on Mango Street* (1984) describe place-centered subjectivities, but
often the places are unhomely. Ultimately, the artists show how landscapes
that are seen as places of violence and alienation might be reclaimed. Writers
such as Cherríe Moraga in "Queer Aztlán" (1993) and Gloria Anzaldúa in *Bor-
derlands/La Frontera* (1999) rewrite their homelands, recoding understandings of the border that currently construct it and its inhabitants as invisible,
dangerous, or disposable. Once free from imperialist symbolic configurations
of the border, writers and artists begin to theorize how we can relate with each
other in new ways.

## Exploring the Interstices, Working the Bridge in "Nos/otras"

> As I use the term, *thresholds* represent complex intercon-
> nections among a variety of sometimes contradictory
> worlds—points crossed by multiple intersecting possibilities,
> opportunities, and challenges. Like thresholds—that mark
> transitional, in-between spaces where new beginnings, and
> unexpected combinations can occur—threshold theories
> facilitate and enact movement "betwixt and between"
> divergent worlds, enabling us to establish fresh connections
> among distinct (and sometimes contradictory) perspectives,
> realities, peoples, theories, texts, and/or worldviews.
>
> —AnaLouise Keating, *Transformation Now!*

*intersectionality
stemming from
recognition of
possibility in
thresholds*

This threshold project emerges at the intersections of three bodies of literature that share a focus on intersubjectivity: Chicana studies, ecofeminist philosophy, and new materialist feminisms. *Intersubjectivity* connotes a sense of

self that moves beyond the bounded, individualizing *I* of the Cartesian rational self. Major works within each of these three fields recognize that we can only understand ourselves through a web of relations to other humans and the more-than-human world, including the natural and built environments through which we move and to which we develop attachments. The following chapters explore how artists, scholars, and activists working in the ecological borderlands deterritorialize problematic representations of the border and its inhabitants while posing new ways to think of the borderlands and our relationships with each other. They center relationalities that address both social *and* ecological justice, balancing the tension between ecological territorialization, or what Devon Peña calls "lococentrism" (1998a, 6–12; see also Kirk 1998, 192–93), with efforts to destabilize rigid identity categories, allowing a more open and relational subjectivity. Such an approach to (inter)subjectivity suggests the need to form more connections (if only partial and temporary) with our surroundings, conceiving ourselves as more fully part of the territories in which we move. Here, readers may find this approach resonant with recent work on material feminisms, including Jane Bennett's *Vibrant Matter* (2010), Stacy Alaimo's *Bodily Natures* (2010), and Alaimo and Susan Hekman's *Material Feminisms* (2008). Each decenters human experience, conceptualizing a posthumanist subjectivity in relation with an agentic material world. While ecofeminism too has long posed the need to see ourselves through our webs of interconnection with the natural world, one of the sticking points of ecofeminist philosophy that has drawn criticisms of essentialism relates to the construction of the categories *woman* and *nature* that are thought to be inextricably linked within ecofeminist logic.[10] In putting this debate in dialogue with Chicana studies and material feminist scholars focusing on the nature of our material connections, this book begins to theorize new directions for ecofeminist philosophy and Chicana feminisms. The aim is not to claim these works for ecofeminism but to take AnaLouise Keating's theories of social transformation to heart: "Commonalities offer pathways into relational investigations of difference" (2013, 19).

In my research, I saw a specific strategy—or what Chela Sandoval might call a *technology of differential consciousness*—at work in Chicana feminist and Mexican American women's art, literature, film, and activism. I name this phenomenon *performative intersubjectivity*—a mode of disrupting/re-creating the self through practices that actively stage relationality. I point to various practices employed by these women that construct, via performative strategies, intersubjective relationships between selves, landscapes, and spirit. In these cases, performative intersubjectivity recognizes continuities between humans

10

and their environment and can help us better understand and enact coalitions for social and ecological justice.

For Judith Butler, performativity describes subjectivity as an effect of discourse. That is to say, there is no "doer behind the deed," but that our identities and sense of selves are created through the reiteration of practices (Butler 1999, 181). Butler writes, "Performativity is not a singular act, but a repetition and a ritual, which achieves its effects through its naturalization in the context of a body, understood, in part, as a culturally sustained temporal duration" (1999, xv). Femininity is not natural, but *naturalized*. The emphasis on "perfecting" oneself through rituals of dress, makeup, diet and exercise, posture, speech patterns, and so on that must be reenacted constantly to keep up the image of ideal womanhood stands as a good example of the fact that "one is not born a woman, but becomes one" (Beauvoir 1953). While one might continue to cite the norm through all of these femininity-producing practices, and this citation of norms is carried out to the point of giving coherence to identities (e.g., this is a woman), one can also *mis*-cite the norm—performing what Butler calls a "performative subversion" or subversive repetition (1999, 185). Norms can be subverted through practices that denaturalize gendered identities and performances, leading to resignification of the norms, of the practices, and therefore, of identity; for example, drag, especially in exaggerated camp performances, can stretch the logic of gender and resignify what it means to *be* a man or a woman (1999, 174).[11]

Critics have interpreted Butler's work as being overly reductionist in its emphasis on discourse and linguistic norms that ignore the ways materiality might exceed discourse and language—indeed, responses to Butler have fueled the recent turn to a more material base in feminist theorizing—as in Karen Barad's "Posthumanist Performativity" (2003), for example. In claiming that subjects are the effects of norm citations and subversions, Butler has also been critiqued for seeming to limit agency to those small spaces of negotiation between working with and troubling the norm; there is no fully intentional and therefore fully agentic subject. Nonetheless, Butler's work has been influential for feminists seeking nonessentialist notions of subjectivity. Further, focus on the citationality of discursive norms shines more attention on the micropractices or individual behaviors of social reproduction and resistance.

In contrast to Butler's performativity theory in which "the doer" emerges from "the deed" as an act of hailing by discourse—that is, you understand yourself as gendered only after the nurse hails, "It's a girl!" (1993, 7–8)—Chela Sandoval theorizes how subjects that develop an oppositional consciousness might themselves hail discourse (2000). Drawing insights from a number of

Chicana feminist and postcolonial studies scholars, she suggests that, as subjects caught between cultures that include competing discourses and norming systems, one begins to recognize the logic and instability of such systems. As a result of being perpetually caught within and between these systems, one learns to manipulate them for survival. The development of this differential oppositional consciousness

> requires a consciousness that perceives itself at the center of myriad possibilities all cross-working—any of which is fodder for one's loyalties. Such loyalties, once committed, can be withdrawn and relocated depending on survival, moral, and/or political imperatives. . . . When the differential form of cognitive mapping is used it is the citizen-*subject* who interpellates, who calls up ideology, as opposed to Althusser's formulation, in which it is "ideology that interpellates the subject." (31)

This is not to suggest that there is a coherent, entirely self-aware and agentic subject, but rather to highlight the possibility of subjects that are constantly in movement, seeking new alliances and temporary identifications, and which, under certain circumstances, can develop an especially sharp critical consciousness. In situating performativity theory within the field of Chicana studies, I highlight the spaces within performativity theory where actors can self-consciously manipulate norms in the name of collective politics for social and ecological justice.

In light of this, some key questions arise: How do we escape from status quo logics, as "new stories must partially come from outside the system of ruling powers" (Anzaldúa 2002, 560)? Can performativity offer a way to think ourselves through relations and practices that diffuse boundaries between the self and its surroundings, enabling what I call *performative intersubjectivity* that is also *ecological*? One that recognizes continuities between selves, landscapes, including human and nonhuman others, and spirits? In subsequent chapters, I respond to these concerns by establishing more coalitional space between environmental and Chicana/o movements for social justice. I do so, in part, by showing their convergences and by reworking their genealogies to show histories and political investments that must be negotiated if a broad coalition for social and ecological justice is to be had. I also show how scholars, artists, and activists create performative subversions in imperial and patriarchal logic that pairs women, and Chicana and Mexican American women in particular, with an "untamed" and "dangerous" nature. While representational challenges are key to reshaping discourse and freeing up space for liberating representations of "woman" and "nature," performative subversions do more than challenge epistemological frames; they encourage ontological shifts, allowing for new

12

(inter)subjectivities, new bodies, new assemblages to emerge. They destabilize not just discourses, but people and movements as well. These performative subversions have real decolonizing potential. → effects on the material world

There are three sites of debate where performative subversions of subjectivity are particularly important to help us become more fully enmeshed or en-*natured* with our surrounding landscapes, including debates on (1) embodiment, (2) the relationship between "woman" and "nature," and (3) spirituality. These three areas are highlighted both because they can help us radically rethink our sense of self and because they call up debates that remain sites of tension within ecofeminism and feminist theory more broadly. The following chapters address this in much more detail; here, we consider how affect structures our relationships and stretches identities beyond our embodied selves.

## EMBODIMENT

One of the virtues of performativity theory is awareness of the body through the repetition of practices. In Butler's *Bodies That Matter*, *matter* is described "not as a site or surface, but as *a process of materialization that stabilizes over time to produce the effect of boundary, fixity, and surface we call matter*" (1993, 9; emphasis in original); bodies are created as effects by regulatory discourses that write themselves on the body (Foucault 1977; Butler 1999). Feminist theorists debate female embodiment to determine whether the body is only *key Q* an effect of discourse and known through language or whether the body precedes and exceeds discourse and can act as a site of knowledge production. Rosi Braidotti and Elizabeth Grosz may be considered predecessors of the turn to new materialist feminisms in their focus on *both* the exteriority *and* interiority of the body (i.e., how the "outside" or discourses shape the inside and how the "inside" or psychic life shapes the outside); their theories are helpful in extending Butler's insights to my own theory of performative intersubjectivity.

Grosz, interested in disturbing binaries of inside/outside and mind/body, writes,

> If, as feminists have claimed, "our politics start with our feelings" and if the very category of experience or feeling is itself problematized through a recognition of its ideological production—if, that is, experience is not a raw mode of access to some truth—then the body provides a point of mediation between what is perceived as purely internal and accessible only to the subject and what is external and publicly observable, a point from which to rethink the opposition between the inside and the outside, the private and the public, the self and other, and all the other binary pairs associated with the mind/body opposition. (1994, 20–21)

Grosz raises questions about the inside and outside of bodies, about the social construction of affect (or feelings, emotions) as well as how feelings might bridge the "inside" and "outside," moving between them and making new connections among bodies. If affect does not exist in some pure form but is understood through social relationships that give it context and a prism through which meaning can be made, then affect is also a product of relations. I'm interested in how affect joins bodies together, destabilizing boundaries between them and one's very sense of self. Affect is productive and connective; through performative repetition, affect can be mobilized to open up intersubjective selves. Teresa Brennan's points on affective transfer are illustrative: "The transmission of affect, whether it is grief, anxiety, or anger, is social or psychological in origin. But the transmission is also responsible for bodily changes; some are brief changes, as in a whiff of the room's atmosphere, some longer lasting. In other words, the transmission of affect, if only for an instant, alters the biochemistry and neurology of the subject. The 'atmosphere' or the environment literally gets into the individual" (1).

The permeable body caught in a web of its surroundings is similar to what Stacy Alaimo calls the "trans-corporeal self" (2010, 2), a subject that is produced as an intersubject through the jobs we do, the food we eat, and other means. Whereas Alaimo emphasizes the shared materiality of subjects, I stress intersubjectivity as a process that is both material and forged through the relay of affect that regulates connections between bodies. Throughout this book I depict embodiment as shifting and reliant on the nature of the practices that produce connections—in emphasizing practices, I emphasize agency. In constantly reproducing the subject through relations of belonging with (human, nature, and spirit) others, there is the potential to hail, as Sandoval suggests, relations that are more just.

These insights do not only belong to material feminisms. Moraga's "theory in the flesh" developed in *This Bridge Called My Back* (Moraga and Anzaldúa 1983) demands consideration of the ways oppressive social systems inscribe the body. It notes the body as a site of political development and consciousness-raising. It also suggests the body can be a site of connection to others and a source of great pleasure. She explains that a "theory in the flesh means one where the physical realities of our lives—our skin color, the land or concrete we grew up on, our sexual longings—all fuse to create a politic born out of necessity" (Moraga and Anzaldúa 1983, 23). Critique as well as the vision for change will come from reflection on "flesh and blood experiences" (23). Moraga's role as a writer, not just of personal/theoretical essays, but also of poetry and plays, connects her to others in a more than metaphorical sense. The bridges in *This Bridge Called My Back* are built on testimonies of hope, betrayal, shared histories, and points of potential commonalities—"*su cuerpo es una bocacalle*" (Anzaldúa 1999, 102). Moraga shares in common with Anzaldúa the belief that change originates in the body and that bodies themselves—their perceptions and knowledges—are not self-evident, but must be negotiated and their signs read.[12] In all of Anzaldúa's work, the performative impulse in her writing and its link among bodies is clear. In fact, writing is a mode of knowing and becoming in the world: "conocimiento is reached via creative acts—writing, art-making, dancing, healing, teaching, meditation, and spiritual activism—both mental and somatic (the body too is a form as well as a site of creativity). Through creative engagements, you embed your experiences in a larger frame of reference, connecting your personal struggles with those of other beings on the planet, with the struggles of the Earth itself" (Anzaldúa and Keating 2002, 542). These examples theorize intersubjectivity as built on bodily awareness, and they posit connections that are not only hard forged but also staged actively through creative and coalitional means. Although the body is at the heart of these connections, its boundaries are potentially vast and porous.

## WOMAN-NATURE

The argument outlined previously directly bears on the question of essentialism in the conceptual connections between "woman" and "nature" put forward by patriarchal discourses and some ecofeminist responses to them. In assuming a self that is constructed by practices of relationality made between the self and its environment, the idea of "woman" is not only destabilized but so too is the idea of "nature." It is important to think of ourselves as en-natured in order to develop an ecological consciousness, and there are ways to do so without reifying stereotypes of femininity and naturalness in the process. Performative subversions that disrupt binaries between human/nature and culture/nature can serve decolonizing efforts. Building on the insights of Moraga and Anzaldúa mentioned previously, consider the following studies that use art and its creation of affective changes in a body to manifest social change.

In "In Here and Out There: Sensations between Self and Landscape" (2003), Amanda Bingley explores boundaries around the self that are negotiated through past memories and current sensations of landscape interactions. Using sand play and modeling along with open-ended questions about the landscapes participants inhabited as children, Bingley's interviewees used vivid language to articulate their relatedness to their natural and built environments—those they currently inhabit as well as their memories of those of the past. This stands in contrast to the less vivid language found in interviews

15

that did not involve the creative and sensory experience that sand play offered. Bingley concludes that, for participants, "it was possible to unravel the intricacy of the relationship between Self and landscape. . . . The moment of perception of landscape was found to be a moment of intersection and interaction between the several elements of subjective sensory experience: various elements of identity, past memories, projections, myths, cultural and personal experience" (343). Creative practices and behaviors oriented toward rethinking relations with others and the landscape produced a change in the embodiment of the subjects—they became more animated, more likely to articulate themselves in relation to the landscapes of their childhood and present, more likely to see relationships in general as constitutive of their being. Interviews and the use of language alone to frame their beliefs and experiences did not bring about new thoughts about oneself or her environment.

Similarly, Bronwyn Davies's *(In)scribing Body/Landscape Relations* (2000) explores coextensive bodies and landscapes and investigates practices that facilitate intersubjective awareness. She writes, "Because of the lack of practice in reading our bodies in this way [i.e., as body/landscapes], I have sought here to develop a new form of embodied writing. I adopted a number of strategies for disrupting my taken-for-granted clichéd ways of knowing my own body/landscape relations" (19). Davies traveled to unfamiliar landscapes and wrote about her embodied responses to such settings, reflectively noting the ways those responses are both bodied and culturally inscribed. She also engages with a process she calls "collective biography": "Here, a group of Australian women explore, through stories of childhood in specific landscapes, the ways in which belonging with/in landscape is achieved in the double sense of becoming appropriate and being appropriated with/in Australian landscapes" (11). In both cases, the act of reflection and writing about embodied/encultured relationships with the natural world does not so much reflect our actual relationships or reveal aspects of our "true selves," but instead represents a performance of *becoming* body/landscape. Through creative subversions of the norm and reinscriptions of ourselves with our environment, we stage new relationships and alliances that may be oriented toward more socially and ecologically just movements. Not to be misconstrued as a new-age effort to get "in touch" with nature, such practices hail us to deconstruct the binary between humans and nature altogether and to see ourselves as coextensive.

Nonetheless, as with all subversions, challenging the norm will not guarantee movement toward justice in itself. In tracking the ways some Chicana and Mexican American scholars, artists, and activists developed practices toward performative intersubjectivity, this book explores the staging of human/

16

landscape deconstructions in ways that do not merely embrace an idealistic ecological intersubjectivity; many of the examples depicted pair performative reconstructions of ecological intersubjectivity with a historicizing critique of the patriarchal, racist, and imperialist ordering of human/landscape relations, pointing the viewer to embrace an openly counterhegemonic positioning. To return to Anzaldúa again, consider the ways she figures herself as part of the borderlands. *Borderlands/La Frontera* tells an economic, political, and environmental history of Mexico/south Texas that is interwoven with the author's personal history and that of her family. Culture clashes within traditional patriarchal, Chicano nationalist, and racist Anglo cultures, all of which are confining in their misogyny and homophobia, shape the new mestiza consciousness that defines possibilities for those that dwell on this border (and possibly others). This consciousness is a heightened level of awareness that can see above competing discourses and their conscriptions and has the potential to rewrite histories, myths, lands, and bodies to make them anew. Although Anzaldúa has been criticized for her revisionist histories and the leeway she takes in myth-making, her aim is not to accurately portray the past, but to change the present.[13] For example, one of the recurring symbols in her mythology is that of a serpent that represents Earth and the natural world. In *Borderlands*, Anzaldúa writes, "Like the ancient Olmecs, I know Earth is a coiled Serpent. Forty years it's taken me to enter into the Serpent, to acknowledge that I have a body, that I am a body and to assimilate the animal body, the animal soul" (48). Focusing on Anzaldúa's return to the region in which she grew up, now challenged with drought, poverty, and a militarizing border patrol, Priscilla Ybarra's ecocritical reading of *Borderlands* makes the performativity of the woman-nature (or body/landscape) connection plain:

> [Anzaldúa] associates the image of a serpent with Earth itself—the natural environment. But she does not stop there. She also extends the metaphor to herself—she finds her bodily materiality in the act of "enter[ing] into the Serpent," and in so doing she realizes her direct connection to the animal world and the greater natural environment. In a book where she dwells on the challenges as well as opportunities presented by boundaries—borders, differences, discriminations—ultimately she breaks down the boundary between humans and the natural environment. (2009, 186)

## SPIRITUALITY

Finally, questions of spirituality mark the third site of debate within ecofeminist literature (the place of religion and spirituality remains contentious in feminist literature more broadly). Perhaps even more so than with respect to

the porous boundaries around embodiment and between woman-nature relations explored above, performative relations couched in spirituality challenge
individuated notions of subjectivity and can open up the self. Although none
of the theorists explored here posit a *natural* body or landscape that can be
fully known prediscursively, there is recognition that the body might exceed
those cultural inscriptions and provides other ways of knowing and feeling
that we are not yet adept at thinking about at the cognitive level. Spiritual
awareness may exceed our frames of understanding and articulation, yet it
often carries affective import and serves as a practice of relationship building.
Although academics in particular may be unaccustomed to thinking of mind
and body together, we are even less accustomed to thinking about the role of
spirit in connection to the mind and body in any nonessentializing ways. This
is one of the shortcomings of new materialist feminisms; despite careful attention to the ways bodies are embedded within ecosystems and social systems
and come to materialize differently because of them, there is little recognition
of the role spirituality may take in facilitating materialization. Taking the role
of religion in individual and collective social action seriously, Laura Pulido's
study of social movements of the American Southwest shows that "spirituality refers to consciousness and connection—our connections as individuals
to our souls, other people, places, nature, spirits, and in some cases, connection to a creator" (1998b, 721); she goes on to argue that spiritual beliefs may
emphasize the supernatural and/or the community, but what is most important is that they enfold us in a power bigger than ourselves and can move us
toward collective feeling, identification, and movement. Within movements,
a strong sense of spirituality can provide energy and fuel resilience in the face
of opposition.

Jacqui Alexander also poses a serious challenge to secular feminisms, asking
readers to think differently about the role of time, memory, and the sacred in
learning about and teaching transnational feminisms. She writes, "In a fundamental sense *Pedagogies of Crossing* moves from the betrayals of secular citizenship and dispossession to sacred citizenship and possession, from alienation to
belonging, from dismemberment to rememory. And it does so not in any discrete, noncontradictory, linear way, not in any way that suggests that there is no
traffic between and among them, but rather as a way to indicate that possession
can be a guided, conscious choice" (2005, 16). For Alexander, the body exceeds
the merely cultural and material. Rather, the body provides the base that knits
the mind and spirit together. Interestingly, this question of subjectivity is also
potentially a question of practices, of performativity: Alexander reveals how

18

practices of "divine self-invention" figure the sacred as performative. Practices that are encoded with spiritual affect link the self to others across time and space through practices of re-membering; they connect selves to a collectivity that is conceived of as divine. Orienting ourselves to the divine may draw us together, refresh us after the exhaustions of resistance, and stage practices of intersubjective collectivity as a response to the social fragmentation produced by empire.

I emphasize spirituality because, in addition to acting as a site of tension in ecofeminist praxis, a tradition of politicized spirituality can be seen widely within the art and literature of Chicana studies. Laura Pérez's study of Chicana art in "Spirit Glyphs: Reimagining Art and Artist in the Work of Chicana Tlamatinime" highlights the recovery of Aztec practices wherein the artist becomes a social healer capable of creating images, or glyphs, that call upon the presence of the natural and spiritual world (1998). In the Aztec tradition that has been re-membered (a cross between recollection and invention) by many Chicana feminists, including Anzaldúa's work quoted previously, art is at once political and spiritual. This memory of the past reworks elements of Aztec culture and hybridizes it with Chicana/o, colonial Catholic, African American, and other cultural heritages. The performative work of the Chicana artist or, as Pérez calls her, a *tlamatini*, draws the audience to see beyond the immediate, material world and to vision it as it *could* be in ways that put spirituality and spiritual healing at the center of one's life and struggles against oppression. Yet this spirit world is not separate from the physical, material world around us. It is also immanent, en-natured, and embodied in a number of ways that are detailed in subsequent chapters. The editors of a recently published book on spiritual activism drive the performative link between embodiment and spirit home: "'to flesh' and 'to spirit' acknowledges that spirituality is something that we do; it is part of creating culture and the production of meaning. . . . As such, to flesh the spirit and spirit the flesh heals" (Facio and Lara 2014, 11). In subsequent chapters, I strive to retain a nonessentializing and nonreductionist orientation to the role of spirituality in performances of ecological intersubjectivity. In particular, I explore how Chicana and Mexican American scholars, artists, and activists working in the ecological borderlands have cited spirituality as a technology or practice of intersubjectivity that both reworks what Davies has named "body/landscape relations" and expands them to body/landscape/spirit relations, offering a comprehensive effort to shift subjectivity from the secularized and individuating practices that are produced by dominant discourses.

## Decolonizing Possibilities

> How do we decolonize ourselves without returning to a
> static and utopic precolonial past? How do these decolonial
> practices (re)claim and create enunciative spaces ... that
> challenge the violence-driven technologies of imperial and
> patriarchal subjection? ... What strategies of decolonization
> allow our struggles for identity to engage in nonbinary,
> nonhierarchic, and nonhegemonic articulations of metiza/o
> consciousness ... ?
>
> —Arturo Aldama, *Disrupting Savagism*

This chapter closes by pondering *deterritorialization* as a potential strategy for decolonization. The term "decolonization" has been usefully deployed to describe a process of attaining autonomy from within the internal, largely unrecognized borderlands colony of the U.S. that relies on hierarchies of gender, race, sexuality, class, and nation in order to exploit Chicana/os, Mexican Americans, and indigenous Americans (Córdova 1998). Deterritorialization can shift the grounds on which colonizing discourses proliferate. The concept of deterritorialization both urges that our problematic representational patterns be dislodged and that we begin to vision new worlds. In focusing on performative micropolitics—those daily practices that push us to new associations with human and nonhuman others—deterritorialized notions of (inter) subjectivity are precisely those that "allow our struggles for identity to engage in nonbinary, nonhierarchic, and nonhegemonic articulations of metiza/o consciousness" that Aldama suggests are necessary for decolonization. This chapter introduced theories of performative intersubjectivity that move us toward new directions in organizing for social and ecological justice; each of the following chapters explores these in a variety of ways.

The first chapter presents activist histories of borderlands environmentalism from the era of Manifest Destiny to the present; it traces the dominant narratives of the mainstream environmental movement, ecofeminism, and the environmental justice movement to see when and how they occlude the environmental activism of Mexican American men and women across the Southwest, from the southern border of Texas to Northern California. I also excavate alternative histories of environmentalism to fill in gaps and realign the status quo stories that have shaped our approaches to environmental conservation, to social movement theorizing, and to alliance-building among organizations and movements. Much of the activism has been misrecognized or miscategorized; it has been pigeonholed as one type of activism—for labor rights, for example. Those of us who would learn from intersectional organizing never see the lessons that have been hard earned by those living and working in the ecological borderlands.

Chapters 2, 3, and 4 investigate ecological narratives in the cultural production of writers, artists, and filmmakers that self-identify as Chicana feminists working in Mexico and the U.S. Southwest. The texts featured in these chapters are tied together by subject matter and era of production: all were produced during the past three decades; this was a fruitful period that saw Chicana studies scholars carve out a rich theoretical foundation in response to white feminists and Chicano studies scholars. This period also saw a great deal of ecofeminist theory emerge to grapple conceptually with relationships of domination that oppressed both women and the natural world. The confluence of the growth of Chicana and ecological feminisms provides a rationale for the era of focus, but the art and writings share thematic matter as well. In each case, Chicana feminist themes of body, nature, and spirituality are present in ways that sometimes converge and sometimes diverge with ecofeminist discussions on the same subject matter. In each case, the ecological threads have been undertheorized in the criticism of those Chicana feminist works—this book brings attention to the environmental themes that are present throughout this body of diverse works.

*[margin annotation: how she is intervening in and/existing scholarship]*

Chapter 2, "Misrecognition, Metamorphosis, and Maps in Chicana Feminist Cultural Production," offers an ecocritical reading of texts that are seldom considered for their ecological import. I look at the widespread theme of cartography as an important way to chart and thus reclaim symbolic space in a nation that would erase Mexican American cultural presence even as it militarizes the border as an attempt to eradicate the physical presence of Mexican Americans. I pay special attention to how the different modes of art production examined (e.g., murals, autobiography, performance art) not only reclaim symbolic space in different ways but also stage opportunities for transformation in the artist and her audience. More than metaphor, these cartographic representations spatialize historical and contemporary relationships among humans, nature, and spirit others, and point the way forward toward a more just social and environmental configuration.

*[margin annotation: ✳]*

Chapter 3 moves from cartography to the related representational strategy of autotopography as seen in Amalia Mesa-Bains's altar installations. The artist is best known for her "domesticana" displays that use the critical juxtaposition of objects on display to tell personal and collective stories. These stories both celebrate and critique the domestic space and other facets of "women's culture." I read both the earlier domesticana altars and Mesa-Bains's later earthworks-inspired installations through an ecocritical lens. My aim is twofold: first, to put more emphasis on a recycling aesthetic in her early work that not only traces its way back to Tomás Ybarra-Frausto's rasquache sensibility but can also be seen in Mesa-Bains's own reuse of altar pieces in later exhibits; juxtaposed with the coinciding display of physical excess and feminine glamour, this aesthetic offers a critique of capitalism that has interesting ecological implications—we have not seen this kind of environmental practice before. Second, I trace how the artist's understanding of "nature" evolves from metaphor to material force over the course of her career. Following insights from object-oriented ontologists and Mesoamerican indigenous worldviews, if we take objects seriously in their own agentic capabilities, Mesa-Bains's altars come alive in new ways. They are historical narratives that trace colonialism's legacy; they are personal narratives of subjugation and resistance; they are spiritual sites of transformation; and they are ecosystems where the natural elements are allowed to act over us—they are sites where object-agents push back against and through us rather than altar-tables where we place the object-tools to be wielded by autonomous human-subjects.

In chapter 4, I move to film and offer an in-depth case study of a single documentary, *Señorita Extraviada*, directed by Lourdes Portillo. In this chapter, the case-study approach allows me to offer an ecocritical reading of a film that has received much scholarly attention, but never from an environmental viewpoint. This chapter builds on insights from the prior chapters on artists' use of affect to create new relationships with their audience, and it merges those discussions with assemblage theory to consider the unique role of filmmaking in the creation of new subjects. I argue that this film creates new subjects within the text (i.e., new readings of the humans, landscapes, and spirit configurations within the film) and that it *can* create new kinds of action-oriented subjects within the human community of spectators that view it. However, in its case-study approach, this chapter also employs reception analysis to look at the effectiveness of filming strategies that could potentially raise social and ecological consciousness. These findings have implications that bear on the other chapters on cultural production as well: How can artists negotiate their portrayal of complicated histories that do not fit within easily recognizable status quo stories, especially to an audience that may already be complicit in the representational trauma artists are combating?

I move from one case study to another; chapter 5 yields an in-depth analysis of a single organization, a women's center in New Mexico that draws women interested in personal skill-building and empowerment as well as those interested in broader change for social and ecological justice. I use ethnographic methods and document analysis of the news stories, brochures, and videos by the center to analyze how narratives about the environment are articulated in the everyday activities of contemporary activists in the U.S. Southwest. Similar to the chapters on cultural production, one of the draws in studying this particular organization is that its mission is *not* explicitly environmental; nevertheless, ecological consciousness is woven throughout the center's focus on women's empowerment in a way that can teach us something new about the intersection between social and ecological justice.

Taken together, each chapter explores strategies that seek to decolonize environmental theory and the academic disciplines in which it is produced. As such, this project is as much about methodology as it is about Chicana feminist approaches to environmentalism. One of its key premises is that feminist thought is limited by the marginalization of ecofeminism and an unwillingness to work through knotty debates that have haunted ecofeminist genealogies, such as disciplinary divides and tensions over essentialisms linked to theories of the body, spirituality, and the character of the woman-nature link. Moreover, the literatures of Chicana studies remain marginal to both feminist studies broadly and ecofeminist philosophy in particular. In bringing the fields of ecofeminist philosophy and Chicana studies together with posthumanist, materialist philosophies that theorize how the connections among the fields might produce new ways of knowing and being in the world, this project aims to join scholarly efforts at decolonization. *Ecological Borderlands* does this by deconstructing given genealogies of activism and theory production and by challenging the disciplinary divide in environmental and ecofeminist research that separates humanities-based approaches from social science approaches of study. In addition to putting pressure on the limitations of disciplinarity in  the academy, these chapters show how writing, art, and activism can produce decolonizing efforts that scale from reworking individual selves toward efforts at remaking movements for ecosocial justice.

The interdisciplinarity of this project is necessary to address what Chela Sandoval theorizes as "inner and outer technologies that construct and enable the differential mode of social movement and consciousness" (3). In highlighting psychic, or inner, technologies and social, or outer, technologies that drive social change, Sandoval proposes that a "methodology of the oppressed" enacts a democratic move toward coalitional consciousness. The cultural production under examination in chapters 2, 3, and 4 critiques modes of representation that currently give shape to thought and that, in turn, materialize our realities. Interventions in colonizing representations challenge us to critique oppressive systems and begin to vision ourselves outside those subjugations—that is, analysis of cultural production demonstrates how we might put "inner technologies" that create oppositional consciousness to work, and how we might performatively create a new self that is recognizably embedded within an array of ecological body/nature/spirit relations. Similarly, investigation of environmental activism in chapters 1 and 5 explores movement politics, including "outer technologies" that create new subjectivities, new communities, and new movements for social and ecological justice.

However, practices that demonstrate "outer technologies" are not entirely distinct from those that employ "inner technologies." In fact, as this introduction suggested, it is fruitful to challenge dichotomies between mind and body, culture and nature, and inside and outside. *Ecological Borderlands* theorizes the interaction between inner and outer technologies in ways that do not place so much distance between the inside of the self and the outside, between the self and the community. For example, cultural production not only shapes how we think about ourselves and our environments (i.e., its interpretation acts as an inner technology), but it also draws us together for collective action and galvanizes movement. Affect can travel among an artist and her audience and can connect the inside of one self with multiple others (e.g., other spectators, the art in question, and the objects, memories, emotions, landscapes, futures, or pasts that it conjures). The chapters on cultural production and direct action relate to each other, but each sets to motion new deployments of environmental feminist thought, and each focuses on different technologies or practices of intersubjectivity that might motivate coalitional activism. The chapters on organizations and social movements (chapters 1 and 5) bookend those on cultural production and you will see that shared themes and practices weave their ways through and across each chapter. My hope is that the commonalities of theme and method as well as the points of divergence (how a film is not like a mural, for example) will serve as starting points for further conversation.

## CHAPTER 1

# Borderlands Environmentalism

## *Historiography in the Midst of Category Confusion*

> The ecopolitical scope of subaltern envi-
> ronmentalism might be impossibly broad
> and diffuse in its political impact: corporate
> accountability, cultural and media criticism,
> worker organization, human rights, indigenous
> self-determination, social justice, international
> solidarity, sustainable development, worker
> health and safety. This is an ambitious wish
> list, but also a necessary consequence of the
> heterogeneity at the grassroots, a heterogene-
> ity which constantly moves toward transna-
> tional spheres of interaction and cooperation.
>
> —Soenke Zehle, "Notes on Cross-Border
>    Environmental Justice Education"

> Category confusion is a crucial component in
> threshold theories. When we enact threshold
> theorizing, we shift "betwixt and between"
> established categories, enacting what I've
> elsewhere described as both/and/neither/nor
> thinking—negotiations between (and within)
> affirmation and negation—that facilitate the
> invention of additional possibilities.
>
> —AnaLouise Keating, *Transformation Now!*

Chicana and Mexican American women's diverse ecological practices might
be understood as a form of subaltern environmentalism that is not readily
grasped through categories of analysis such as *ecofeminism* or *environmental*

*justice*, but if we begin inquiry within the category confusion that ensues, we may find new directions for building ecological alliances. While mainstream environmentalism has focused on issues such as climate change and wild-life preservation, and the environmental justice movement has critiqued the largely white and middle-class bias of the mainstream movements and organi-zations (e.g., Greenpeace, Sierra Club), the environmental justice movement is overdetermined by a focus on toxicity. This focus stems from the origin of the environmental justice movement, which began as a response to the place-ment of landfills and burning facilities in the communities of people of color. Ecofeminist literature shows a broader array of concerns, such as the gendered effects of toxicity; the fact that women are more likely to live or be employed in areas that are ecologically fragile; women's efforts to create spiritual connec-tions to the land; and representations of women's connection with the natu-ral environment in art and literature. The environmentalism of the activists collected here encompasses ecofeminist and environmental justice concerns and enlarges them. It raises questions regarding the devaluation of ecological knowledge that is based on a long-standing awareness of the land and wild-life that many communities in the Southwest have tried to retain. As Zehle's epigraph shows, a diverse movement toward epistemological and ontological modes of decolonization is emerging in this environmental praxis. This chap-ter makes its way through category confusion in the ecological borderlands and positions activist histories through an interdisciplinary lens that better captures the multiplicity of Chicana and Mexican American women's envi-ronmentalism in the Southwest.

To tell decolonizing histories, this project details not just the stories that have been told about Chicana and Mexican Americans' environmental activ-ism but also probes alternative sources and movements for new points of con-nection across environmental histories. This effort takes up Emma Pérez's call to multiply and fracture groups in ways that resist their easy consolidation into a monolithic, reified entity such as the "Chicano community" (1999);[1] it does the same with the notion of "environmentalism" as it disrupts the narrative of America's history of environmentalism. To this end, I discuss the limitations of mainstream environmental movements for their exclusions of Chicana/o and Mexican American activists and perspectives. I then address how ecofeminist and environmental justice movements may have improved on some of the failures of the mainstream movement but still fail to recognize Chicana/o and Mexican American struggles in their complexity. Finally, I turn to alternative sources from which to understand these struggles. Using an interdisciplinary framework, this chapter looks at activism such as participation in marches, boycotts, and justice-oriented organizations *and* at cultural production and the stories artifacts tell about communities and their relationships with the environment and more-than-human world. Ecofeminist studies often focus on social science approaches or humanistic approaches to study, but rarely do scholars bridge the disciplinary divide in theorizing women's relationships to their environment. Environmental justice researchers, on the other hand, have been largely preoccupied with social science approaches to human-nature relations and miss the role of cultural production in the construction of ecological subjectivities.[2]

In addition to consulting sources from varying sites of activism, this historical review is also a regional one that highlights Chicana/o and Mexican American activism in the U.S. Southwest, including Texas, New Mexico, Arizona, and California—states that border Mexico and that comprise the region from which Chicana/o borderlands theory grows. These states also share ecological characteristics to which their populations have struggled to adapt under changing political and economic conditions. Borderlands theory may be useful to understand ecoactivism in the region if it is seen not only to refer to the symbolic and material conditions of life on the border, but also to displacement from ecological belonging and strivings to reroot. Laura Pulido exhorts the importance of regional histories such as this; she notes that several processes intersect to shape people's lives and their relationships to this land in particular: "economic restructuring, internationalization, and immigration" (2009, 280). These processes shape both the relationships possible among people and those between people and the land, yet they also yield unique directions for resistance. Given a history of forced displacement across the region, this chapter concludes with an analysis of strategies that affirm a sense of community without reification. It affirms a sense of place-belonging without incurring either lococentric xenophobia or loss of a transnational framework that can strengthen and enliven environmental movements.

## Limitations of Mainstream U.S. Environmental Movements

American environmentalism, like American feminism, is told through a wave model of historical advancement: the first wave tracks the progressive conservation and preservation movements of the late 1800s, which emerged as a response to the overhunting of big game and the massive deforestation from development. These movements led to the formation of national parks and the forest service. The second wave of the contemporary environmental movement gathered momentum in the 1960s and 1970s with a focus on

27

environmental toxicity, which broadened the conservation scope of the earlier movement. The third wave began in the 1980s with the recognition of an increasing number of hazards (e.g., acid rain, ozone depletion, poor air quality, and accelerating species decline and extinction). This era saw a fracturing and diversifying of the mainstream environmental movement. Diversification has occurred in both the specialization of organizations (e.g., campaigns to save endangered species, clean up water pollution, or slow climate change) and in ideological orientation. More radical movements such as deep ecology, ecofeminism, and environmental justice challenge and in some cases expand the work of mainstream environmentalists.[3] The proliferation of environmentalisms does not represent a failure of solidarity. Rather, "this increased diversity has allowed environmentalism to fill (and create) many niches within our society and, as in nature, increased diversity may lead to greater resiliency in social movements" (Dunlap and Mertig 1992, 7). Resiliency is important to note, although we should disrupt the narrative that situates *all* environmental activism as an outgrowth of mainstream efforts. The mainstream environmental movement bolstered American identity by exclusion, protecting the well-being of middle- and upper-class white citizens while invisibilizing and exploiting indigenous, working-class, immigrant, and racialized communities. While the wave model offers a starting point to understand current environmental activism, a historical context that starts with the lives and histories of those living in the borderlands during these historical shifts paints a different picture.

## EMPIRE THROUGH WESTWARD EXPANSION AND CONSERVATION

The history of westward expansion across the United States is popularly framed as inevitable, as Manifest Destiny—a rightful claiming of land and its riches—yet it was a fraught process in which tensions about gender, race, class, and sexuality were tied to the land. Antonia Castañeda's frontier history in California reviews the records that were drafted by popular historians of the time (bankers, lawyers, and other elites). The records reveal racialization at work: they narrativize Mexican men as lazy and dangerous; women were largely absent from their accounts, yet when present, there were clear demarcations between "Spanish" women, elites who were seen as "morally, sexually, racially pure," and "Mexican" women, who were "immoral, and sexually and racially impure" (1990, 9). These stereotypes reflect the social Darwinism of the time that used biological and social claims of inferiority to legitimate war and expansion. Simultaneously, such representations constructed a counter-ideal of white Victorian femininity and, although Castañeda does not note it, of white masculine virility and work ethic. Women were racialized and sexualized differently depending on the needs of Anglo settlers; marriage into wealthy "Spanish" landowning families required the deracination of some women against the hyperracination of others. The racialization of indigenous and mestizo populations in the Southwest provided ideological justification for westward expansion and the integration of Texas; it reinforced a consolidated post–Civil War American identity against the new *other*. Castañeda writes that the second half of the nineteenth century, from the signing of the Treaty of Guadalupe Hidalgo onward, marks Mexican Americans as dispossessed, suspect citizens in a new nation, made "foreigners in their native land" (2001, 120).

In effect, the signing of the treaty, the dispossession and seizure of lands belonging to Mexican Americans, and the westward migration of white settlers during the Great Depression reterritorialized the American Southwest, erasing the history and presence of existing indigenous and mestizo communities. In so doing, white settlers rescripted the land as the "rugged West" to be dominated and developed by incoming settlers. This action also included setting certain areas aside to maintain controlled zones of "pure wilderness." In fact, the reterritorialization of the Southwest is an effect of legislation that is often perceived to represent the earliest roots of the U.S. environmentalist movement: programs to set aside national parks and wildlife areas (Ybarra 2007, 2). The wilderness ideal is criticized by contemporary scholars for its rural focus that renders urban spaces unimportant to the environmental movement, but is less often recognized for the role it played in "Americanizing" the West through the dispossession and othering of Mexican and indigenous Americans.

The second and third waves of environmentalism can also be reoriented by virtue of their exclusions. The second stage of the environmental movement emerged in the 1960s and 1970s with a focus on environmental toxicity, and the 1980s onward saw a further fragmentation and diversification of environmental movements. Occurring alongside new social movements such as the women's liberation movement, the antiwar movement, and nationalist movements such as the Black Panthers and the Brown Berets, activists borrowed strategies and rhetoric from other movements of the time and those that preceded them, such as the civil rights movement. However, little sustained critique of the classed, raced, and gendered nature of environmental security reached the mainstream organizations at this time. African Americans, Native Americans, and Latinos were organizing in grassroots efforts rather than participating in mainstream environmental organizations (Freudenberg and Steinsapir 1992). "Racial-ethnic activists involved in environmental issues did not always articulate them as such ... and others were simply opposed to the environmental movement itself, seeing it as a challenge to civil rights activism" (Pulido 2009, 276). There are many reasons for this, one of which is the antipathy toward the perceived protection of "nature" and the continued ignorance of human suffering based on racial, ethnic, and class oppression in communities populated by people of color. Especially in the case of the Southwest, the protection of the land came at the cost of stripping indigenous and Mexican American people from their rights to land.

## EMPIRE AND THE NIMBY MENTALITY

Although many conservation-based organizations continued to grow throughout the past several decades, grassroots activists increasingly focused on human health problems. The 1962 publication of Rachel Carson's *Silent Spring* galvanized environmentalism at the time. It exposed the dangers that pesticides pose to human and ecological health, greatly increasing the visibility of the movement. Following the explosion of interest in *Silent Spring*, Carson and others made advances in research that showed the dangers of incinerators, chemical runoff from industrial sites, and other hazards. With this new information, environmental organizations made concerted efforts to reduce or relocate toxic hazards such as pesticide spraying, incinerator or nuclear-plant placement, and so on; this environmental approach has come to be known as *not in my back yard* or *NIMBY*. Activists in the environmental justice movement argue that race and class backgrounds of populations matter tremendously in the ability to prevent toxins from entering a community. A consequence of the NIMBY mentality is the relocation of toxins from the neighborhoods of those with relatively more privilege and power to communities that have fewer resources to defend themselves. Benjamin Chavis has called this *environmental racism*—"racial discrimination in environmental policy-making and the enforcement of regulations and laws, the deliberate targeting of people of color communities for toxic waste facilities, the official sanctioning of the life-threatening presence of poisons and pollutants in our communities, and the history of excluding people of color from leadership in the environmental movement" (qtd. in Adamson, Evans, and Stein 2002, 4). Perhaps the two most important examples of environmental racism across the borderlands region include the industrialization of agriculture in the U.S. Southwest and the maquiladorization along Mexico's northern border.

The industrialization of agriculture in the United States, including the advancement of pesticide technologies, coincided with the implementation of the Bracero Program (1942–64) that encouraged Mexican immigration to meet the needs of agribusiness in the United States. Federal policies like the Bracero Program encouraged Mexicans to immigrate under conditions that increased their vulnerability (Peña 2005, 97). The othering process that continued through the Bracero Program produced an exploitable labor force even as it produced areas of the West as either wilderness/conservation zones or development zones. Development zones subject both the earth and the laborers to toxic chemicals while the workers labor long hours in backbreaking conditions. The Bracero Program may have ended in 1964, but Mexican Americans and immigrants from Mexico and Central America continue to be exploited and poisoned in agricultural fields across the Southwest. Without an immigration system in place that formally welcomes workers, immigrant laborers may have even fewer protections now than in the past when the Bracero Program was a recognized government policy. The concealment of agribusiness and its laborers, along with the concentration of pesticide use in farming that largely employs vulnerable populations, should be considered part of the NIMBY mentality; the costs of environmental degradation are distributed differentially, fostering security for privileged citizen-consumers and invisibilizing the land and bodies that bear the brunt of costs.[4]

In addition to agricultural production, the maquiladorization of the border zone as a result of the Border Industrialization Program and the North American Free Trade Agreement (NAFTA) reflects the NIMBY mentality. The ecological destruction and violence against women on the border is unprecedented. Locating production on the northern border of Mexico separates capital from labor, removing the social, economic, and environmental costs of the production of goods consumed in the United States and elsewhere (Biemann 1999); production does not occur in America's backyard, but in the free-trade zone just across the border. Maquiladoras primarily draw young women from other regions of Mexico for employment that supports not only their own livelihoods, but those of their families as well. While industrialization of the border and the subsequent economic and physical violence to women and the environment is a product of the political and economic relationship between the United States and Mexico, similar phenomena can be witnessed across the globe. This phenomenon has caused physicist and environmental activist Vandana Shiva to ask, "Are we going to move into a[n] era of environmental apartheid, where the North becomes clean and stays rich while the South stays poor and becomes the toxic dump of the world?" (qtd. in Platt 1998, 142).

# Interrogations of Environmental Justice and Ecofeminist Activism

## ENVIRONMENTAL JUSTICE

The environmental justice movement critiques the NIMBY mentality by recognizing the roles that race, class, and (to some extent) gender play in environmental issues. *Environmental justice* is broadly defined as "the right of all people to share equally in the benefits bestowed by a healthy environment. We define the environment, in turn, as the places in which we live, work, play, and worship" (Adamson, Evans, and Stein 2002, 4). Unlike mainstream environmental organizations, the environmental justice movement draws a more racially and class-diverse group of constituents together and is largely mobilized by grassroots efforts responding to specific local harms, such as high levels of toxins in a local water source. Despite greater attention to the role of privilege in one's experience of environmental security, the movement has its limitations (or, at the least, popular genealogies of it do).

The literature of environmental justice most closely associates the movement with African American grassroots activism. Genealogies of environmental justice that primarily situate the movement as an outgrowth of the civil rights movement (Bullard 1999; Bullard and Wright 1992) and studies that exclusively highlight the burden of ecological devastation borne by African Americans (Bullard and Wright 1992; Taylor 1989) serve an important function—they make clear how health and environmental well-being has always been a racial project and they show how civil rights rhetoric and organizing strategies such as boycotts and protests helped stage successful campaigns. However, these genealogies risk reifying the movement and excluding other histories because they situate the movement solely within a U.S. national context, occluding struggles that occur outside the United States as well as a *transnational* perspective such as that foregrounded by Vandana Shiva. Last, a strong focus on equal human rights to a healthy environment emphasizes the movement's anthropocentrism.

Aside from its historical framing, another limitation of the literature is its disciplinary narrowness. Until recently, the literature of environmental justice has almost exclusively derived from the social sciences (Sze 2002; Peña 1998a). Undoubtedly, the justice movement has legitimized itself through studies such as the Commission for Racial Justice's report (1987) that revealed evidence that communities of color are disproportionately burdened by the placement of hazardous waste. In wielding the epistemic authority of quantitative data toward social and environmental justice aims, grassroots activists and their allies have influenced policy and coerced corporations to work with them to improve waste output from the production process. Chicana/o and Mexican American grassroots activists have used these strategies and others to raise their concerns and earn allies. However, efforts that do not fit the narrowly sociological mold or demonstrate active resistance through protests, picketing, political pressure, or litigation are not easily recognized as belonging to the movement. Chicana/o and Mexican American activists have deployed a variety of strategies toward the aim of public education and community-wide resistance, including the use of theater of the oppressed (e.g., Houston and Pulido 2005), literature (e.g., Viramontes 1996), and murals (e.g., Hernández 2003), for example. The multiplicity of these struggles—that they cannot be easily identified by disciplinary eyes as belonging to a Chicana/o nationalist, workers', or environmental movement; that they employ a variety of tactics to subvert oppressive interlocking systems of racism, classism, sexism, and coloniality—situates them in the interstices of movements and disciplines. This interstitial borderlands environmentalism is easily misrecognized.

Finally, much environmental justice literature remains androcentric. Some authors note that women make up a large percentage of the activists in the movement (Visgilio and Whitelaw 2003; Prindeville 2003; Peña 1998a), but gender analysis is not yet mainstreamed despite the significance of gender asymmetry in the effects of environmental degradation. Platt summarizes,

> [There is] extensive damage that many toxins cause to women's reproductive systems. In the Third World, occupational divisions of labor created by invasive "development" programs have different effects on women than on men. Women are less likely than men to profit from the introduction of a cash economy and more likely to experience increased manual labor. And in the move from a rural to urban environment necessitated by environmentally destructive development, women are more likely than men to have to turn to prostitution as the only form of employment open to them. (141)

Platt's concerns are important for the U.S. context—including what U.S. third world feminists have called *internal colonies* (Córdova 1998)—and they remain relevant for the developing world, requiring a transnational understanding of development and its effects. As in mainstream environmentalism, women's voices and perspectives are marginal to the literature of the environmental justice movement; where present, they are portrayed as a special case study (i.e., the Mothers of East Los Angeles) rather than incorporated into the body of the environmental justice movement, reorienting its interests and analyses.[5]

# Ecofeminism

Unlike the environmental justice and mainstream environmental movements, ecofeminism has always taken as its object of study the gendered nature of environmental degradation and the linked oppressions of women and the natural environment. However, its association with white Western feminism has turned some women of color away. For example, Gwyn Kirk's "Ecofeminism and Chicano Environmental Struggles: Bridges across Gender and Race" (1998) develops a social constructivist position that sees environmental activism as an extension of the care and subsistence work that women in general, including the Chicanas in her study, already do. Kirk also specifically addresses the connections between spirituality and politics in order to create more coalitional space between Chicana studies and ecofeminism as well as to mitigate against the too-easy dismissal of theories that address spiritual concerns: "Many Native American, African American, and Chicano environmentalists do not seem to polarize spirituality and politics as some ecofeminists do" (179). In addition, she warns against the folding into ecofeminism of some women of color who do not claim this position for themselves. In efforts to appear more inclusive, such attempts erase the implicit and often explicit criticisms of racist and classist false universalisms some see within ecofeminism.

Although there is a dominant theme in ecofeminist theory that poses a relationship between the oppression of women and that of nature, such theories cannot be universalized. As just one example, borderlands environmental theories would take into consideration the specific ways that Mexicans, Mexican Americans, Chicana/os, and Native Americans have been constructed in policy and in historical and literary narratives as primitive and "natural" in contrast to more developed, cultured Anglos. These representations differ from the construction of white Euro-American women as closer to nature. Though it does not attend to environmental concerns, Castañeda's work (1990, 2001) begins to do this, showing how populations are racialized in opposition to each other, which, in turn, has ecological consequences.

Because this racialization is linked to the production of hierarchicalized labor relations, working-class Chicanas and Mexican American women continue to stand in different relationships to the landscape than do white, middle-class women that may be protected by their privilege. Devon Peña, in his essay "Los Animalitos: Culture, Ecology, and the Politics of Place in the Upper Rio Grande," details the roles that Chicanas have played in both the capitalist economy as well as in their communities as workers on family subsistence plots, canners, and cultivators of healing herbs, noting that knowledge of the cultivation and use of plants is passed down through female oral traditions. Thus, while attending to the many roles women play that bring them in contact with the nonhuman world, Peña asks, "Ecofeminism posits that women have a special, harmonious relationship with the natural world. To what extent do the experiences of Spanish-Mexican women affirm or reject this interpretation? What are the lessons that ecofeminists might learn from Mexicanas?" (1998b, 52).

Looking at Chicana and Mexican American women's activism from a strictly ecofeminist perspective may yield recognition that women *are* engaging in *ecological* activism, which is a perspective that mainstream environmental and Chicano studies have not highlighted in reading such struggles solely through an anthropocentric social justice framework. However, the full meaning of such strategies is hidden without greater attention to the broader context of Chicana and Mexican American women's activism for both social *and* ecological justice, including the ways in which they overlap and are conceptualized as one and the same. Activist Teresa Leal, who is known for her participation in campaigns for the United Farm Workers and for her membership in the Southwest Network for Environmental and Economic Justice coalition (SNEEJ), elaborates on the politics of naming and categorization: "People who are barely surviving can rarely have the luxury of haggling over terms. They can't afford to call it 'just' an environmental movement or 'just' a social movement.... Our movement was interconnected with human rights, labor rights, gender rights, and environmental rights and this reality—of interconnectedness—still guides our actions and campaigns today" (Adamson 2002, 47). This is an important point; in telling stories of mainstream environmentalism, the environmental justice movement, and ecofeminism, we must both relay and disrupt those narratives. I am not suggesting that there are firm boundaries around them nor am I suggesting that a borderlands environmental model is separate and different from each of those movements. In fact, as Anzaldúa was thinking through her own theories of the borderlands and new tribalism, she was following ecofeminist developments and found the symbolism of women healing the earth useful (Steele 2008). Rather, I ask what new perspectives on the environment become available if we begin theorizing out of the specific location of Chicana and Mexican American women's activism and art in this region. standpoint - theory approach

## Sources of Borderlands Environmental Activism

### LAND AND WATER USE

Since the acquisition of Mexican territory in 1848, lands in the U.S. Southwest have become fragmented—some were retained by land grants, some were privatized and sold to encroaching Anglos, and some were appropriated for public use such as national parks and railroads. Fragmentation disrupts human communities and regional ecologies because the border was drawn with political and economic interests in mind rather than with an awareness of the demands of bioregions. From the colonial era onward, "development" has dramatically altered social and ecological relationships in the borderlands. Railroads and commercial development displaced land-grant heirs and those too poor to hold on to their homes at the same time that they displaced species evolved with specific roles in the ecosystem. Irrigation and a shift from ranching to industrial farming is drying up the Rio Grande and the Colorado River and threatens the acequia water-management systems that have long sustained communities in the Southwest. Militarization of the border and the construction of border fences have led to violence at the hands of border patrols and vigilante militias like the Minutemen Project. They have also led to risky crossings and numerous human deaths even as they prevent migratory animals from making their journeys back and forth across the region. Militarization of the region has other impacts as well; land grants, which cannot be sold, are often leased for private use, which may include extraction of minerals or the production of weapons and energy. Uranium mining, for example, has had devastating impacts on the health of native communities.[6] Borderlands environmental activism has grown out of all of these concerns; to get a better picture of movement strategies, I focus on just a few.

Water availability is a keystone in the stability of a bioregion, and the Southwest (especially California) is experiencing years of record-breaking drought brought on by climate change (Seager et al. 2007). Concurrently, the number and severity of wildfires is increasing across Arizona, Colorado, and New Mexico. Acequia water systems are one of the more sustainable water-management strategies in the region. Communities in the Southwest have maintained acequia irrigation systems since Spain colonized Mexico. Today, New Mexico has more than one thousand acequias that are overseen by local communities that determine how water is used. These systems are important both for their ecological and cultural functions. Demonstrating centuries of adaptation to the local ecosystem, those that employ acequias have developed cultural norms and traditions that support and correspond to the natural world; thus, threats to acequia systems disrupt both human and nonhuman communities. Unfortunately, fragmentation of the land from commercial and suburban residential development has had a profound impact in the region. Peña describes what is at stake as a result of the land and water fragmentation and misuse occurring in the region:

When places are violated in this way, by the destructive forces of industrial extraction and other forms of maldevelopment, local people feel the changes intimately and personally as a loss that touches their sense of being in a most deeply troubling and disquieting manner. One farmer, Adelmo Kaber, even described this loss as a type of *susto*, a term that refers to an illness defined in ethnomedical folklore as a form of fright so intense and profound as to lead to the "loss of the soul." . . . Ecological devastation is the same as the malaise of "soul flight," susto. (2002, 66)

The deeply felt loss of a relationship to the land reflects the important role of embodied epistemologies as well as the role of affect that moves through the body (of the individual, of the community) to charge people toward change efforts. As a result of these geographic deterritorializations, activism has taken several different forms in the region, all in an effort to preserve the ecosystem and develop a tighter sense of belonging in place.[7]

The land-grant movement aims to reclaim lands given to families by Spanish and Mexican land grants prior to the U.S. annexation of Mexico. Success of the movement requires that Congress transfer lands from the U.S. Forest Service and U.S. Bureau of Land Management to land-grant heirs. While the movement continues today, it received attention in the 1960s as a civil rights struggle led by Reies López Tijerina that was connected to the symbolic reclamation of Aztlán, the Aztec and Chicano homeland of the Southwest. Protests and incendiary speeches brought the movement to the attention of many and helped fuel a separatist dream among Chicano nationalists (Rosales 1997). Interestingly, this strategy relies on liberal philosophies of the importance of legal mechanisms to guarantee rights as well as a radical notion of cultural separatism that refuses the authority of Anglo political power. As such, Tijerina's movement resisted the imperial logic that has ordered relations between Anglos and Chicana/os and Mexican Americans for nearly two centuries. This strategy acts out what Chela Sandoval (2000) has theorized as differential consciousness, the tactical switching among activist registers to outwit a ruling power.

If we hold on to Sandoval's theory of differential consciousness, it may be easier to understand why some communities have relied on culturally essentialist ideas to attain land rights. Laura Pulido's examination of Hispano grazing in New Mexico investigates the tactical appropriation of logics that position Hispanos as "naturally closer to the land" and less civilized than Anglos among grazing activists in the Southwest. The community used the tourist rhetoric that commodified their culture and redeployed assumptions about the "natural" and "unchanged" nature of their culture and relationship to the land to stake claims of land ownership and responsible use. Among the potential problems, Pulido warns that "the reification of cultural difference that

37

seems to exist beyond, or independent of, economic structures also has the potential to reproduce the existing social formation" (1998a, 135), yet she also notes that it is "difficult to imagine a strategy of resistance that does *not* use the master's tools" (137). The reification of cultural difference has the potential to isolate communities and mitigate against coalition because of calcifying "us/them" logics, but here this was not the case. The Hispano community created alliances with Navajos who supported their politics and they were able to challenge dominant ideas about poor land management among Hispanos and native peoples in the region.

Both efforts rely on claims of land belonging and an inherent connection between social and ecological justice to make their cases, although they use different tactics to do so. Both showcase flexibility and diversity in how communities reconfigure relationships among people as well as relationships between people and their environments. Similar tactics are put into play while addressing environmental workplace concerns in agribusiness in the Southwest and maquiladora industrialization along the U.S.-Mexico border. The struggles are localized and arise from different conditions, but what they share in common is a devaluation of the land that degrades or destroys the local ecosystems, replacing it with a monoculture (whether it is a maquiladora plant or a strawberry field). These labor cultures also rely on a devalued and easily exploitable workforce that is poisoned on a regular basis and expected to work hard for long hours at little pay; in both the factory and the field, the social, political, and economic conditions produce disposable laborers and environments.

## AGRICULTURE AND FACTORY LABOR

The agricultural industry in the United States has relied on the labor of Mexican immigrants and Mexican Americans from the time of the Bracero Program (1942–64) to the present. The program replaced many American laborers who left for service during World War II. This was also the era of pesticide development; as such, it brought Mexican nationals across the border into fields that they did not yet know to be poisonous. In the final years of the Bracero Program, César Chávez and Dolores Huerta founded the United Farm Workers (UFW) to secure higher pay, health insurance, retirement benefits, and freedom from pesticides for many workers. The UFW is still active today, but it is notable for its visibility and influence in galvanizing the Chicano nationalist movement throughout the 1960s and 1970s. Although the UFW works toward economic justice, it articulates those aims with environmental concerns that differently impact men and women laborers. As farm workers, women are at greater risk of facing sexual harassment, earn less money than their male counterparts, and come home to perform the majority of the reproductive labor. They also bear the harms of pesticide use in their bodies to a greater extent than men. Female farm workers have suffered miscarriages (Saxena et al. 1981); cancer of the breast, ovary, and cervix (McDuffie 1994); and natal problems, including giving birth to children with malformed or absent limbs and facial clefts (Nurminen 1995). Further, evidence shows that children are more susceptible to pesticide poisoning (Zahm and Ward 1998) and women, who are primarily responsible for the care of children, are more likely to be burdened with the emotional, financial, and physical labor of caring for children living with environmentally induced disabilities and illnesses.

There are historical links between factory and farm labor pools in the American Southwest. The maquiladorization of the border began in 1965 with the Border Industrialization Program—a political agreement between the Mexican and U.S. governments that would create new jobs in Mexico to replace U.S. jobs lost by the cessation of the Bracero Program. Even in 1965, before the escalation of the free-trade ethos that brought about NAFTA in the 1990s, the aim was to draw investment to Mexico and to provide jobs for workers while creating cheaper goods for American consumers. Jobs were especially scarce in the areas around the northern border, where the population swelled due to deportation efforts by the U.S. government (Tiano 1985). Feminist development scholars critiqued the program and NAFTA's extension of it for failures to bring economic benefits to the workers and the Mexican state. In addition to the fact that such work environments produce cheap labor, the working conditions are notoriously bad, including poor ventilation, long hours and lock-ins, and constant surveillance of workers' bodies and behaviors that includes control of their dress, comportment, and reproduction through pregnancy tests, sexual harassment, and assault.[8]

In addition to the violence brought upon women workers, maquiladorization degrades the environment and these harms are also gendered. Chilpancingo *colonia* provides a good case study. Chilpancingo is a neighborhood near Tijuana that was once inhabited by Metales y Derivados, a U.S.-based battery-recycling company that is now abandoned. Chemicals that seeped into the ground and water supply are having a pronounced effect on those who live in the town, and the owner of the company moved back to the United States and is avoiding arrest warrants charging him with "gross environmental pollution" (Sullivan 2006, 102). Linda Christensen, speaking with an activist who works with women on both sides of the border to protest human and environmental health hazards, summarizes what she has learned: "Lourdes described children born without brain stems, children whose parents slept

39

with them at night, fearing they would drown in their own blood from spontaneous nose bleeds, maquila workers who suffered miscarriages and birth defects, neighbors with abnormally high rates of cancer" (2006, 97). Women may be particularly susceptible to toxins because of the gendered nature of disease and reproduction as well as the socially constructed responsibilities of child care; because they comprise the majority of the cheap and flexible workforce, they are also more likely to be exposed to toxins for longer periods of time than their male counterparts. As a response, some of the factory workers formed the Chilpancingo Collective for Environmental Justice to pressure the U.S. and Mexican governments to clean up the factory site. They worked with other environmental groups on both sides of the border to hold factories in the area accountable for the poor health of the residents. After being featured in the documentary *Maquilapolis (City of Factories)* (Funari 2006), the collective joined the Community Outreach Campaign—a larger association of organizations that "includes dedicated activists on both sides of the border, mediamakers committed to social change, and most importantly a group of women factory workers struggling to bring about positive change in their world" ("Maquilapolis Community Outreach Campaign").

Attention to borderlands environmental struggles reveals parallel problems of toxicity and the development of monocultures that have gendered effects on those that work in the fields and in the factories. Activists in each of these sites combat these problems, but they do so by taking different approaches that grow out of their regional needs; direct action, as can be seen with activists in Chilpancingo, shows that because the problem is a transnational one structured by economic and political policy, activists do well to engage with women and organizations on both sides of the border. In contrast, activists in land and water struggles that focus on long-standing relationships to the land may find that localizing their activism is more effective. In each case, these struggles usually fall outside the purview of mainstream environmentalism, ecofeminism, and—given the specific gender focus—environmental justice. Borderlands environmentalism often exceeds the frames of interpretation that those movements bring to their conceptualization of environmental activism.

## Strategies of Borderlands Environmental Activism

This section focuses on the capacity to connect struggles to a multitude of movements and actors. This relational feature can enliven activists and avoid the reification of the movement and the identities of those that comprise it. Four technologies of intersubjectivity characterize this rhizomal borderlands environmentalism;[9] they include the use of spirituality, coalition-building, "translocal" and transnational framing, and cultural production as movement resources.

## THE PLACE OF SPIRITUALITY IN MOVEMENT POLITICS

Ecofeminism has been one of the few areas of feminist praxis to embrace spirituality (albeit unevenly) as a guide for ordering human and human-nature relationships. Spirituality has also been an important part of the environmental justice movement. The "Principles of Environmental Justice" from the First National People of Color Environmental Leadership Summit (1991) "affirms the sacredness of Mother Earth, ecological unity and the interdependence of all species, and the right to be free from ecological destruction" ("Principles"). In struggles for land, water, and workers' rights, activists deployed spiritual language and representations to several ends. UFW organizers incorporated images of the Virgin of Guadalupe in the organization's literature and protest art. Dolores Huerta, cofounder of the UFW, describes the Virgin as "a symbol of the impossible, of doing the impossible to win a victory, in humility"  (Wolfteich 2005, 163). Further examples of the integration of spiritual, social, and environmental politics in the farmworkers' struggles can be seen in their modes of protest. For example, to initiate a strike against grape growers, farmworkers met in the church of Our Lady of Guadalupe to cast their votes for the strike. Banners of the Virgin were carried alongside banners for the UFW at the head of marches. The most visible march involved thousands of farmworkers and allies in support of the grape strike; the walk, which Chávez named a pilgrimage, lasted several days and covered two hundred miles before concluding in Sacramento on Easter Sunday. According to Chávez, "We wanted to be fit not only physically but also spiritually, and we wanted to stress nonviolence even more, build confidence, and have more visible nonviolent tactics" (qtd. in Wolfteich 2005, 165). The ritualized pilgrimage marked the workers and the land they traversed as sacred. Such an act both highlights the farmworkers' struggles as spiritual and follows other traditions in Chicana/o activism of reclaiming public space through theater, muraling, and other acts of protest.

Fasting also played a large role for Chávez, representing an act of sacrificial penance and a commitment to social change ("Story of Cesar Chavez").  Hunger strikes have an ancient history around the world, but the visibility of Chávez's actions created a legacy for other Chicano activists, including faculty and students fighting for greater Chicano and comparative ethnic studies support at UCLA in 1993 and Stanford University in 1994. At the University of Southern California, supporters seeking rights for cafeteria workers cited the

UFW though ritualized fasting and the passing of Chávez's personal crucifix among protesters. Houston and Pulido note how this performatively links to a cultural memory of legitimized activism and spiritual wealth:

> Chávez's cross represented such a "technology of memory" that linked the USC workers to "past performance" of regional labor politics. Specifically, it represented the historical exploitation of Mexican workers and acknowledged the extent to which they are no longer confined to the agricultural sector, but are central to the manufacturing and service industries. In short, the staging of cultural memory became a strategic site of political intervention and praxis. (2005, 336)

There is also a rich history of spiritual activism along the U.S.-Mexico border. I address this in more detail in later chapters, but here I will give two examples. Border organizations such as Voces sin Eco protest the murders and the devaluation of women in Juárez by painting the city with crosses, resacralizing the land and women in the region while claiming rights that were denied by NAFTA's lax standards for human and environmental protections. Further, organizations such as the Women's Intercultural Center (WInC) in Anthony, New Mexico, were started by nuns in support of women in the region and the daily issues they face, such as threat of deportation and lack of education about rights, violence, and environmental degradation. WInC's daily morning meditations supported women's spiritual leadership in the community and encouraged personal reflection and social consciousness-raising through prayer. Moreover, WInC and other organizations in the area hold an annual mass at the border to recognize those who have died in the crossing and to protest the militarization of the border and the economic and political conditions that create deprivation and environmental degradation in the region.

The importance of spirituality in guiding movement politics and revitalizing activists cannot be understated. In this book's introduction, I defined *spirituality* as it is understood by activists as "consciousness and connection" (Pulido 1998b, 721). Huerta, in speaking of the use of spiritual tactics in the UFW protest, also frames spirituality as a relational energy: "I consider nonviolence to be a very strong spiritual force because it's almost like an energy that goes out and it touches people" (Harding). Spirituality acts as a technology of connection; it is a way to acquire a sense of ourselves as intersubjectively connected to human- and nature-others through affective work—constructing shared histories, shared emotions, shared visions for just futures. While the interhuman connections of the movements for workers' rights have been highlighted in much of the Chicana/o studies literature, connections between workers and their environments remain at the heart of these struggles, and the effort to resacralize both workers and their environments should not be ignored.

## THE PLACE OF COALITION IN MOVEMENT POLITICS

The use of coalitions is another common element in ecosocial justice organizing. Coalition-building has a long history in Chicana/o studies, articulated in Gloria Anzaldúa's (1999) sense of *facultad* or mestiza consciousness that enables a critical consciousness derived from crossing borders and that can facilitate the creation of alliances. Similarly, Moraga and Anzaldúa's *This Bridge Called My Back* (1983) represents one of the most comprehensive attempts to create coalition among women of color writers in the United States. These writings on the praxis of negotiating a sense of home, crossing borders, and building coalition across difference come from the lived experiences of women who not only have felt themselves to be bridge builders in their daily actions, but who have also seen the benefits of working collaboratively across organizations and movements. This section underscores the potential of developing alliances across a series of borders, including those that are identity-, issue-, and region-based.

In addition to mobilizing affect through the cultivation of spiritualized subjectivities, another reason the farmworker movement has been successful is its ability to make connections across the positionalities of its participants and allies and to point to the intersectionality of movements and issues. The UFW led several grape boycotts in the 1970s and '80s that received national and international attention. In 1986, Chávez initiated the Wrath of Grapes campaign "to draw public attention to the pesticide poisoning of grape workers and their children" ("UFW Chronology"). One of the most effective strategies of the boycott was to point out that farmworkers *and* consumers are affected by pesticide use. In describing the connections between the UFW struggles and ecofeminism, Ellen O'Loughlin uses an ecological concept to look at the many places women are in this system of production and consumption (in the field with pesticides, in the grocery store, in agribusiness management) to see how women are networked but nevertheless have different access to cultural, political, and economic resources based on differences of class, race, nationality, gender, and so on (150). In highlighting the relationalities among women (and men) with respect to the production and consumption of grapes, O'Loughlin shows how the UFW successfully broadened the scope of their protest and acquired new allies. Moreover, she writes, "by incorporating information about resource and environmental pollution into the arguments about worker health, the UFW specifically allies itself with more conventional environmental and conservation causes. This type of argument is meant to break down walls of classism and racism and evoke a true sympathy between farm workers and the rest of us" (152). The movement of affect (O'Loughlin calls it *sympathy*) connects people to each other and to the earth, which motivates and mobilizes this coalition.

The Southwest Network for Environmental and Economic Justice (SNEEJ), founded in 1990, is another coalition at the forefront of environmental justice activism in the Southwest. SNEEJ describes itself as "a people of color, intergenerational, multi-issue, regional, bi-national organization comprising 60 grassroots community-based, native, labor, youth and student groups and organizations working for environmental and economic justice in the southwest and western U.S. and northern Mexico" (Southwest Network for Environmental and Economic Justice). They also emphasize interculturality as central to their ability to challenge epistemologies that order social and ecological relations: "Overcoming cultural barriers has been essential to allowing us to impact policy beyond the local level" ("About Us"). This multicultural and multi-issue coalition relies on diversity to inform their decisions on regional and national initiatives; that is, this shifting, transversal epistemological stance balances the social and ecological concerns of constituent groups.[10] This group critiques mainstream environmental organizations that focus on conservation at the cost of addressing the marginalized populations that have been displaced in the name of conservation efforts. In centering knowledge production based on epistemological border crossing, it also suggests fluidity between subject positions (and the frames of reference that construct them) in a way that relies on a deep sense of relationality.

Las Comadres collective is another example of a multi-issue, multicultural, binational coalition that, among those surveyed here, offers the most explicit gender analysis of border issues. In addition to these coalitional elements, Las Comadres rely on interrogative forms of activism (i.e., theater of the oppressed and other forms of performance art); such performances invite spectators to question their own identities and access to privilege. Performances incite consideration of our relationships to social and ecological problems and the people that most directly bear the brunt of those problems. Their "1,000 Points of Fear—Another Berlin Wall?" campaign publicized the dangers of border militarization and anti-immigrant retrenchment by flying a banner across the border. They challenged the consolidation of artificial borders around racial fears and posit instead something like Anzaldúa's ideal for a border inhabited by the "new mestiza"—they sought a "transborder culture

44

of cross-pollination and non-dualism" (Berelowitz 1998, para. 14). In addition, Las Comadres critiqued NAFTA for exacerbating harms against women and the natural environment in the border region and regularly worked with groups such as SNEEJ to bring about changes in the borderlands. Although they aimed to *de*territorialize spectators through performances such as the "1,000 Points of Fear" protest that challenged spectators' ideas of belonging to a land and culture, Las Comadres' desire to *re*territorialize subjects in terms of Anzaldúa's mestiza consciousness shows awareness of the links between social and ecological justice and the need for coalitional efforts to address them.

## PLACE-CENTEREDNESS AND TRANSLOCALITY IN MOVEMENT POLITICS

I highlighted the role of place, including ecoregions and regional politics, earlier in this chapter; instead of an essentialist or universalizing representation of the borderlands, I pointed to the different social and environmental histories in Texas, for example, than in California or New Mexico. Here, I focus on the place-making strategies of activists: how do they position the movement as complex and locally situated while also communicating within a broader national and transnational context? In assessing strategies of scholars and activists, I employ the notion of "translocality" to explore meaning-making across multiple spatial scales in the name of ecosocial justice. I argue that translocal framing potentiates coalitional consciousness by expanding the notion of self and community, opening up multiple forms of belonging. In their article "Translocal Subjectivities: Mobility, Connection, Emotion," David Conradson and Deirdre McKay explain the concept of translocality as it is taken up by social geographers:

> Appadurai coined the term "translocality" to describe the ways in which emplaced communities become extended, via the geographical mobility of their inhabitants, across particular sending and destination contexts. Social communities that were once relatively localized become internationalized. A translocality is thus a place whose social architecture and relational topologies have been refigured on a transnational basis. At the same time, the term recognizes that localities continue to be important as sources of meaning and identity for mobile subjects. (2007, 168)

The field of Chicana/o studies emphasizes the migratory histories of borderland inhabitants and the artificiality of the border—for many, their families have lived in the area for generations before the border crossed them. As such, translocality is an apt concept with which to understand place-making efforts in the Southwest. Translocality negotiates the primacy of localization within diasporic populations, but it lacks a concrete sense of how locality is also linked to a specific bioregion. Borderlands environmentalists can contribute to the field of social geography through their work on ecological belonging in a translocal context.

Ecologists stress bioregional models of place-centeredness because of the boundedness of the ecozone that includes relatively stable relationships between plants and animals that, in turn, are connected to the soil, air, and water qualities of the zone. Deep ecologists argued for bioregional models of human environmental practice, yet environmental justice activists note that deep ecology sometimes fails to account adequately for how man-made social hierarchies evolve over time to give groups of people differential access to land, water, and other resources. In contrast, Peña offers a model of place-centered ("lococentric") subjectivity in which identity is tied to locality and ecosystem. Peña argues that, prior to the colonization of the Southwest by Spain and the United States, indigenous communities developed a coextensive, supportive relationship with the flora and fauna of their region in addition to preserving the soil and water quality (1998a, 2005). As mentioned earlier, degradation of those environments led to a disturbance of the bioregion as well as a profoundly disturbing deterritorialization of human subjectivities that disrupts the intersubjective relations between humans and their environments. Despite the benefits that place-centered philosophies provide over bioregionalist models that ignore the human social elements of a landscape, lococentrism comes with its own potential pitfalls. First, it raises questions about how one can develop place-centeredness, especially in a setting of migration, displacement, and privileged mobility that characterizes the translocality of the borderlands. Second, how can place-centered philosophies avoid the problem of xenophobia or the NIMBY mentality detailed earlier? Gwyn Kirk advises, "A sense of place needs to become a much wider concept that encompasses a sense of being connected to the whole planet so that I am not tempted to respect my place at the expense of yours" (1998, 193).[11]

Examples of place-centeredness in the work of Chicana/o and Mexican American artists are plentiful and, since I dedicate several chapters to them in this book, I highlight just one here: Juana Alicia's 2004 mural *La Llorona's Sacred Waters* on the theme of women, water, and globalization. The mural shows not just how our immediate spaces shape us, but also how transnational capitalism, infused with gender, race, and class hierarchies, shapes subjectivities and environments. Alicia's mural reclaims the San Francisco neighborhood where the mural is painted with the help of the community and, in so doing, marks out Chicana feminist symbolic space. In addition, she links the symbolism of the Aztec goddess of water, Chalchiuhtlicue, with a female figure often associated with a response to Spanish colonialism, La Llorona; the figures preside over scenes depicting water-related environmental struggles across the world, including antidamming struggles in India, water-privatization struggles in Bolivia, and activism against maquila industrialization and femicide along the Rio Grande. Situating her mural within the place-specific mythology of conquest in the Southwest, Alicia comments on the connections between colonialism and neocolonialism. A logic of domination links different regions and eras together and, in mapping them out, she invites her audience to think coalitionally of resistance. Lastly, in painting the mural, including women's bodies, in watery blues, Alicia underscores our inseparability from nature; her work clearly depicts how social relations shape our access to water, which in turn impacts our bodies and our livelihoods.

We can also explore two cases of activist histories cited earlier for their translocal dimensions and ability to deterritorialize subjects toward intersubjective, ecological belongings. The UFW makes connections to how the immediate locality of the fields extends into private homes across the country through the consumption of pesticide-treated fruit. The grape boycott linked farmworkers and consumers, establishing coalitional activism through recognition that the pesticides that afflict the farmworkers in the fields sit on the grapes as they make their journey into private homes, thus connecting the space of the field with the space of the home, and the materiality of the pesticide with that of the grape, the farmworker, and the consumer. Border activism is similarly translocal; the border is constructed, in part, through negotiations among the U.S. and Mexican governments and the corporations that inhabit the free zone. NAFTA increased migration to the border—pulling workers from all regions of Mexico, driving the repatriation of an earlier generation from the Bracero Program, drawing some across the border to seek a home in the United States and others to the border to protest the U.S. nationalism that militarizes the border. Transnational frames of activism are particularly important here because they avoid a NIMBY mentality—instead of moving an incinerator (or in the case of Chilpancingo, a battery factory) from one location to another, activists argue for a change in the politics of production.

Borderlands activists have been adept at balancing transnational analysis and alliance with a perspective on the specific local histories of struggle. The examples mentioned earlier illustrate negotiation among site-specific subjectivities, the environments that construct them, and the broader transnational processes that increasingly rework and reconstruct them in conjunction with other spaces and subjectivities. As a result, actors from different regions and different positionalities may become deterritorialized and then reconstituted as subjects more likely to understand their intersubjective coextensions with others (i.e., the human-others that make their clothes and electronics and pick their fruit and vegetables; the nature-others such as the degraded ecosystems where production occurs).

## Cultural Production and Chicana/o Environmentalism

Cultural production has already been mentioned briefly in some of the previous examples and is discussed extensively in other chapters for the role it plays in drawing attention to social and ecological injustices. From the perspective of Chicana/o studies historians, cultural production has also been important in reconceptualizing the way stories about the past have been told. For example, status quo stories of mainstream environmentalism that omit the role of race politics in setting aside large tracts of land for "conservation" remain important in that they establish trajectories that later historical narratives and cultural representations have not been able to shake off entirely. In line with current understandings of the performativity of identity, contemporary scholars and activists must wrestle with working within and troubling the subject positions that circumscribe Chicana/os and Mexican Americans that are created by these narrative sedimentations. These histories need to be deconstructed and rewritten in order to create possibilities for decolonial futures. One way to do so is to look to alternative historical sources such as the cultural production of marginalized groups to tell a counterhegemonic story.

Examples of cultural production that rewrite the history of Mexican American women's work for social and environmental justice include Helena María Viramontes's novel *Under the Feet of Jesus* (1996), which focuses on migrant workers in California's toxic fields from the perspective of its adolescent female protagonist; Juana Alicia's mural *Las Lechugueras* (1983), which depicts women lettuce pickers, some of them pregnant, working in the fields while pesticides are sprayed above; the performance art of Las Comadres mentioned earlier; and Vicky Funari's *Maquilapolis (City of Factories)* (2006), a documentary on border activism against the devaluation of women and the land along Mexico's northern border. Cultural production can be a critical tool of popular education—this is one of the reasons the UFW employed Teatro Campesino and so many other Chicana/o artists for their cause. According to community organizer Teresa Leal, "if the issue is introduced in a way that is simple, yet highly,

highly informative, it often triggers people's concerns and activism. That has been a concern for me, that writing about the natural environment and on contamination and globalism continues to be very, very elitist and inaccessible" (Adamson and Stein 2002, 25). Community-based art, murals, short stories, and theater invite spectators to grapple with issues that might otherwise be inaccessible to them, offering individuals new ways to understand their relationships to each other and to their environments outside of the narrow purview of academic discourse or the exclusions of mainstream environmental activism. Spectators are called, through an affective encounter with art, to rethink themselves with respect to their current human and nature-based communities and to reorient themselves through a reworked history of their past.

*potential for transformative experiences*

## Conclusions, Deterritorializations

This chapter explored historical accounts of the "victory narrative" of Manifest Destiny alongside early environmental efforts that fragmented lands inhabited by Mexican and indigenous communities. In revisiting early histories of conservation and conquest in the Southwest, I disrupted these status quo stories to show nation-building around the consolidation of a white, masculine national identity. The histories of the ecofeminist and environmental justice movements were also destabilized, pried open to see how they created their own exclusions; although much more work on this subject needs to be done and other genealogies could be drawn, this one traced how dominant historical narratives have misrecognized the histories of Chicana/o and Mexican American environmental activists. This chapter aims to set scholars of both ecofeminism and environmental justice into new motions to explore what is at stake in the genealogies of each movement as well as how each movement might shift to better recognize alternative epistemologies and activist strategies. Finally, this chapter highlighted Chicana/o and Mexican American epistemologies and activisms to draft, from an interdisciplinary perspective, a partial history of borderlands environmentalisms and the work they do toward decolonization. In contrast to mainstream environmentalism, ecofeminism, and environmental justice, which can be enhanced through deterritorializations that push them into new directions, the latter half of this chapter emphasized the deterritorializing nature already present in borderlands environmentalisms. These are environmentalisms that challenge how movements are conceptualized; rather  than seeing movements for workers, women, indigenous rights, and environmentalism as separate, such an approach is holistic and relational. Taking a closer look at the diversity of struggles, one also sees a more profoundly deter-ritorializing move in effect: an enactment of technologies of intersubjectivity. These technologies, such as the role of spirituality, translocal framing practices, coalition-building, and cultural production, challenge discrete categories of identity and emphasize processes of *becoming* that move toward more just, intersubjective understandings of the self. The supposedly bounded, autono-mous self is opened up to intersubjective human/nature/spirit relationalities.

# CHAPTER 2

# Misrecognition, Metamorphosis, and Maps in Chicana Feminist Cultural Production

It began with a dream where I was physically transformed. I was no longer body and flesh, eyes, hair, and teeth, but hills, valleys, orchards, forests. I had metamorphosed into a mountain range with eyes and volcanoes and bodies of water surging through me. As I extended my arms, I was a whole coast, and then I stretched into a continent. I was my own continent with many geographies. I could see lush forests, fields of abundance, the sands of desert terrain that were me. This was my physical landscape.... My writing has been a way to name the landscapes of emotions, to recognize those layers of experiences that have sculpted my ecosystem and have chiseled my herstory. As well, writing has been a path to forging my spiritual cosmology.

—Elba Rosario Sánchez, "*Cartohistografía: Continente de una voz*"

In the epigraph, Elba Rosario Sánchez's subjectivity unfolds as a landscape, a territory that is natural and earthy, shifting and eroding, and one that is constructed through the process of writing. Sánchez understands herself through her relations with her landscape, and she notes how becoming oneself is an ecological, cultural, and spiritual process. Moreover, writing is not an individual endeavor, but in writing herself and discovering her landscape, Sánchez invites others to recognize themselves in her poetry: "In this encuentro between writer and reader/listener, ser a ser, there occurs the possibility of a powerful process" (24). The writer develops a collective sense of self that is in relation with both the natural and built environment as well as with her human allies. Sánchez calls this writing "cartohistography"—more than autobiography, the author is explicitly drawing out an ontological (not merely symbolic, but actual, material) connection between her personal experiences, her intersubjectivity with others who may recognize themselves in her work, and the "physical, material space with its own geography, ecology, and cosmology" that she lays claim to in the materialization of herself through writing (26). The writing of self into history and onto the land can be seen in much of the literature in the emerging canon of Chicana/o studies, but it does not often get read as an ecological aesthetic so much as a strategy of belonging in the United States at a time when the increasing number of profiling laws (e.g., Arizona's SB 1070) make all Latinos suspect. While cartohistography does grow out of historical concerns about one's place in the nation, the notion is also illuminating in the ways it draws embodied relationships to the landscape and to spiritual forces: Sánchez expresses a desire for the self to grow coextensive with human, nature, and spirit others, which is further evidenced by her invitation to others to see themselves in her writing.

Questions of embodiment, spirituality, and the woman-nature link (or the relationship between humans and their environments) have been contested terrains within ecofeminist theory for the ways that some writers have drawn criticisms of essentialism; in this chapter I suggest that, while these themes have been dismissed as some of the most problematic elements of academic ecofeminism, the art and literature under study provide new ways to think about human-nature relations. In order to understand the representational strategies employed by the artists and writers studied here, we first need to recognize the ecological import of their work. The failure to fully recognize ecological narratives in Chicana feminist cultural productions occurs across Chicana/o studies, as Priscilla Solis Ybarra explains: "Chicana/o literary study has been complicit with overlooking Chicana/o writers' environmental insights, largely because the environment has been perceived to be a lesser priority than the seemingly more immediate needs of social equity" (2007, iii; see also Parra 1999). To be clear, there is a strong presence of Chicana/o and Mexican American scholars and activists in the field of environmental justice, as chapter 1 showed. However, scholarship in the field is largely situated in the social sciences and has a strong policy orientation. By bringing an ecocritical lens to visual and narrative cultural production in Chicana studies, we create more dialogue between social scientists and humanities-based researchers and better navigate the disciplinary divide—a divide that has already been bridged by Chicana/o artists and social-movement activists who have a long history of collaboration. Further, the discursive distance between Chicana/o studies and ecofeminism in the academy inhibits greater understanding of each of the fields, yet much can be gained by putting them into closer conversation.

To illustrate the problem of ecological misrecognition, consider Renato Rosaldo's response to Sánchez, in which he writes, "I'm not enamored of carto-histography as an organizing concept for your essay. I know what you mean by the term and I know how much you like to hold opposites in tension (like hot/cold, death/birth), but mapping a landscape and grasping a history/herstory do not fit together very easily as activities or forms of understanding" (2003, 53). Rosaldo grasps this concept as a metaphor only and fails to understand the ontological drive behind writing oneself into being and history through the legitimizing trope of the land. Moreover, such writing does not just use the trope of a "natural" self tied to the land to legitimize a subaltern voice, but also stakes territorial claims in a neo/colonial landscape. Sánchez's en-natured self is just that—one that is connected to the land and to other writers and readers, and not merely a symbol of becoming visible through writing. *Carto-histography* shares much in common with Gloria Anzaldúa's term *autohistoria*, which serves as a *testimonio* of her own personal history and tells a collective story that is rooted in the geography of the Southwest (and the psychological and metaphorical space of the borderlands more generally). While Rosaldo does not see how "mapping a landscape" and "grasping a history/herstory" fit together, for the writers and artists in this chapter, mapping the landscape—its political, ecological, and spiritual dimensions—is critical to developing self-awareness and to transforming both oneself and the surrounding landscape.

Rosaldo goes on to say, "Your concept of histocartography is more cerebral than your wonderful poem 'Me siento continente/I Feel Myself a Continent,' which is so sensuous and womanly" (53). In this, a number of Sánchez's key points are misrecognized: her struggle with multiple and conflicting identities (recognition of her whole self rather than just a gendered identity); her sense of continuity with others and the nonhuman world that is facilitated through her writing; and her coming to political consciousness as an activist in support of the United Farm Workers resistance to poor wages, toxicity, and environmental damage as a result of intersectional racial, gender, and classed injustice. Although she details these drives in the same essay, he has drawn links between "woman," "nature," and sexuality that he directly contrasts with the "all-too-cerebral" understanding of self that Sánchez has arrived at through reflection on her experiences. While people of color—and especially women—have been naturalized in colonial narratives, in the vein of social eco-feminists who aim to deconstruct the logic of domination, Sánchez plays with and destabilizes a number of binaries, including self/other, human/nature, culture/nature.[1] In exclaiming "I could see lush forests, fields of abundance, the sands of desert terrain that were me" (19), she names the multiplicitous aspects of herself that defy simple categorization while she gives us an account of her life that allows the reader to historicize and contextualize her en-natured approach to storytelling. Bringing an ecocritical reading to bear on the notion of cartohistography illuminates Sánchez's efforts to deconstruct the colonialist ordering logic that poses an individuated Cartesian subject separate and above nature and human others, and it challenges the notion that women of color are imbricated in nature without access to culture—the very process of writing self and land into being, of charting history through writing, as cartohistography suggests, points to this fact. Of course, while this exchange is exemplary, Rosaldo is not alone in his misrecognition. The remainder of this chapter emphasizes the ecological impulses behind place-making; it highlights strategies for ecosocial justice from artists and writers transforming interpersonal relations at the local, regional, national, and transnational scales—a metamorphosis that refigures body/landscape/spirit relations, mapping new selves, new lands, and new futures.

## Ecological Themes in Chicana/o Literature

Chicano writers strongly emphasize their places in the built environment and just as strongly resist displacement through tenacity and a strong map of landscape and memory. They inscribe their belonging not only in maps of the imagination but also through their writing.

—Tey Diana Rebolledo, "Landscaping a Poetics of Belonging"

Chicana literature has consistently offered alternative methods of conceptualizing space not only by noting how social change must be spatialized but also seeing and feeling space as performative and participatory, that is, by refusing a too-rigid binary between the material and discursive.

—Mary Pat Brady, *Extinct Lands, Temporal Geographies*

### AZTLÁN: PLACE-MAKING IN THE CHICANO NATIONALIST MOVEMENT

From the beginning of the Chicano nationalist movement, artists and writers have been called on to help unify the community, build a political identity, and envision new futures. In the early 1960s, artists were recruited by the United Farm Workers (UFW) to create posters, banners, and other artifacts to draw allies and support for farmworkers who work long hours, are paid little, and work in dangerous and toxic conditions. Building on the successes of the UFW and the growing politicization of Chicana/os and other marginalized groups throughout the 1960s, *El Plan Espiritual de Aztlán* was drafted in 1969. This manifesto reiterated the UFW's insight that toxicity and degradation of the environment were related to the oppression of those who worked it. Representations of the land continue to serve an important function in Chicana/o activism and cultural production since *El Plan* voiced a connection between contemporary Chicanos and their spiritual and cultural ties to indigenous communities that have long lived in the territory now defined as part of the United States. In the declaration that "Aztlán belongs to those who plant the seeds, water the fields, and gather the crops and not to the foreign Europeans," movement activists stake a claim on territory and citizenship in the U.S. Southwest (*El Plan* 1969). The manifesto points out the artificiality of the U.S.-Mexico border and the injustice of colonization that renders Chicana/os suspect with regard to American citizenship status. Indeed, the editor of a collection of essays on landscapes in Chicano literature notes that "even before the Treaty of Guadalupe Hidalgo was signed in 1848, Chicanos were experiencing a life of constant struggle for the land they had inhabited for centuries and a continuous erasure of their cultural landscapes" (Martín-Junquera 2013, 3). She continues, "The ongoing problem of displacement and deterritorialization suffered by Chicanos dates as far back as the big migration of the Aztecs from the old mythical Aztlán to the area where Cortés met and subjugated them in the sixteenth century" (3). By claiming an alternative form of belonging to the land that predates Spanish and U.S. imperialism as well as a continued closeness to the land based on daily interactions and a spiritual connection to the forefathers, *El Plan* offers a model of nationalism rooted in the land. Yet, as Martín-Junquera's anachronistic use of the identifier *Chicano* signifies, tying a sense of belonging to the notion of indigeneity raises new questions about identity, authenticity, and what it means to belong to both a land and a culture.

During the Chicano movement, indigenist iconography and mythology emphasized territorial belonging and memory that function outside colonialist histories of the United States. As such, Aztec cultural and religious symbols were heavily featured in movement literature and art. Feminist scholars have criticized this strategy for a number of reasons. First, such images were patriarchal, with stereotypical depictions of heroic men and passive and sexualized women. Second, the appropriation of indigenous imagery to make claims of territorial belonging relied on colonialist logics that pair Native Americans with nature as a means of oppressing both racialized human-others and nature-others. Third, in excavating Aztec symbols and mythology, the movement ran the risk of pointing back toward a recuperated glorious past while simultaneously erasing extant native communities. Chicana artists strived to reclaim an indigenist aesthetic, but offered an "alternative to the previous notions that indigenism could only be articulated through the body, culture, and the history of the male Indian" (Latorre 2008, 26). Chicana-identified writers and artists pointed out the erasure of women's experiences in the nationalist movement and began to produce texts that were more relevant to women's lives, yet the theme of place continues to loom large and complicated in their cultural production.

## BORDERLANDS AND AMBIVALENT BELONGING

Gloria Anzaldúa's *Borderlands/La Frontera* (1999) is a noteworthy example that considers the relationship between subjectivity and place in a complicated way that evades essentializing identitarian claims. Her borderlands subjectivity is of a specific place and time in history—southern Texas at a time when the region is experiencing economic and ecological drought and increased militarization. Shaped by the effects of living in that region, living among a number of different cultures yet not comfortably belonging to any of them, Anzaldúa looks to Aztec stories to make sense of life in the borderlands and to imagine a more inclusive way forward; Coatlicue features prominently in the text. An earth goddess and mother of other deities in the Aztec pantheon, Coatlicue is associated with the serpents that made up her skirt. For Anzaldúa, the "Coatlicue state" is tied to the earth goddess's ability to create and take life; Coatlicue signals disruption, transition, and coming to consciousness. This transitory state is expressed as Anzaldúa's struggle to know herself as a border dweller living with cultural and sexual ambiguity—"You're changing worlds and cultures, maybe classes, sexual preferences" (2000, 226). In a later essay, "now let us shift," Anzaldúa moves through a Coatlicue state as she wrestles with a diagnosis of diabetes. She experiences a war with her body and dissociates from it before she achieves consciousness and moves toward healing: "You urge yourself to cooperate with the body instead of sabotaging its self-healing. You draw a map of where you've been, how you've lived, where you're going. Sorting and resorting, you go through the trauma's images, feelings, sensations. While an internal transformation tries to keep pace with each rift, each reenactment shifts your ground again" (2002, 553). Interestingly, as she works through this state, Anzaldúa's reflections also shift from her own bodily trauma to other traumas, including the genocide of Native Americans, the devastation brought by the slave trade, and "the loss of connection to the Earth, a conscious being that keens through you for all the trees felled, air poisoned, water polluted, animals slaughtered into extinction" (553). A play between personal and collective storying is visible here and throughout *Borderlands/La Frontera*; she pays attention to the specificity of the trauma, but insists on considering their connections nonetheless. In this last example, her collectivism expands beyond human belonging to account for nature others.

As a way out of the Coatlicue state, Anzaldúa draws on another Aztec deity: Coyolxauhqui. Moon goddess Coyolxauhqui was murdered and dismembered by her brother, the war god Huitzilopochtli. For Anzaldúa and other Chicana feminists who have found resonance with the myth, Coyolxauhqui is a "symbol for the necessary process of dismemberment and fragmentation . . . it is also my symbol for reconstruction and reframing, one that allows for putting the pieces together in a new way" (2009a, 312). Coyolxauhqui is a valuable resource for cultural producers because she shows the value in creative expression: in writing the story differently, one makes oneself and one's community anew. Under the guidance of Coyolxauhqui, the story of a return to Aztlán can be retold as an account of dwelling in the *Borderlands* to make space for those who were excluded in the earlier nationalist account.

Indigenist imagery in Anzaldúa's work is not necessarily an effort to reclaim an indigenous past. Rather, it serves as a way to imagine a new, contemporary nation through the recovery and reinvention of goddesses that were lost as both the Aztec and later Chicano movement patriarchs upheld masculinist warrior figures. Norma Alarcón's analysis of Anzaldúa's native appropriations suggests that, in claiming the diversity of deities (Coatlicue, Coyolxauhqui, and the many others) as facets or representations of Chicana subjectivity, indigeneity is a strategy to destabilize and defer categorical identity claims: "The effort to pluralize the racialized body by redefining part of their experience through the reappropriation of 'the' native woman on Chicana feminist terms marked one of the first assaults on male-centered cultural nationalism on the one hand . . . and patriarchal political economy on the other" (1999, 66). Together these examples show that, while rooting her writing in Aztec mythology, Anzaldúa does not claim a narrow sense of kinship to an essentialized cultural identity nor does she offer a straightforward sense of belonging to the land based on that identity. Indeed, in contrast to the position taken in *El Plan Espiritual de Aztlán* that the land belongs to those who work it (a position closer to that of ownership), Anzaldúa seeks a connection to nature that expresses co-being—a planetary connection.[2] She not only claims a multiplicitous racial and cultural belonging but sees herself as *of* the natural world.

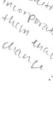

57

## QUEERING AZTLÁN

As with Anzaldúa, Cherríe Moraga reflects on the possibilities for personal and communal transformation. The essay "Queer Aztlán" opens with an explanation of how Moraga became politicized through the recognition of her lesbianism. She writes, "Coming to terms with that fact meant the radical re-structuring of everything I thought I held sacred. It meant acting on my women-centered desire and against anything that stood in its way, including my Church, my family, and my country" (1993, 146). "Queer Aztlán" critiques the racism of the mainstream women's movement and the homophobia of the Chicano movement, as well as the sexism of gay Chicanos and their refusal to yield male privilege. Within the Chicano movement that seeks a homeland in Aztlán, issues of sexuality and concerns grounded in women's experiences have been subordinated to class and race. Thus, remembering the insights of earlier activists such as Sojourner Truth and the women of the Combahee River Collective, Moraga suggests that no movement will be successful unless it accounts for all *others*. Her vision of liberation through the creation of a "Queer Aztlán" goes far in breaking the silence around Chicana/os and queer desire.

Yet Moraga shows as much concern for nature-others as for human-others. She writes, "*The earth is female* . . . like woman, Madre Tierra has been raped, exploited for her resources, rendered inert, passive, and speechless . . . *how will our lands be free if our bodies are not?*" (172–73; italics in original). Moraga notes the interlocking nature of systems of oppression and insists that until the most disenfranchised and voiceless among us is included, social *and* ecological justice will remain out of reach. She resists the human-centeredness that, in concert with colonial and capitalist endeavors, has ravaged the earth and its nonhuman inhabitants. She concludes by suggesting that Chicana/os return to indigenous roots (reenacted and remembered selectively) where an alternative socioeconomic structure and inclusive mode of community-building support more responsible relations among people and between people and the nonhuman world. In her vision, indigenous religions support this cultural model by honoring female deities alongside male deities: "Religions that grow exclusively from the patriarchal capitalist imagination, instead of the requirements of nature, enslave the female body. . . . Bring back the rain gods, the corn gods, father sun, and mother moon and keep those gods happy" (172). Following *El Plan Espiritual de Aztlán*, her conclusion is part of a tradition of decolonization through the imagining of alternative futures and the resignification of the past in ways that propel us toward that future.

And like Anzaldúa's, Moraga's ecological connections are strategic rather than essentialist; they underscore the link between women and nature because indigenous spirituality offers women a position of authority through association with nature goddesses and the land, and therefore would authorize women as the privileged founders of a new land, a Queer Aztlán. Moreover, founding that land as a *queer* space for queer citizens troubles an essentialist reading and opens the door to readings that find a multitactic differential consciousness at play (Sandoval 2000). Moraga's own name for her analytic framework, "theory in the flesh," helps us see her antidualism at work; her refusal to separate mind from body, reason from emotion, culture from nature, human from landscape is apparent: a "theory in the flesh means one where the physical realities of our lives—our skin color, the land or concrete we grew up on, our sexual longings—all fuse to create a politic born out of necessity" (Moraga and Anzaldúa 1983, 23). In this, Mary Pat Brady surmises, "Moraga offers a different concept of spatiality, in which land and bodies blend in both metaphysical and real senses, in which perception and living cannot be distinguished so easily" (2002, 139).

Although Moraga wants to claim Aztlán as a space that fosters celebration of Chicana/o identity and culture, she also recognizes the dangers of nationalism: "Its tendency towards separatism can run dangerously close to biological determinism and a kind of fascism" (Moraga 1993, 149). In its place, this utopia would embrace the multiplicity of its inhabitants' positionalities. In short, while the nationalist call for a return to Aztlán may exemplify a deterritorialization of the current hegemonic social imaginary of the U.S. Southwest in order to reinscribe and *reterritorialize* it through an indigenist heteromasculinist mythology, Moraga disrupts that utopia once more while keeping its borders more open, more inclusive.[3]

Chief among the strategies employed by Sánchez, Anzaldúa, Moraga, and other writers is the notion that identities and their rootedness in place are both deeply felt *and* malleable. The need to articulate one's experiences, yet avoid exclusionary and essentializing personal and collective identities is grounded in a particular historical moment and geographical location. Specificity of land-based, politicized identities does not necessarily signify claims of authenticity or an essential sense of oneself and surrounding world; it does not foreclose openness. As Maria Antònia Oliver-Rotger suggests, "The interrelated, real social conflicts that Chicanas describe have given rise to images of space that challenge geographical, cultural, and social divisions. The simultaneity of discourses that constitute the spatial power relations of society is the basis for a new aesthetics forged by hybrid subjectivities committed to multiple issues" (2003, 18). Moraga exemplifies this: her critique of Chicano nationalism points to both its sexism and homophobia, and she also challenges her allies to take up anticapitalist and spiritually invigorated resistances that can enfold care of the land into the struggle. Herein lies the transformative coalitional impulse of this work that links ecological justice to other social concerns and that opens intersubjective relationality not just to human-others but to nature-others as well.

## Ecological Themes in Chicana Feminist Visual Culture

> Concretizing our spiritual lives through words and image, and in turn, spiritualizing our material lives, allows us to paint a fuller picture of our realities. This work resists dominant western thought that would have us split our bodies, our flesh and bones and cells, from our spirits—the invisible yet felt aspect of our beings that is part of our life force—as if they were separate or opposite.
>
> —Elisa Facio and Irene Lara, *Fleshing the Spirit*

The writers studied here use metaphors of mapping as well as indigenist imagery and spiritual mythology as a means to express spatial and temporal relationships among humans and between humans and the borderlands environment. They reimagine our ecosocial relationships as nonhierarchical while providing a clear, historically grounded critique of the unjust present. In this section I extend that analysis to notions of time, place, and identity as they emerge from Chicana feminist visual culture, including the community murals of Juana Alicia, the paintings of Yreina Cervántez, and the digital arts of Alma López; in each of the works, the artist might be said to map a political and economic history of ecosocial social relations while pointing forward with a critique that performatively motivates metamorphosis—a change in the current situation. The art under analysis shares the distinction of not only building from the prior work of Chicana feminists that responded to the Chicano nationalist movement and the mainstream feminist movement but, like Sánchez, Moraga, and Anzaldúa, these artists are also responding to politics in the U.S. Southwest after the institutionalization of globalized and militarized capitalism in the region and across the world post-NAFTA.[4]

### JUANA ALICIA'S MURALS: SACRED SPACE, COALITION-BUILDING, AND WOMAN-NATURE LINKS

Murals are particularly suited to the development of politicized and place-specific identities because they are painted in strategic public places. The site of their construction matters in terms of both public access and their surrounding environment. The creation of art that draws the community together in both production and reception of the mural can stimulate "a sense of responsibility toward the place, its community, and its environment" (Latorre 2008, 15). In effect, the mural not only builds community but also reclaims space that has historically been denied Mexican Americans from Manifest Destiny to the contemporary moment where anti-immigrant sentiment remains strong and Chicana/os are figured as always already noncitizens.

The production of murals is just as important as their site specificity. Execution takes time and is often a community effort, requiring the participation of many to complete the project. While a primary artist may conceptualize murals, community volunteers help shape that concept and bring it to visual life; thus the creation process is coalitional from the start. In the process people come together to learn new skills and to create an object of aesthetic value for their community. Due to the political drives of the mural, volunteers can also undergo a process of transformation. Latorre clarifies, "Spiritual transformation also took the form of political revelation, whereby all those involved underwent a radical process of what Paulo Freire would call *conscientização*, or 'conscientization,' through which they became conscious of their own oppression but also of their own potential and power to bring about change at an individual and collective level" (2008, 8). I draw attention to murals in the San Francisco Bay Area that are especially representative in their ability to reclaim space and build a politicized community: Juana Alicia's *La Llorona's Sacred Waters* (2004), *Las Lechugueras* (1983), and *The Spiral Word: El Codex Estánfor* (2012).

*La Llorona's Sacred Waters* shares many themes in common with ecofeminism in that it notes colonialism's legacy of devastation of both peoples and the natural environment while drawing clear links between women and nature. The mural brings together two icons that are associated with water, La Llorona and Chalchiuhtlicue, and surrounds them with women protestors from around the world. Chalchiuhtlicue is an Aztec goddess of lakes and rivers and a patron of childbirth and fertility. La Llorona is associated with Mexico's Spanish colonial period and is sometimes coded as having drowned her children in revenge for her husband's unfaithfulness. An ambivalent figure that has accumulated a diverse spectrum of significations, she has also been recouped by Chicana feminists, as in Sandra Cisneros's "Woman Hollering Creek" (1991); La Llorona has been resignified as a woman who not only resists patriarchy but also colonialism.[5] Because of her association with water, La Llorona has been linked with Aztec nature goddesses, creating a hybrid figure with indigenous roots that emphasizes resistance and empowerment (Latorre 2008). Below the two central characters, the mural depicts women engaged in water-related protests that include Indian women's struggles against damming projects in the Narmada River valley, Bolivian women's resistance to the privatization of their water, and women's protests against the murders in Juárez along the Rio Bravo. Further, rather than seeing these struggles as primarily human ones and the environment as distinct from humans, Alicia recognizes the continuity between humans and the nonhuman world, between bodies and landscapes. The entire composition is painted in watery blues punctuated by vivid reds. On the left side of the mural, rivers rolling down from the mountains blend with rising tides flooding the Narmada Valley and the women are holding signs: "Damned! Doomed! Drowned." Nearby, waves and wind gusts surround Bolivian protesters standing off against the police and a violent figure, perhaps a personification of the Bechtel Corporation, which sought to privatize Bolivia's water. On the right, storm clouds gather over a barbed-wire wall that traps mourning women outside of a maquiladora—the wall recalls Anzaldúa's borderlands as a "thin edge of barbwire" (1999, 25); as a military helicopter flies overhead, rain pours over and through the women and nearby nopal cactus, pooling at their feet. At the center, waterfalls wash down Chalchiuhtlicue's jade skirt, and a tear falls from her eye as well as from La Llorona's. Alicia explains: "This moment is one where women are leading environmental struggles and carrying the weight of poverty on their backs and in their bodies, which are made mainly of water" (Hernández with Alicia 2003).

The two sacred figures appear to be weeping at the scenes of social injustice in which corporate globalization backed by militarizing states degrade the environment and make women insecure. Art historian Latorre suggests that Chalchiuhtlicue is shown with a scroll from her mouth that implies "she is speaking against these social conditions" (2008, 209). She further remarks that despite the era difference between the emergence of the two sacred figures, Alicia makes them both relevant to contemporary events and links them to an expanded need for *transnational* justice "to underscore the negative effects of globalization on marginalized communities across the globe. . . . The onset of globalization . . . has ushered in the realization among many Chicana feminist artists that the struggles of the Third World and women of color across the world bear striking similarities; thus, their approaches to activism and resistance are also comparable" (210). While the parallels are strongly present in the mural, I argue that the mural is not only suggesting that the struggles are similar and therefore the resistances might be too—in that case, strategies can be borrowed from one context to the other in ways that leave resistant groups essentially isolated from one another. The coalitional impulse is deeper. The previous chapter about activist histories discussed the strong tradition among borderlands artists and activists to draw support and alliance across groups and movements, and here we see an example of the transnational impulse in cultural production. In fact, the mural maps relationships between third world women of color across a variety of geographies and suggests not only a common logic of domination (Warren 2000) and a common struggle against neoliberal capitalism but also a *call for alliance* against it—themes in the work of decolonization scholars such as Chela Sandoval (2000) and Chandra Mohanty (2003). Indeed, although another scholar, Clara Román-Odio, offers a thorough analysis of the mural and makes a number of good points, her reading of La Llorona misses something key that can help us better understand the artist's goals. She notes that La Llorona, pictured at the foot of the mural and depicted sheltering a young black boy, is "extending her hand to aid third world women who are victimized by neo-colonization and transnational capitalism" (2013, 45). However, the women in the mural are all pictured behind La Llorona, out of sight and active in their resistance. La Llorona is not facing the activists, but the audience—those of us in the street gazing up at her; she crouches near and reaches a hand out to us to join them all. This point is crucial because the art does not just tell a story but offers an invitation for transformation as well.

In order to understand the *invitational* decolonial impulse, we can also read this mural as a means to map transnational relationships as well as temporal ones. *La Llorona's Sacred Waters* can be seen as a map of colonized lands and bodies in the past—referenced by precolonial Chalchiuhtlicue and colonial La Llorona—and their links to the present, represented by contemporary protesters. Further, it points toward a *future* of alliance-building rather than as a representation of parallel activisms. As such, it becomes possible to see how the mural cartographically depicts relations of power that incite viewers toward engagement. Linking narratives of women's social and spiritual leadership with the specificity of territorial belonging and sense of responsibility to the environment, Alicia creates opportunities for viewers to raise their consciousness and join in transnational alliances that will intervene in the injustice to heal *both* the community *and* the land.

*La Llorona's Sacred Waters* is not Alicia's only mural that draws connections between social and ecological justice. That mural was painted over the fading *Las Lechugueras* (1983), which featured women lettuce pickers under the toxic threat of pesticides. One woman in the mural is transparently pregnant (the fetus is visible through her clothing), suggesting that both the natural world and its human inhabitants are at risk from agribusiness *and* that women are at the heart of these struggles. The mural is closely tied with Alicia's own experiences. As a teenager she met César Chávez and was inspired to move to California and work with the UFW. During her time as a farmworker, she experienced pesticide poisoning, which shifted her consciousness in a visceral way. Awareness of how social and ecological problems intertwine and impact communities on a bodily, social, and spiritual level resonates throughout her work. In an interview, she explains:

> I'm interested in the rights of all living beings and the earth, and nature itself, not just specific political ideologies. I think that all life forms are quite threatened at this point. Having had a personal struggle with cancer recently, I feel that cancer is an environmental issue. I've worked a long time in the area of environmental justice, with my images, and I feel that we are at a critical moment: we've hurt the planet in a way that is irreversible, in ways that our children and our children's children will be coping with for a long time. ("On Art, Activism, and Social Justice")

While women's bodies and their productive, reproductive, and spiritual labor are shown as connected to the natural world in important ways in these two murals, Alicia's more recent work aims for a more complete, more ambitious accounting of history and the possible future.

*The Spiral Word: El Codex Estánfor* is a series of four murals composed for El Centro Chicano, Stanford University's Chicano/Latino student center. Completed in 2012, Alicia was inspired by "the history and literature of multiethnic latinoamerica" (Alicia 2016). A codex is a pre-Columbian folding cloth book on which Mayans encoded their stories through glyphs. In the Mayan tradition, glyphs, which were drawn by the priestly class, more than represented that to which they refer; rather, glyphs *evoke* that which is represented (L. Pérez 1998). Writing and translating the glyphs is a sacred process with transformative potential. As such, glyphs demand more than an epistemological shift—they incite an ontological shift, a metamorphosis. They do not offer a representation, but that which they create or evoke is meant to alter reality. In naming the mural series a *codex* and inscribing it with glyphs, Alicia tells a history of people in the Americas (in the tradition of Coyolxauhqui, she puts the history together anew and emphasizes the place of women within that history) and she pulls us toward a new direction.

The first panel, *Mayan Scribe*, features a bare-chested woman adorned with tattoos who is creating her own codex. She sits on a tree trunk at the center of the panel with a Mayan stone figure behind her and an urban landscape of city buildings to her left. The scribe is flesh-toned in front of the other elements of the composition, which are painted in shades of red. Alicia describes the image as follows: "Among the ruins of Mesoamerican culture, stone sculptures and ancient masks whisper into her ears. The ruins of the barrios of our continents, from Sao Paulo to the Bronx, sit behind her as well, echoing the immigration stories of sacrifice, survival and triumph" (Alicia 2016). Another panel, *Codex del Centro*, unfolds a series of images, including a section titled "Creation" that depicts a Mayan creation story and features a sacred Jaguar breathing into a conch-shell trumpet and other scenes from the *Popol Vuh*. The creation scene blends into another composition titled *Conquest and Slavery*, which gruesomely reminds viewers of African and American indigenous men and women who died from the Middle Passage, slavery in fields and mines, and lynching. Above these scenes, a speech scroll/breath from the scribe depicted in the first panel joins the hand of Sor Juana Inés de la Cruz as she "inscribes her observations of injustice, penning the revelations of the first feminist writer of the colonial Americas" (Alicia 2016). As a response to these traumas, the panel blends into the next scene, *Resistance and Revolution*, featuring singer Mercedes Sosa speaking/breathing her resistance. She is adorned in a cloak bearing images of varied cultural workers and activists from across Latin America. Next to her, "the Ollin butterfly, the Aztec symbol for movement and balance, holds out against the forces of war, nuclear destruction, the fireball of Fukushima and the melting icebergs of our current moment" (Alicia 2016). The final panel of the frieze is aptly titled *El Futuro* and it centers a young woman facing left toward the previous scenes as she writes history, connecting her work to those who came before her. The mural was completed in 2012 at the end of the Mayan calendar, and the final panel signals a new beginning and the chance to create a more socially and ecologically just world: "The future holds a vision of reforestation and ecological renewal, with mycelium fungi reclaiming toxic waste sites" (Alicia 2016). In the image, trees grow in a chaos of abundance, twining their trunks and their roots together and weaving into the rest of the scene, curling like the speech glyphs that connect the scenes. Text and earth are bridged as the glyph calls this hoped-for future into materiality.

The first two murals are capped off by a ceiling composition, *Nopal de Resistencia,* and the frieze directly below it, *Raices*. *Raices* translates to *roots* and, like the tree system in *El Futuro* and the blooming tree in *Creation*, the root system is extensive. In this panel, the connection to speech glyphs is even more explicit as the scrolls/roots of the lower frieze give way to the nopal cactus that grows directly from them in the adjoining mural. Just as the *Creation* mural featured a jaguar, an image sacred to the Mayans, Aztecs, and Incas, the nopal is representative of the present-day inheritors of those traditions. Alicia's nopal is reminiscent of Pat Mora's desert flowers that grow to be beautiful in harsh conditions. Alicia explains their growth as the "joyful energy of resistance and the blossoming of ideas and culture"—twinning the growth of plant life and the growth of decolonial cultural production in the same way that Mora's gardening metaphors speak to the cultivation of Chicana feminist writing.[6] Inspiration for resistance and change come from history, represented by the speech scrolls, and from the earth, and the two are seen as *coextensive*.

Juana Alicia's murals sketch relationships among subjectivity, time, and place in a number of important ways. There is an emphasis on embodiment and a relationship to the land: *La Lechugueras* focuses on the gendered and racialized exploitation of women's labor and the effects of pesticides on the bodies of women and their children as well as on the land; *La Llorona's Sacred Waters* focuses on women's bodies in specific regions of the world resisting the violence of neocolonial globalized capitalism. Across all the compositions in *The Spiral Word*, women's bodies are tattooed or cloaked in the glyphs and images of their histories; moreover, women are seen as the scribes and history makers—their embodied experiences are the grounds on which to re-member the past and to vision the future. Indigenist imagery has a pedagogical function that recalls a past that has been lost to many present-day Chicana/os and Latina/os and it carries the weight of a spiritual invocation, one that spurs metamorphosis and, as Facio and Lara's epigraph advocates, it spiritualizes the material and materializes the spiritual elements of our lives. Moreover, the place where the murals are painted is significant. *The Spiral Word* inspires the Chicana/o and Latina/o students of Stanford University, a place where Alicia has taught in the past and one with its own troubled history with respect to students of color, as protests mentioned in chapter 1 show. *La Llorona's Sacred Waters* and *La Lechugueras* are large-scale works on a very public street in a multiethnic community. Their sheer scale has a visceral impact in the viewers. This impact and the affective response it creates is important in challenging viewers who might otherwise remain complicit or whose politics might remain narrowly nationalist. In both critiquing hegemonic economic and political practices that are detrimental to women and their environments *and* posing an alternative move forward based on transnational coalition-building and healing, the murals by Alicia and her collaborators enact a performative move that exposes ruling logic and resists it at the same time.

## THE BODY POLITICS OF YREINA CERVÁNTEZ: NEPANTLA AS A *BECOMING OTHER*

Yreina Cervántez's self-portraits may appear more personal and autobiographical than Alicia's murals, yet Cervántez too draws connections between the personal and the political, the individual and the collective, the past and the present, the subject and her environment. The works discussed in the following emerged during a time when Chicana artists utilized self-portrait to become "directly visible on their own terms, reclaiming their own bodies and presences as subjects to be defined and expressed by themselves, as opposed to being circumscribed whether by Chicano or mainstream society," according to art historian Holly Barnet-Sánchez (2001, 130). The self-portraits are multilayered and pedagogical—they show the artist as multiplicitous, fracturing the viewer's understanding of the artist and the histories that shaped her. As such, the images prod the viewer to raise questions about how *we* see and know the world.

For example, the first panel of the *Nepantla* lithograph triptych (1995) shows Cervántez's face juxtaposed with competing representations of Chicanos. Organized along the left side of the composition, the viewer finds news clippings about Proposition 187, which prohibited undocumented immigrants from using public services (e.g., health care, public education) in California. There are human skeletons down on all fours and a depiction of a Euro-American-styled American Indian man standing next to a "partially civilized" American Indian and another who is understood to be "wild," suggesting the social Darwinism behind the Manifest Destiny ideology as well as the continued repression of Chicanos through the erasure of their histories and language in schools. A news article on Chicana protesters at UCLA closes out the left portion of the image: the copy reads "In an effort to escape nepantlism, even while amid the dangers that continue to threaten its onset, the Chicanos' response and their aims are to define their identity as a base from which to orient their actions and their interactions, and thus to make their demands heard." The glyph of *ollin*, signifying movement, brings a spiritual charge to this activism and links the state of *nepantla* experienced by present-day Chicana/os with indigenous populations under the threat of colonization. This message is underscored by the inclusion of a passage from Miguel León-Portilla's *Endangered Cultures* (1990) at the center of the composition; it highlights the role of cultural violence against indigenous traditions as León-Portilla mentions the *nepantla* state, a term that references both "the land in the middle" and a mode of "remaining in the middle" or being in the process of becoming something else. This process is thought to have characterized survival during the colonization of Mesoamerica. On the right, Cervántez includes another juxtaposition: Albrecht Dürer's diagram of the mathematical model of perspective applied in Euro-American artistic traditions and a pre-Columbian life-death mask. Their pairing at the top right of the composition juxtaposes different artistic traditions and, by extension, ways of looking at the world;

while Dürer's perspective orders the world in a linear and mathematical way, the mask shows the Aztec worldview that pictures materiality as a duality and cycle.[7] This panel marks the difficulty of navigating a *nepantla* state where one is trapped between competing cultures, worldviews, and limiting representations of women both in the mainstream American culture and in the Chicano nationalist movement even as it highlights the *nepantla* state experienced by indigenous communities caught between their traditions and the cultural and spiritual impositions brought on by Spanish colonizers. The citation of particular cultural and historical symbols reveals the power behind social, political, and educational institutions and their historic patterns of repression that continue into the present, thereby offering a performative subversion of the ruling logic. In addition to the exposure and critique of ruling logic, Cervántez introduces her own visage into the work. The largest figure in the composition, she sits at the lower right of the piece, gazing directly at the viewer and holding a sprig of sage, often associated with women who perform *curandera* or healing work.

The second panel of the triptych, *Mi Nepantla*, shows Cervántez's face in the center of the panel. With eyes closed in reflection, she is surrounded by images and text that suggest a more personal understanding of her (new) mestiza consciousness: cherubic Christian images juxtaposed with Aztec symbols and glyphs and the hybridized Guadalupe sit next to the poem "Come Union" by Gloria Enedina Alvárez translated into both Spanish and English. Below, a passage on the "New Mestiza" from Anzaldúa shares the same space as a figure bound up in ropes and caught within Dürer's rendering of perspective. The transposition of this diagram of perspective over her forehead with the words "de-colonization" suggests a personal struggle to find oneself outside of harmful logics and foreign perspectives. The jaguar—Cervántez's animal spirit and an animal sacred among Mesoamerican cultures—points to a continued effort at decolonization and the calling up of spiritual energies to heal the self, a reading bolstered by the inclusion of another sprig of sage and the glyphs on her cheeks of Coyolxauhqui's bells. The doubling of her self-portrait and the citation of Coyolxauhqui on one of the artist's two faces recalls the role of the Aztec moon goddess to writers like Anzaldúa—she represents fragmentation and dismemberment as well as recuperation and re-membering, calling forth a selectively remembered past to vision a better future.

The third panel, *Beyond Nepantla*, suggests progress toward that future. The lithograph shows a spiraling feathered serpent, "the glyph of Quetzalcóatl, man-God representing both wisdom and the arts, the unity of the spiritual and material" (L. Pérez 2007, 44). The serpent is surrounded by natural elements such as shells and a feather, a mortar with herbs to be ground, and Cervántez's self-portrait, including the sprig of sage. The bottom of the panel features an essay about "two Americas" (the America of ancestors and the America of today) and another diagram of Dürer's model of perspective with images of the "evolution"/assimilation of the American Indian caught within its geometry. Laura Pérez reads this last panel as a mode of reframing perception and suggests that colonialist representations "may be transformed in viewing them from the nonhierarchical, circular perspective of traditional American Indian, and other, cultures" (2007, 44). Cervántez's use of images reframes the viewer's understanding of historical and contemporary events. In drawing on indigenous artistic practices, Cervántez creates not just images, but also glyphs that evoke that which is represented. She invokes a change in perspective and a future that moves toward transformation by forging new connections and relations among humans and between humans and their environments. They manifest visions into more just realities. Further, although the title *Beyond Nepantla* suggests decolonization beyond "the middle ground" and it signifies an end to process and to states of *becoming* that characterize *nepantla*, the inclusion of a glyph of *ollin* troubles the idea of linearity implied by the title *Beyond Nepantla*. For scholars of Aztec metaphysics, *ollin* "defines the *shape of coming-into-life, of cyclical completion, of life energy* generally. Indeed, it defines *the shape of life or living* per se" (Maffie 2013, 190; italics in original); *becoming decolonial and the continual process of creation is the goal*. With this example, Cervántez demonstrates the performative enactment of working within and between logics, contesting and stretching them to the point of incoherence or hybridizing them to generate new directions. *Beyond Nepantla*, rather than signifying an end point in the struggle, reaffirms the process of *becoming decolonial*.

The *Nepantla* series shows Cervántez working through a process of decolonization and, as an artist and a healer, establishing an alliance with her viewers toward decolonization on a broader scale. *Big Baby Balam* (2000) focuses on Cervántez's body as a contested history. If, as Foucault suggests, bodies are the sites upon which relations of power discipline us, they are also the first sites of resistance.[8] In this watercolor self-portrait, Cervántez's face is tattooed with the marks of a *balam* (jaguar) and Aztec glyphs representing elements from the natural world, such as water. In contrast to earlier images of Chicanas in which women were sexualized in the movement or depicted as maids or factory workers in mainstream media, Cervántez creates a new way to represent the Chicana body in a manner that defies objectification. The figure staring back at the viewer resists the male and colonial gaze and creates a counterhegemonic subjectivity through the citation of indigenous codes that are illegible to the uneducated viewer. The artist retains a certain degree of distance: neither Cervántez nor her image will be easily consumed. Moreover, the symbology of the jaguar reveals a human-animal synthesis that defers an essential identity and defines Cervántez as a fluid subject in the process of "becoming-animal" (Deleuze and Guattari 1987). Daniel Perez argues that this creates a "new feminine," one in which "she represents herself as both animal and human capturing the unsocialized and socialized natural self. Cervantez [sic] addresses the de-humanization of women, gender-cultural stereotypes, and bridges social identity, culture, and the self-realization of female empowerment" (2013, 7; see also L. Pérez 2007, 85). *Big Baby Balam* disrupts colonial paradigms that position the nonhuman world as other to humans; instead, Cervántez presents her own perspective as more in line with an Aztec worldview wherein the natural environment of flora, fauna, and the elements are co-arising with the cultural world of humans and the spiritual world of the gods. Here, the body resists the colonial order and, figured as a conjunction of the spiritual merging of human with animal, acts as the foundation for alternative knowledges. Indeed, although there are fewer signifiers in *Big Baby Balam* than in the *Nepantla* triptych, the fact that the artist painted her eyes different colors brings extra attention to questions of perspective and draws the viewer's eyes up to Cervántez's gaze to linger on questions of vision and worldview.

Both the *Nepantla* triptych and *Big Baby Balam* make connections between the body as text, the individual in relation to her historical and geographical context, and the spiritual nature of the self that can motivate change. The codex form is key to understanding Cervántez's intent to create art that raises consciousness not only on the issues that constrain Chicana/os in the present period, but by educating about heritage and indigenous culture as well. Cervántez's self-portraits show that she sees herself as fulfilling the role of more than an artist; she is also a codex reader. In the indigenous tradition, she understands the role of an artist to be an interpreter and teacher who enables her audience to achieve a critical consciousness. Thus, like the tradition of autobiography with works such as Cisneros's *The House on Mango Street*, Mora's *House of Houses,* and Sánchez's "*Cartohistografía*," self-portrait is not just a reclaiming of the self and a writing of one's own narrative, but is also the writing of a collective story and a means to draw others into a politicized awareness.

## The Cartohistographic Landscapes of Alma López

Among the artists reviewed, Alma López's digital compositions offer the most direct critique of globalized capitalism's efforts to racialize and gender women in order to exploit their labor. Although not as explicitly ecological as the works of Alicia and Cervántez, who forged connections among humans and between humans and their environments, López's compositions concern themselves with the role of place and time in Chicana/o politics. Her works draw together desert landscapes and the Los Angeles skyline as linked by the im/migrations of women, by the labor they perform, and by the neocolonial political maneuverings that structure their lives. López's use of maps is particularly important and we can draw a connection between the mapping strategy of *California Fashion Slaves* (1997) from the series *1848: Chicanos in the U.S. Landscape after the Treaty of Guadalupe Hidalgo* and the notion of cartohistography introduced by Sánchez earlier in the chapter.[9]

In *California Fashion Slaves* López layers a map of Mexico with the words "Manifest Destiny" written in an arrow that points to an image joining the Virgin Guadalupe and 1848, the date of the signing of the Treaty of Guadalupe Hidalgo in which northern territories of Mexico were claimed by the United States. The map also features an image of a border-patrol vehicle chasing a man south. Lastly, an image of Coyolxauhqui is layered onto the map, which, as it does in other visual and textual narratives created by Chicana feminists, signifies that López is participating in the practice of re-membering Chicana history and culture by pulling together disparate experiences and histories— those that are repressed and silenced in dominant historical narratives. Over this spatiotemporal representation of the racialized history of the borderlands in the 1800s, López tells stories of the present. *California Fashion Slaves* shows seamstresses positioned as a border between the map of northern Mexico and the Los Angeles skyline. Laura Pérez suggests that the image of the seamstresses "effectively conveys the hidden presence of female garment workers in Los Angeles, one of the many garment-production capitals of the world, whose superprofits are built upon unseen superexploitation" (2007, 173). Like Almudena Carracedo's 2007 documentary *Made in L.A.*, *California Fashion Slaves* shows that women are not only concentrated in the more visible border maquiladoras but also that migration across the border is shaped by a need for cheap labor in the United States where economics and anti-immigration sentiment conspire to create conditions of exploitation for Chicanas and Latina immigrants. Additionally, although López *is* sketching connections between colonialism and capitalist neocolonialism, the placement of women's bodies *onto the map* also rewrites history to include the experiences of women, suggesting that women have always been implicated in the process of colonization and that colonialism itself is a gendered process.

Reading *California Fashion Slaves* from an ecocritical lens provides additional insights into representations of women and the landscape. Geographically, two regions are represented. The lower half of the image (i.e., representing the southern cardinal direction) features a map that is itself antiqued in the color of sand, reinforcing desert imagery. It shows a nearly empty landscape save for a single man chased down from the north. The logic of Manifest Destiny relied on just such notions of an empty landscape to sanction westward expansion. In contrast, the upper (i.e., northern) half of the image displays the Los Angeles skyline as densely packed skyscrapers; opposite the antiqued, sand-colored map of the Mexico and the U.S. Southwest, the city and sky above them are in full color—as if López is signaling a colonialist history of economic and social progress that has been built on the backs of women. We can also read women as *part of* the landscape because many of them are pictured in the same hue as the map (one woman, López's mother, is in full color). López acknowledges, "This digital print portrays my mother as a seamstress, and as a part of a working poor community racially stereotyped and vilified for allegedly draining the United States economy" (2002, 90). The bridge of women highlights white fears of overpopulation and resource extraction even as the artist turns the tables in her critique. She shows how women's labor and their bodies are exploited in the same way natural resources are exploited in this and other ages. Women are dehumanized and their labor is naturalized by drawing a host of dichotomies into action (mind/body, intellectual labor/physical labor, men's work/women's work, whiteness/racialized other, human/animal). After all, the exclamation "GOLD!" overlaps López's mother as well as the open space of the map's landscape, pointing out the role of the gold rush in facilitating westward expansion as well as the money to be made off of women's bodies in the fashion industry today.

Nearly all the artists and writers explored in this chapter summon the past to reframe the present and López is no different. She also shares a strategy of showcasing an indigenous knowledge system in which time is not linear, but is repetitious or cyclical. However, it is also useful to read López's spatiotemporal understanding as a decolonial "third space." Emma Pérez (1999) explains the idea of a "third space" as that interstitial space where the gaps and silences around the histories of Chicanas can be found and articulated (xvi). As López illustrates, the decolonial imaginary is also that space between colonialism and the postcolonial period, the processual state of being "beyond *nepantla*" to which Cervántez's triptych aspires. The *nepantla* state mapped so clearly here shows how time and space are unified—not just a middle land or middle ground, *nepantla* is also an era of growth, change, and synthesis.

The concept of a *nepantla* or "third space" and the transition to a decolonial imaginary that creates a place for a postcolonial landscape returns us to this chapter's opening. Elba Sánchez summarizes, "As cartohistography, my writings explore the longitudes and latitudes of an ever-shifting map of life, where my conciencia is affected by physical elements and vice versa. My landscape is at times eroding, but rebuilding as well, always renewing, changing once again. Each time I or we write and chronicle our real and imagined spaces, we are consciously naming, putting on the map, so to speak, previously unknown territory" (2003, 27). Like Sánchez, López depicts personal and communal histories in nonliteral and nonlinear ways. *California Fashion Slaves* pays close attention to the space in which such histories occur and, while documenting dominant histories that reproduce events in a singular and linear manner, López also offers histories from the margins. The bodies of women are layered onto and become coextensive with the colonized cityscape and desert she depicts. In so doing, her cartographic aesthetic may be said to do as Sánchez suggests: she summons space to imagine how these landscapes and the lives of the humans and others that occupy them may be reshaped.

## Conclusion

Ecological themes abound in Chicana feminist art and literature, yet they are often misrecognized while criticism attends to a more anthropocentric focus on social concerns divorced from their environment. Turning an ecocritical gaze on these works shows how patriarchal, racist, and capitalist norming logics figure the natural environment *and* women, working-class, and racialized others as exploitable. The artists and writers explored show how ecological narratives produced in the borderlands can reframe major debates in ecofeminism; in particular, artists and writers create performative subversions of ruling logics by reworking understandings of the body, the relationship between women and nature, and spirituality. Counter to essentialist understandings of these themes that buy into the paradigm that women or "Indians" are closer to nature, the writers and artists employ elaborate iconography and narrative elements to destabilize our given understandings of historical and contemporary social, political, and economic systems; in so doing, they disrupt our sense of selves and orient us toward critical reflection and the formation of new (inter)subjectivities. As a borderlands environmental aesthetic, cartographic representations spatialize and temporalize relationships among communities and their environments by: (1) showing the coextension of women with their environments and the coextension of women across space; (2) analyzing the transnational nature of oppression; (3) mapping a way to alliance with others for ecosocial justice; and (4) citing spiritual forces to guide representation toward transformation, making word and image real in the world.

2. Juana Alicia, *La Llorona's Sacred Waters*, mural, Twenty-Fourth and York Streets, San Francisco, 2004. Courtesy of Juana Alicia.

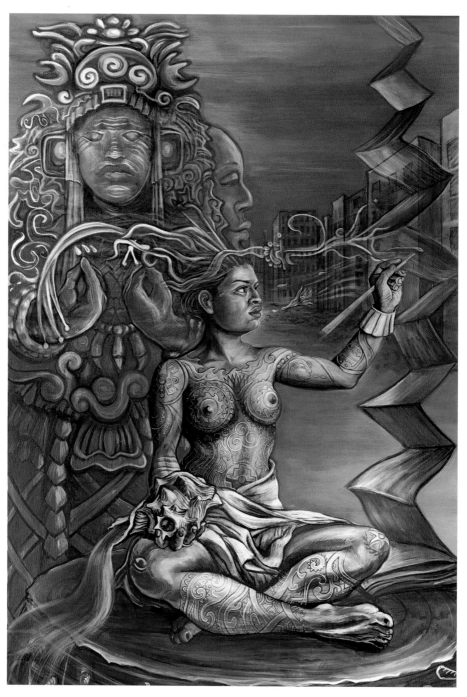

3. Juana Alicia, *Mayan Scribe* in *The Spiral Word: El Codex Estánfor,* mural, El Centro Chicano, Stanford University, 2012. Courtesy of Juana Alicia.

4. Juana Alicia, *El Futuro* in *The Spiral Word: El Codex Estánfor,* mural, El Centro Chicano, Stanford University, 2012. Courtesy of Juana Alicia.

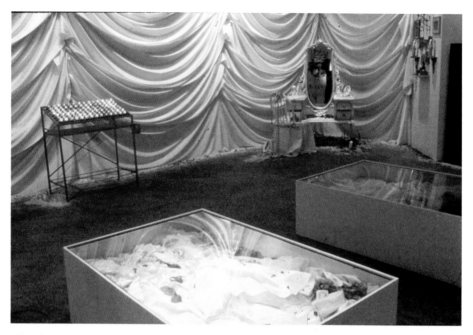

5. Amalia Mesa-Bains, *Venus Envy Chapter I: First Holy Communion Moments before the End*, installation, 1993. Courtesy of Amalia Mesa-Bains.

6. Amalia Mesa-Bains, *The Virgin's Garden* in *Venus Envy Chapter II: The Harem and Other Enclosures*, installation, 1994. Courtesy of Amalia Mesa-Bains.

7. Amalia Mesa-Bains, *The Virgin's Closet* in *Venus Envy Chapter II: The Harem and Other Enclosures*, installation, 1994. Photo courtesy of Amalia Mesa-Bains.

8. Amalia Mesa-Bains, *Vestiture . . . of Branches* in *Venus Envy Chapter III: Cihuatlampa, the Place of the Giant Women,* installation, 1997. Photo courtesy of Amalia Mesa-Bains.

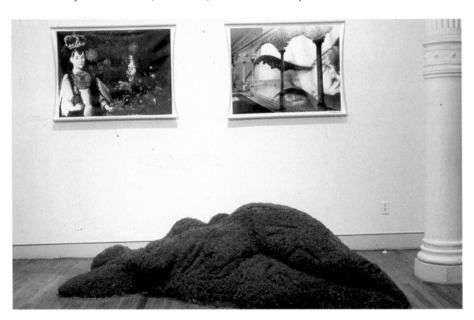

9. Amalia Mesa-Bains, *Cihuateotl (Woman of Cihuatlampa)* in *Venus Envy Chapter III: Cihuatlampa, the Place of the Giant Women,* installation, 1997. Courtesy of Amalia Mesa-Bains.

10. Amalia Mesa-Bains, *Private Landscapes/Public Territories,* installation, 1996.
Courtesy of Amalia Mesa-Bains.

11. Amalia Mesa-Bains, *The Curandera's Botanica,* installation, 2008. Courtesy of Amalia Mesa-Bains.

# CHAPTER 3

# Allegory, Materiality, and Agency in Amalia Mesa-Bains's Altar Environments

I would say that even beyond our own capacity to individually remember, or the capacity of a community to sustain memory, there is actually a way that nature itself remembers.

—Amalia Mesa-Bains, *Homegrown*

Vital materialists will thus try to linger in those moments during which they find themselves fascinated by objects, taking them as clues to the material vitality that they share with them. This sense of a strange and incomplete commonality with the out-side may induce vital materialists to treat nonhumans—animals, plants, earth, even artifacts and commodities—more carefully, more strategically, more ecologically.

—Jane Bennett, *Vibrant Matter*

What does it mean for nature to remember? Nature bears witness to human struggles and it has agency in its own right. It imposes cycles of life and death and, immersed within a spiritual worldview that bridges Mesoamerican indigenous and Catholic traditions, nature heals and guides humans who are attentive. For installation artist Amalia Mesa-Bains, who has become famous for her altars, "ceremonial work is linked to our struggle for our land and our cultural life" (qtd. in Gaspar de Alba 1998, 85). She has been preoccupied with questions of memory, place, and community throughout her five-decade-long career. Her altars include natural elements such as rocks, moss, soil, and twigs in which the natural elements and the trope of "nature" serve a number of functions. As seen in Day of the Dead *ofrendas*, Mesa-Bains uses flowers and fruit to remember and commune with the dead. Herbs signify *curanderismo* for personal and communal healing. Soil stands sometimes as a symbol for the Aztec homeland of Aztlán, sometimes as a crossing point along the U.S.-Mexico border, and sometimes as the detritus of an archaeological dig. Antlers point not just to the animal that bore them, but to Frida Kahlo and her legacy as a symbol of power and creativity among Latinas. Although signs of the natural world are everywhere in the artist's work, her environmentalism has been undertheorized by feminist and art critics. Using a key idea from one of the foremost scholars on Mesa-Bains—*autotopography* (González 2008)—we can better appreciate the artist's understanding of the "natural" world and, by extension, her environmentalism.

Chapter 2 considered the genre of *autohistoria*, a term coined by Gloria Anzaldúa and deployed by other Chicana feminist writers.[1] Autohistoria weaves together personal and family stories within a wider social history of Chicana/os; frequently, such tales also include facts and imagery of the *places* where community is built or uprooted. Elba Sánchez adapts the genre to her own needs with the development of "cartohistography" to describe her poetry: "Each time I or we write and chronicle our real and imagined spaces, we are consciously naming, putting on the map, so to speak, previously unknown territory" (2003, 27). The term is explicit in the relationship between Sánchez's identity and experience growing up and living close to the land; Sánchez describes herself as a landscape—her subjectivity unfolds out of the geographies that shaped her and it folds into the lives of others who may share some of her experiences or ideas. When Jennifer González uses *autotopography* to describe Mesa-Bains's installations, it resonates with the work of the aforementioned writers, yet manifests in a material form with its own mappable spatial dimensions. "Its own form of prosthetic territory," González explains, "this private-yet-material memory landscape is made up of the more intimate expressions of values and beliefs, emotions and desires that are found in the private collection and arrangement of objects, used to anchor a life narrative" (2008, 145). Autotopography uses organization and juxtaposition to convey its narrative and relies on viewer literacy, whether the viewer is a saint drawn to the altar or a visitor viewing the altar in a private home or museum.

Writers use autohistoria and cartohistography to provide a historical framework for their audiences, and they engage them with personal testimonies that provide a bridge to readers' own experiences. Readers are invited into

the spaces and subjectivities drawn out and are encouraged to become allies
in the work of decolonization. Autotopography works in the same way, yet
physical objects serve as a bridge between the artist and viewer. Because the
installation is staged as an altar, it also acts as a threshold, joining the material
and spiritual worlds. Moreover, when composed in a museum, the altar connects the space of the museum to other spaces represented in the installation
(a boudoir or sitting room, a private garden). Traditionally, altars are uniquely
gendered and personal spaces created by women to maintain the family's ties
to the spirit world and to loved ones. Kay Turner's oral histories with Mexican
American *altaristas* show the practice to be one in which women are empowered through their spiritual practice; by layering the altar with objects of deep
personal significance—photos and mementos that record family history and
the *altarista*'s relationships to saints or deities—the woman's power lies in the
interplay between the items, the unique story they tell, and in her performance
of prayers: "Through speech and gesture, she performs the expectation and
certainty of having her needs met. The self-created altar becomes a vehicle for
self-creation, a place for manipulating and shaping consciousness, for making the world the way the altarista wants the world to be" (Turner 2008, 195).
Much of the altar work done is in the service of protecting one's living family
and maintaining relationships with those in the spirit world. As such, the altar
is a site where women ritualize their work to support and transform social
relationships. Altars bring the material and spiritual world together and they
tie personal empowerment with the care of family and community so that the
personal is both political and spiritual. This collection of photos and artifacts,
like the layering of images that occurs in the work of Alma López and Yreina
Cervántez explored in chapter 2, represents an act of *re-membering* and documenting the past in ways that stand against the erasure of Chicana/o communities within (neo)colonial narratives. Not only does the juxtaposition of
images and other meaningful objects offer an affirming history of Mexican
American families, it also writes against narratives of the heroic patriarch that
featured heavily during the height of the Chicano nationalist movement.

Ethnographic research with *altaristas* depicts home altars organized as top-
ographic connections between the individual and her family and community;
artists such as Amalia Mesa-Bains adapt that layered aesthetic in their own
work. Indeed, the artist relies on her viewers' knowledge of home altars in
order to decipher her art: The altar format provides a certain lexicon from
which to interpret the inclusion of particular objects in an installation—there
is a "rhetoric of objects" (González 1999, 185) where one can read the codes
and interpret the artist's meaning(s). As such, "the installation re-creates a

space in which the subject is enshrined by the objects that represent the subject's absence . . . material culture is used to point elsewhere, beyond the thing-in-itself to the social rank, cultural role, or invisible community that a real or imaginary subject inhabits" (200). In this view, the artist places the objects into position and they get busy telling stories. Or maybe stated another way, agency shifts too much from artist to object. In the previous chapter I argued that the ecological consciousness embedded within Elba Sánchez's work is misrecognized when we consider her description of herself as a landscape in a metaphorical sense only. Similarly, consideration of the altar installation's objects only insofar as they must point elsewhere, beyond themselves as signs in an overarching discourse, limits the scope of what is possible by attending to objects in their full materiality—what agency does the thing have, especially if that thing carries spiritual significance? Items in an altar installation can be both objects and signs, "things-in-themselves" and human arguments with rhetorical sophistication. Recognizing this multiplicity allows us to see human identity and memory as deeply, thoroughly entangled with the objects, places, and spirits that codevelop with us. This stands in contrast to a vision of autobiography or autotopography in which objects are organized and conceived of as separate from humans, tools employed by us to narrate our personal and communal histories. Social constructivists note that autobiography is not an objective account of a person's life that reflects a singular subject wholly known to herself; in conversation with new materialist feminisms, we may also see how humans themselves are composed of individually acting and intra-acting substances whose agencies, unknowable as they may be, give rise to our own.[2]

The object-oriented interpretation of human/nature (and spirit) intersubjectivity has roots not only in new materialist feminisms, but also in Mesoamerican indigenous cultures and their appropriations in Chicana feminist writing.[3] For Anzaldúa, nature's agency is all around and it took a lifetime to learn to see and listen for it: "The connections are there, the signs I read in the environment—if a snake crosses my path when I'm walking across Lighthouse Field, it means something to me. I'll look at that tree silhouetted by the sun, and its design says something to me, to my soul, which I then have to decipher. We get these messages from nature, from the creative consciousness or whatever you want to call the intelligence of the universe" (2009c, 74). In a conversation with bell hooks, Mesa-Bains echoes the sentiment: "We know there are many things in the landscape that are sacred, and many artists have struggled to capture them. Sometimes in our art we have sought to document our labor, our work, and our worth, while claiming a spiritual tradition that can exist only in that geography" (hooks and Mesa-Bains 2006, 101). Artists like Mesa-Bains, who speak of a deep connection to the environment and who include natural elements in their work alongside a number of other human-created mementos, blur the boundaries between nature and culture, human and more-than-human, subject and object. Mesa-Bains raises a number of questions: "What is 'nature'"; "how does oppression become naturalized"; "what does a representational strategy look like that does justice to the intertwining of human, nature, and spirit in all their complexity"; and "how are representation and materialization co-arising processes?"—a question of the utmost importance in the decolonial work of building new futures. In the next section, I sketch some biographical detail of Mesa-Bains's relationship with the more-than-human world to better frame her autotopographical approach before turning to the shifts in interpretation of objects and nature that have occurred during her career. This shift traces Mesa-Bains's view of nature as trope to nature as agent. While it is important to note the artist's intentions, I am reminded that we are not wholly known to ourselves, and our agency is not solely our own in a world where spirits and objects are active; this chapter leaves space for the objects to live on their own, outside the artist's own published interpretations.

The use of home altars in Mesa-Bains's installation art follows the traditions of her grandmother and mother even as it joins in a larger movement among artists to explore and reclaim aspects of indigenous Mexican culture.[4] As the daughter of a working-class immigrant family—her father worked as a farm and ranch laborer and her mother as a maid—the artist experienced a migratory life across the San Joaquin and Santa Clara Valleys in California. This childhood was deeply impactful, and the traces of it can be found throughout her work. She recalls her earliest memories, including "the smell of the earth, and the smell of the pitch pots, where the smoke goes out to keep the insects away from the trees" (hooks and Mesa-Bains 2006, 100). As a young artist, Mesa-Bains participated in the first Chicano art show during the United Farm Workers' grape strike in the 1960s. The difficulties of migration, questions of belonging, and an awareness of the injustice of working the land as a poorly paid, often poisoned farmworker sat alongside recognition of the beauty and potential healing capacity of the land. Likewise, her mother's work as a maid presents important tensions that reveal themselves in Mesa-Bains's work: the contradictions of living in relative economic precarity and working with beautiful, expensive items in the homes of wealthy people; the domestic sphere as a private domain controlled by women and one in which women are employed as laborers in the service of others.[5] Although Mesa-Bains has written on these topics, scholarly criticism has minimized or omitted the biographical details of her parents' lives and their potential influence. I emphasize them here because they provide insights into the artist's relationship with the natural world and her development of an ecological consciousness.

## Venus Envy and Other Domesticana

> The home or domestic space interrelates with Chicana labor, historical agency, communities, and bodies, disrupting the artificial dichotomy that links female, domestic, and private as distinguished from male, civic, and public.
>
> —Theresa Delgadillo, *Spiritual Mestizaje*

### DOMESTIC INTERIORS, PSYCHIC INTERIORITY, AND PERFORMATIVE EXCESS

Mesa-Bains uses the neologism *domesticana* to describe her installations. As a play on *domestic* and *Mexicana* (referencing both a woman of Mexican descent and the cheap tourist items bought from a shop), it names a specifically feminist take on the Chicano art of *rasquache*. *Rasquache* describes anything from yard altars to street theater that presents a survivalist, irreverent, and creative attitude of making the most from the least (Ybarra-Frausto 1991). It celebrates a working-class sensibility while critiquing dominant culture through parody. However, while *rasquache* politicizes the cultural and economic marginalization of Chicanos, domesticana responds to the silencing of women in the Chicano movement. Domesticana offers a feminist *rasquachismo* that also defies  high- and low-art distinctions and is rooted in the working class, and in addition it addresses the domestic sphere where patriarchy is also interrogated. Mesa-Bains explains, "Chicana rasquache . . . has grown not only out of resistance to majority culture and affirmation of cultural values but from women's restrictions within the culture . . . Techniques of subversion through play with traditional imagery and cultural material are characteristics of domesticana" (2003, 305).

All of these elements are at play in the *Venus Envy* series, a multichapter and multiyear exploration of the places and roles open to Mexican American women. It is worth noting that, in addition to her arts training, Mesa-Bains earned a doctorate in clinical psychology; in this and other installations, we see a concern with the force of external values upon the psyches of young women and the struggle it takes to create oneself according to a different set of terms. Here, the title *Venus Envy* is a play on (and parody of) Freud's psychoanalytic emphasis on penis envy—the desire by girls to obtain the social position and power afforded to men in a patriarchal society. These works displace the patriarch, celebrating women in his stead. *Venus Envy Chapter I: First Holy Communion Moments before the End* (1993) was installed in a large room with three related areas. The first area, the *Hall of Mirrors*, holds an array of mirrors in which the museum visitor sees themselves alongside pictures of women who are important to the artist, including Sor Juana Inés de la Cruz, a scholar, poet, and proponent for women's rights in seventeenth-century Spanish colonial Mexico. The second area, the *Museum of Memory*, consists of cases in the center of the room. The cases hold communion, confirmation, and wedding gowns that highlight the paradoxical expectations to which women are held: a sexual double bind derived from the interlinking patriarchal institutions of the Church and the family (L. Pérez 2007). The cases hold other items as well, including a rosary, dried flowers, and personal mementos, including those belonging to Mesa-Bains and to other artists whom she considers to be *comadres* in art activism. The emphasis on the gowns reminds us of the role of the body in the work of becoming properly feminine according to social norms—womanhood is a dress that one must be fit into; one wears different dresses for different life stages and rituals of femininity.

The ritual or performative aspect of femininity is enhanced with the third area, the *Boudoir Chapel*, which shows an ornate vanity adorned with statues of the Virgin Mary, angels, and photos of Mesa-Bains and women who appear to be her family. The vanity and chair are also littered with rosary beads, dried flowers, and feathers. Glitter, candles, and dried flowers are scattered on the floor surrounding the vanity. The vanity's mirror reflects a mask of the Aztec mother deity Coatlicue, suggesting a struggle with identity and consciousness. Gloria Anzaldúa's Coatlicue state is a negotiation of personal, familial, and social histories—it is a state of disruption and discomfort that may lead to transformation (1999, 2002). In naming this altar area the *Boudoir Chapel*, the place at which one makes oneself up is also a place of worship: transforming oneself is spiritual work. The glamorous elements of the vanity—feathered fans, beads, perfume, a mask half hidden in a drawer—signify care of the self; "it is an altar where reverence for the otherwise devalued, racialized, gendered self, and what is important to the self, is cultivated" (L. Pérez 2007, 101). This reflects both on the artist's prior work, including an *ofrenda* to glamorous film star Dolores del Río, and interview comments in which Mesa-Bains discusses her love of beauty and style (hooks and Mesa-Bains 2006). However, the glamour and excess do not just signify care of the self against a cultural backdrop in which women are devalued; as Judith Butler's work on performativity reveals, it also exposes the artificiality of femininity (1999). That is, in Mesa-Bains's installations, the spectator may see both the ways in which institutional forces such as the patriarchal family and Church subject women, and the ways in which women create performative subversions to actively negotiate their own subjectivity. The artist works against essentialist notions of identity by pointing to the historical and contemporary social limitations with which Mexican American women have been constructed. Through ritualized altar-building, she re-creates herself and her relationships to others within the past and the present. The ritual element exposes the performativity of identity as shifting and constituted through repetitive and meaningful acts—sitting down at the vanity/altar to make oneself up.

In this installation, the most visible natural elements are the dried flowers: petals sprinkled across the white gowns and the bouquet of flowers on the vanity chair, which likely represents a wedding bouquet. The fact that the flowers are dead, desiccated, and made to resemble blood in their coloring and display reflects upon part of the work's subtitle: *Moments before the End*. The flowers confer femininity and refer to the drawing to a close of a life cycle. This cycle is also reflected in the mask of Coatlicue, an earth goddess who brings both life and death. As Coatlicue presides over the vanity, nature bears witness to the personal transformations that are enabled there as the altar/vanity serves as a connecting mechanism between the human and spirit worlds. Moreover, as an earth goddess, Coatlicue is both a mother and a sexual being. The tension between the roles allocated by the Catholic Church (virgin, nun, mother) and those modeled by Coatlicue play out in the minds of women seeking their own paths, but Coatlicue and the other women admired by the artist, all of whom are framed within mirrors reflecting the gaze of the viewer, act as spirit guides offering alternatives.

The second chapter in the series, *Venus Envy Chapter II: The Harem and Other Enclosures* (1994), is situated in a gallery room made to look like a family room or dining room in the artist's home. As a subtitle, *The Harem and Other Enclosures* names a specifically gendered and sexual trap. Clearly, Mesa-Bains draws a parallel between the harem and the household, both seen as a mode of confinement for women that marks them as gendered and racialized just as *domesticana* with its play on *domestic* and *Mexicana* does. However, while the domestic space is confining, it is also understood here as a place of creativity and resistance. Much like *Chapter I*, there are three related scenes: *Sor Juana's Library*, *The Harem*, and *The Virgin's Garden*. In one corner of the room, a desk/altar is marked as a desk in Sor Juana Inés de la Cruz's library and is littered with photos, scientific instruments, globes, and natural elements (a skull, feather, and starfish, for example). As a well-read poet and scientist during the Spanish colonial era when women were not permitted to study,

Sor Juana advocated for a women's right to education. Eventually, the Church silenced her and confiscated her books and instruments, but she is still celebrated as one of the earliest published philosophers of the Americas. The convent in which she is cloistered and the political and religious dictates of her time served as her enclosure; the convent gave her some degree of freedom (the freedom not to marry, for example) yet it ultimately curtailed her ability to pursue her studies. In citing her, Mesa-Bains calls forth a little-known history of women's achievement. She also draws her into a pantheon of female heroes whose artifacts decorate the room (including images and writings from Chicana artists and Mesa-Bains's family). The walls are lined with mirrors to emphasize perspectivalism and to return the spectator's gaze in a way that undercuts attempts at voyeurism and an uncritical visual consumption of the spectacle: the spectators are made aware of their own presence in the scene as they walk through it.

*The Virgin's Garden* is staged across the room. Resembling a yard shrine, it features a fenced-in area with a bench and other garden decorations. On the back wall, the artist has hung a copy of the painting *The Little Garden of Paradise*, created about 1410 by an artist known as Upper Rhenish Master. The painting places the Virgin Mary in an enclosed garden, surrounded by a low fence not unlike the one created for the installation by Mesa-Bains. The Virgin sits on a bench reading while the child Jesus plays at her feet. Saints circle the two figures. The painting is known not only for its devotional subject matter, but also because it was rare at the time for its careful and naturalistic depiction of plants and animals, which served an educational purpose to viewers.[6] The space to the left of the painting houses a wardrobe with cloaks and cherubs hanging above; mosses, fruits, antlers, twigs, and candles spill out of the closet and onto the museum floor beneath. A small figurine of the Virgin Mary, dwarfed by the closet's size, stands at the center of the greenery. In dialogue with the painting nearby, the clothes themselves appear to be made of a rich brocade fabric associated with the Renaissance. While the painting offers an idyllic garden enclosure that protects mother and child, the wardrobe multiplies our understanding of "garden." The cherubs add additional evidence to suggest that *the garden* represents Eden—cherubs are tasked with protecting the entrance to Eden once Adam and Eve have been removed after Eve's betrayal. The fruits and flowers that litter the ground reference the Tree of Knowledge. If Eve's quest for knowledge, both sexual and intellectual, is blamed for the fall of man, then the fact that the garden is given over to the Virgin shows Mesa-Bains giving space and subjectivity back to women. As the convent served as both a space of confinement and possibility for Sor Juana, the garden is a place of protection and possibility *and* a space regulated by a heavenly patriarch wielding the threat of retribution. Like Sor Juana, the Virgin acts as a guide for women to see themselves out of cultural enclosures. Further, in centering the scene around *The Virgin's Closet*, Mesa-Bains equates

✳ cultivation of the self with cultivation of a garden where the closet becomes an altar on which to create oneself and one's guiding histories anew. Drawing equivalencies among the Garden of Eden, the safe domestic space of the Virgin Mary's garden, and the gardens and yard shrines created by Mexican Americans brings the spirit and material worlds together, validates Mexican American families, and sacralizes women, who are always suspect and surveilled under Catholic dictates.

## DOMESTICANA AS ECOTRANSFORMATION? PLACE-MAKING AND RECYCLING AESTHETICS

Mesa Bains's domesticana offers rich opportunities to explore feminist art activism; here I draw out just two themes in this body of work that bear on ecological understanding in particular. First, I explore the ontological drive within this work that creates new understandings of the self and its relationships to others and to place. As noted earlier, Mesa-Bains's art reveals the multiple subject positions to which Mexican American women are hailed and seeks to create new, more liberatory subject positions for viewers to inhabit as they walk through the installation and take with them the cultural critiques that works like *Venus Envy* offer. Identity is performative and open to change; the specific form of art invites an understanding of identity as both nonunitary

✳ and *relational*. The installation and its organization position the spectator to see how one's sense of self derives from the relationship to historical and contemporary *others*. Mesa-Bains models this relationality through semiautobiographical installations that speak not only of personal history, but also of social history more broadly. Related, the element of ceremony and ritual involved in

✳ altar work codes domesticana as an instance of personal and social healing that further mobilizes the ontological impulse in the work. In fact, Mesa-Bains and other artists often use words such as *transfigure* to describe the function of art in the Chicana/o community: Art does not just re-present some aspects of the world around us; it should transform it.

This strategy of personal and social storytelling relies heavily on the understanding of space and the relationships between humans and objects in space. Consider the first two chapters of the *Venus Envy* series, for example. Employing an autotopographical strategy, both use objects strategically not just to raise critique or to pose epistemological questions regarding the nature of history and self but also to lay the ground for new relationships and new futures. Mesa-Bains disrupts spectators' sense of time, self, and place: "The viewer is drawn against limitations of the temporal and spatial. Interior and exterior are challenged in the use of organic materials such as earth, leaves, twigs, and waste. Mirrors, broken and fragmented, act on the viewer to fissure illusion and gain states of receptivity" (Mesa-Bains 2003, 311). By emphasizing closed-in spaces and installations that spectators walk through and explore, that relational self is very much called to be a self-in-space, conscious of how one's environment shapes sense of self.

In addition to emphasizing transformation and the relational subjectivity that arises from these examples of domesticana, a second ecological theme is present in the *Venus Envy* series and earlier domesticana works such as *Ofrenda for Dolores del Rio* (del Río was an actress whose career was split between Hollywood and Mexican cinema in the 1940s and 1950s): the link between femininity and consumerism in figuring relationships between the self, humans, and more-than-human others. *Chapters I* and *II* rely on an "aesthetic of accumulation" (Mesa-Bains 2003, 307) seen in *rasquache*, but that here takes a unique form related to the distinctly feminine interpellation to consumerism. Mesa-Bains populates her altars with family photos and hyperfeminine depictions of glamorous Latina movie stars that may sit next to plastic flowers or a wedding gown. The juxtaposition of objects on the altars exposes the paradoxical status of women. The altars are simultaneously characterized by accumulation, display, and excess, as González points out, *and* a recycling aesthetic. The glamorous and hyperfeminine elements contrast with signs of a debased and shattered glamour (broken mirrors, dried flowers, tissues smeared with lipstick). We can read the spectacle of excess against the anticapitalist representations in Chicana feminist cultural production as seen, for example, in Alma López's *California Fashion Slaves* (1997), which critiques the system of garment production that renders workers invisible and exploitable producers of goods in the neoliberal market. Indeed, many of the cheap goods and garments found on home altars and deployed in Mesa-Bains's art have been made in the maquiladoras that come under critique.

While displaying a survivalist aesthetic, the nod to glamour and excess might read as capitalist yearning rather than anticapitalist critique. The play of juxtapositions, however, challenges simple binaristic readings. This is a particularly interesting area for *eco*feminist analysis. The critique shows consumerism as linked to a classist and racist beauty standard; the performative excess of the autotopographical arrangements does not deny the feminine interpellation to consumption but criticizes it while rewriting consumption through a recycling aesthetic that speaks both to the structural poverty within many communities of color and, perhaps, the damage that capitalist production schemes place on the environment. This tactic privileges creative reuse, which builds a community aesthetic that respects the need to keep goods out of dumpsters and limits demand for factory goods. The contradictions surrounding femininity are emphasized through the performative excess of domesticana—glamour is celebrated and critiqued; spirituality is embraced but with a historicizing eye on its colonial and present-day traumas; and the collection of objects is both a statement of abundance within a proud working-class culture and a practice to be rethought for its role in destructive forms of subject-making. Indeed, Mesa-Bains lived with these contradictions long before they manifested in her art. Reflecting on the development of her aesthetic voice, the artist notes that it probably "sprung from a home in which my mother had spent her formative years living among wealthy people and handling extremely expensive items [as a maid]. It also came from the church" (hooks and Mesa-Bains 2006, 18). While much has been written about the critique of the Church in her work, less has been written about the excess materiality and critique of capitalism seen in these examples.

## Gardens and Other Bodies of Nature, from Allegory to Agent

From my grandmother's earliest corral, or backyard plant gathering, to my parents' home gardens and my own years as a cannery worker, I came to know and respect the place of nature and plants as nourishment and healing.

—Amalia Mesa-Bains, "Nature and Spirit"

Nature is not a site that is subjected to human signification; it is present to the senses and, most importantly, it appears in its resistance to being subsumed into representation.

—Amanda Boetzkes, *The Ethics of Earth Art*

### PRIVATE LANDSCAPES/PUBLIC TERRITORIES

*Private Landscapes/Public Territories* was exhibited at the Fresno Art Museum in 1996 and features mostly exterior landscapes. It recalls other gardens in the artist's work, including *The Virgin's Closet* from *Venus Envy Chapter II*. The lower half of the walls are painted in variegated greens dappled with gold to appear as a dense border of decorative bushes. Carved topiaries are placed around the room in organized clusters with glass beads tucked into their foliage. Some of the topiaries are made entirely of the beads held in moss-covered planters—a playful reversal of "natural" and artificial materials. These shrubs are mingled with leafy shrubs carved into constraining, highly controlled shapes. Here, none of the signs of nature is free from human manipulation. Privileged with the space of the center of the room, there is a symmetrical parterre (an ornamental garden) carved into a mossy mat. Topiaries stand just outside the mat at each of the four quarters. The parterre developed in France during the European Renaissance around the same time Columbus made his journey to the New World; this work, along with some of her other pieces, responds to celebrations of the quincentennial of Columbus's arrival that took place in 1992. In addition, inclusion of the French-style garden draws viewers to another historical moment, one that is often lost in the focus on Spain's colonial influence in Mexico: the period of French intervention in the mid-nineteenth century. In her writings on the exhibit, Mesa-Bains informs viewers that her great-uncle fought on behalf of France's installed emperor Maximilian, which troubles straightforward critiques of a European presence in the Americas and shows her own family genealogy as bound up with key historical moments in Mexico's history.[7]

The installation recycles the wardrobe from *Venus Envy Chapter II*; here, the closet is caught between the central parterre and the artificial border of bushes painted along the wall. Its placement magnifies Mesa-Bains's family history of migration. The artist traces her family's migration to the United States after the Mexican Revolution. Hometowns on both sides of the border are written on the walls of the wardrobe. The closet is painted green and dappled with white and gold, reflecting the marigolds draped over the doors and sprinkled across the floor; marigolds mark the altar's participation as a Day of the Dead–like memorial to departed family members and invites their spirits to inhabit the space. The closet is also occupied with a figurine of the Virgin Mary in full color; she is surrounded by other female attendants that are painted over with a green, mossy surface that syncretizes the Catholic saints with the more earthly deities of indigenous Mexican spirituality. Personal pictures, letters, and mementos are stuffed within the drawers of the wardrobe along with fruits and flowers. The wardrobe is set on a carpet of moss, marigold petals, and dirt; in contrast to the parterre that sits in front of it, the boundaries of this land are uneven, seemingly stretching out or receding of their own accord. A mix of clearly artificial beaded and "natural" trees surrounds the wardrobe, and three glass bottles are filled with sand and set in front of the wardrobe to signify the importance of land, including the need to keep a sense of it with you.

On the other side of the gallery, a beaded topiary is placed in front of the wall painted as bushes. On the wall behind the shrub, the artist uses gold paint (a reference to the colonial quest for gold) to quote political geographer Edward Soja: "We see how space can be made to hide consequences from us, how relations of power and discipline are inscribed into an apparent innocent spatiality of social life, how human geographies become filled with politics and ideology." The quote acts as a framework to help us understand the installation. Soja's work posits that all spaces are constructed and not even "nature" is innocent; within this installation, nature is highly manipulated—the parterre and topiary reveal colonial Europe's aspirations to see, know, and control the world. Soja is also known for his concept of third spaces—those that are both real and imagined. With the construction of Mesa-Bains's wardrobe, she builds a third space that is caught within and resists the colonial order. As an altar adorned with fruits, flowers, and Catholic and earthly figures, it makes room for a spiritual presence. As a wardrobe borrowed from *Chapter II*'s *The Virgin's Closet*, it invites room for embodied ways of being and knowing in the world. As a space of relatively unrestrained natural elements (in comparison to the parterre, at least), it makes room for nature's resistances. The materialization of spirit, embodied identities, and nature shifts over time through historical contingencies that are traced on the walls of the wardrobe and in the garden carvings. Both representational and "real," this geography elucidates the comediating influences of the private landscapes and public territories for which the work is named.

### VENUS ENVY CHAPTER III

*Venus Envy Chapter III: Cihuatlampa, the Place of Giant Women* (1997) marks a shift in Mesa-Bains's work. It shares a number of themes with her early altars and the other two chapters of the *Venus Envy* series while giving a stronger presence to the earthly materials brought into her installations. In some ways, it is less intimate in its presentation of space than *Chapter I* and *Chapter II*, which focused on dimly lit enclosures such as the dressing table in a bedroom or Sor Juana's desk staged in what looks to be a living room. The installation is spread throughout a large museum room, the spaces are relatively open and free-flowing, and the aesthetic of accumulation is pared down. The centerpieces of the installation are three large figures that signify the female body. *Vestiture . . . of Feathers* is a large and colorful feathered gown; *Vestiture . . . of Branches* is a large, translucent coppery and golden gown with branches stuffed in the neck and arm pieces of the dress. The third piece, *Cihuateotl (Woman of Cihuatlampa)*, is a large, curvaceous, moss-covered body inscribed with Aztec markings and sprawled on the floor. Mesa-Bains explains, "Every element was to compose a picture of nature because it [the installation] was about a place, not just a people." The artist also notes that, in centering themes of "woman," "nature," and the construction of place, she hoped to make "an intervention in 'mother nature'" to disrupt the paradigms that link primitive/nature/female and civilized/culture/male (Steinbaum Krauss Gallery 1997).

With each of the three main figures, Mesa-Bains points to the ways in which women's bodies are culturally inscribed with meaning through costume or literal inscriptions (e.g., through glyphed tattoos). Yet here the artist takes special care to use elements from the natural environment (moss, feathers, tree branches) to embody women. Given their juxtaposition with the very unnatural environment of the museum as well as their placement across from a large mirror (ringed with seashells) and a shelf featuring feminist literature, the artist intertwines nature and culture. In framing the room with an altar and through the use of glyph-like markings, the artist draws spiritual energies from the earth goddesses, the giant women of Cihuatlampa. And rather than yielding a clear and essentializing link between "women" and "nature," Mesa Bains sacralizes both women and nature through the performative use of symbols and the staging of a ritualized scene in the museum room. She also raises questions of "naturalness" and performance by attending to the kinds of performances that are considered inappropriate for women: the sheer size of the bodies in the room, along with a list of descriptors written on the wall— "massive," "excessive," "transgressive," and other negative terms assigned to women who are too large or too much in a society that wants them to be small and silent. The artist creates a new place in which exuberant and powerful women thrive.

This installation does not present as an altar in the straightforward fashion of earlier exhibits. Laura Pérez argues that, by the time the artist completes the third and last chapter in the *Venus Envy* trilogy, "Earth, indeed the cosmos, is the vanity table/altar" (2007, 101). As an earth altar, the ritual seems to have as its purpose the birthing of new kinds of subjectivities. Cihuatlampa is the place in the Aztec afterlife where the souls of women who have died in childbirth gather and are celebrated as warriors. Mesa-Bains hangs an image of a large warrior woman titled *Amazona Azteca* next to a giant dress and a similarly oversized pair of high-heeled shoes to remind us of the oversized women/goddesses that reside here. Their world is a matriarchal place free from men and their control. As such, signs of the natural world and the theme of reproduction are called upon not to claim women's inherent *naturalness* or biologically determining capabilities, but rather women's role in constructing new social realities. Spectators are (undersized, outsider) witnesses in this spiritual labor of social transformation in which categories of sacred/profane, natural/artificial/cultural, public/private, human/more-than-human/spirit are challenged and opened up to support possibilities for counterhegemonic subjectivities and a vision of alternative futures.[8] The installation of gowns moves us from rigid gender (and human) identities toward *becoming-nature* and *becoming-spirit*, an intersubjective stretching of the self. This is modeled by the giant moss-covered woman reclining on the museum floor; like Elba Sánchez does in her poetry, the rolling curves of the oversized woman seem to stretch into hills and mountains. It is likely not a coincidence that the moss-covered sculpture also resembles the *Siluetas* of Cuban-born artist Ana Mendieta, whose earthworks explored the links between the female body (or at least her own body), matter/nature, and spirit—key themes for a woman whose early life was structured by a series of displacements, first from Cuba and then from a number of foster homes.[9] Mesa-Bains acknowledged her influence: "If I could name one person that has really been pivotal to me, that I've never known, it's Ana Mendieta. The whole excavation of the body, the translation of human geography and the land, and the things growing, these primordial mythologies of women as mother earth, as fecundity, she has everything and she took every conceivable risk" (Griffith 2002, 40).

*Venus Envy Chapter III* was exhibited in 1997, a time when the backlash against ecofeminism had gained momentum, which may explain why so few critics engage with this installation as a turn to earthworks or a focus on a "woman-nature" connection and instead focus on the textuality of the series. After all, Mesa-Bains does describe all three works as "chapters." It may be the case that the semiotics of an aesthetic of accumulation are seen as more layered, complex, and literary; the danger of drawing links between "woman" and "nature" has been seen as too risky or embarrassingly out of step with the ascendancy of poststructuralism in the academy. Scholars of this work tend to focus on the piece titled *Archeology Table* that sits away from the three large-scale figures (the gowns and the mossy woman). The table displays mementos from Mesa-Bains's life along with dirt, a magnifying glass, bones, and other items that signify a sorting through of personal history. Given its nearness to the area staged as Cihuatlampa, it also suggests an excavation of women's histories outside of the colonial order. At the opening of the exhibition, Mesa-Bains describes herself as "an archeologist who comes across this place" (Steinbaum Krauss Gallery 1997), but *archaeology* also functions in the Foucauldian sense of uncovering the evolution of discursive regimes that give shape to the present. Certainly, much of Mesa-Bains's work has been archaeological in this way, including her critique of museum collections and the broader art world for their role in perpetuating colonial narratives.[10] Yet we need not assume that the individual components of the installation are all—and only—signs asking us to think about the silencing of a matriarchal world and what was left to present-day women because of it. Rather, in her excavations, Mesa-Bains is materializing a new world, perhaps in the vein of Aztlán or Cherríe Moraga's "Queer Aztlán," yet this one is already peopled with women: Mesa-Bains herself and the feminists she admires and whose works are displayed on a shelf in the room. The earthly elements form the land base that has been part of the Chicano movement even as the spiritual project of *becoming landscape* shifts from the patriarchal Aztlán to the possibility of living an en-natured life according to a new set of rules in the matriarchal territory of Cihuatlampa.

The accumulations on the *Archaeology Table* and its focus on a semiotics of juxtaposition stand in a productive tension with the excessive materiality of both the land and women's bodies imagined by the three large centerpieces. As this section's epigraph suggests, nature is not (only) a sign; it always exceeds human representations and resists our physical and discursive efforts to contain it. Amanda Boetzkes describes the antirepresentational capacity of nature and earth art as a question of "perceptual excess," which acknowledges the limitations of humans to see and know all of nature's secrets and potential (2010, 12). I have described the autotopographical impulse within Mesa-Bains's aesthetic of accumulation as a question of "performative excess"—the strategic fracturing and multiplying of personal and collective histories to defer racist, classist, and sexist colonial narratives and create grounds to materialize new selves. Taken together, there are two kinds of agencies at work in these frameworks: Mesa-Bains harnesses, to the extent possible, the rhetorical and spiritual power held within objects interacting together, with the audience, and with the artist. As spectators, the objects grab our attention and create new relationships with us and any others they may also call forth (e.g., the factory producers of the object, the film stars we admired, the gardens we played in, the deities we pray to). The artist allies with the natural world in search of alternative ways to organize social and spiritual life; in so doing, she finds new ways to defer significations that have confined her in the past even as they have confined how we have understood "nature," "woman," and "place" in their materiality *and* signification.

## THE CURANDERA'S BOTANICA

Finally, I examine how Mesa-Bains's work *The Curandera's Botanica* (2008) shows her evolving relationship to place and nature. This installation was created in response to a period in the artist's life that she describes as marked by "many years of trauma, death, and loss," including her own debilitating back injury (2011, 46). In the corner of a gallery space, one wall is painted pine green with sparse green variegated shrubbery painted low on the wall. Its color evokes a forest, which is further emphasized by cuts of pine branches that are scattered at the base of the wall. The gallery floor is made of wood boards and the area around the installation is covered with lavender; a border edged in sand separates the wood flooring from the lavender. As a healing herb, lavender is known for its soothing properties. The scent of the herbs and pine enter the body immediately as one comes into the space, reminding viewers that they are using their whole body to experience the exhibit, rather than reading the installation from a distant, rationalizing perspective. Above the lavender and pine, a glowing lightbox of Mesa-Bains's paternal grandmother is hung on the wall; as an *altarista* and avid gardener, she has been an inspiration in all of Mesa-Bains's work, serving as a muse along with other women such as Sor Juana and contemporary Chicana feminists writers and artists. In her position of prominence, Mesa-Bains honors her and invites her spirit to the altar.

A stainless-steel medical or laboratory table/altar with two levels is set to the right of the portrait. The top level displays instruments of Western science, including beakers, Bunsen burners, and distillation equipment, although the surface is not solely dedicated to these objects. The artist also displays prayer candles, a clear glass skull, and a red glass heart. The glass heart and skull conjure the body to be healed, but the heart has other connotations as well. Resembling a sacred heart, it joins the Catholic idea of Jesus's compassionate suffering from redemptive wounds and the Nahua idea *yolteotl* (heart of God)—the notion of a creative power connecting with the spirit or force of the world. As such it represents a point of syncretism between the Spanish colonizers' Catholic worldviews and indigenous worldviews (Montoya 2016; Villaseñor Black 1999; Broyles-González 2002). Last, an open book is set to the side on the top level, as though it was placed there as a kind of recipe book to be consulted. Mesa-Bains explains, "The traditions of *curanderismo*, which include the inseparability of the mind and body, the connection between the natural and supernatural, the collective cure, and the power of the soul through family narratives are attested to in the Healing Book" (2011, 46).

The glass heart and the Healing Book are points of connection between the upper level of the table and the lower level, which is adorned with earthly elements to be used in *curanderismo*. The artist includes peace lily flowers to introduce harmony into one's relationships. Eggs are nestled among the mosses and are often used in *limpias* (ritual cleansings). A large set of antlers lies at the front of the table, and while they may be used to ward off spirits, they also recall Frida Kahlo's self-portrait *The Wounded Deer* (1946) and her struggle with pain and injury from a childhood accident.[11] By including Kahlo at the table, Mesa-Bains sanctifies her and recognizes their shared struggle both as artists working as cultural activists and as women struggling with the limitations of their bodies. The two levels of the table bring together Western and indigenous healing traditions and, while acknowledging their separate  genealogies and worldviews, the artist recognizes that they may be brought together creatively as she searches for ways to heal (1) personally from her injuries and (2) culturally from the *nepantla* state that shapes the experiences of many Mexican Americans.

The final piece of the installation is a medicine cabinet set adjacent to the green wall. The cabinet follows Mesa-Bains's work on the *wunderkammer*, or cabinet of curiosities; such cabinets emerged during the European Renaissance to catalog objects collected during the "age of discovery." Cabinets were used to sort the artifacts of the world's non-European cultures as well as the flora and fauna characteristic of those foreign geographies, and they were marked as spectacular objects of wonder. The collections served as the precursor to natural history museums, ultimately characterizing the people and  environments outside of Europe as essentially *other* and separating them as "nature" to be observed, understood, and ultimately controlled by Europeans in rooms designated as sites of "culture"—first hosted in the homes of the aristocracy and, later, in museums. Here, the cabinet references that history, but Mesa-Bains gives it over to a new function: "In this chamber I deliberately combined the natural, artificial, and miraculous in a gesture of recovery from the Eurocentric separation of objects that would fit into such categories" (Mesa-Bains 2013, 49). These items include a photo of United Farm Worker cofounder César Chávez, an image of Juan Soldado (the folk saint of migrants crossing the U.S.-Mexico border), and containers of dried beans and corn that grow across the Southwest and Mexico. Shells, fruit, photos, shoes, and other personal memorabilia also line the shelves.

As a medicine cabinet, Mesa-Bains finds all of these items to be necessary for the kind of personal and social healing she seeks. In this piece, she is interested not just in critiquing the imposition of a Eurocentric worldview, but also in selectively incorporating what may be useful into an indigenous approach to wholeness. In this, Mesa-Bains negotiates what Gloria Anzaldúa calls "mestiza consciousness" that shifts out of dualist and oppositional thinking. She writes, "At some point, on our way to a new consciousness, we will have to leave the opposite bank, the split between the two mortal combatants somehow healed so that we are on both shores at once and, at once, see through serpent and eagle eyes" (Anzaldúa 1999, 101). For Mesa-Bains, this approach to healing integrates the material and spiritual, the "natural" and supernatural; humans are part of that super/natural wholeness rather than separate from it as both the Western scientific and religious paradigms have separated men's rationality from the bodily and religious realms.

*The Curandera's Botanica* was conceived during a time of intense pain and trauma in the artist's life. Confronted with the limits of the human body, its inability to control the world around it, and its ability to make sense of loss, Mesa-Bains immerses herself in a space of healing that bridges the human with the super/natural. The natural elements of the installation are mingled with the artificial in a way that respects nature and recognizes its continuities with other objects; here and elsewhere, there is not such a strict separation between the so-called natural and the human-made world. Despite this, the artist recognizes that natural objects hold a power that is not fully known and cannot be fully controlled. The *curandera* listens to, respects, and works with that power, and she considers the human-made objects (candles and the statues of saints, for example) as equal players in her healing efforts. *The Curandera's Botanica* presents an opportunity to read the accumulated objects as signs and stories of personal and collective healing even as the objects themselves exert their materiality and do the work of healing. Between the human agency of signifying through performative excess and the super/natural agency of objects, including their alterity *and* entanglement with humans, the work oscillates in the tensions between altar as allegory and altar as agent: the metaphor can manifest the "real," but the material is never only reducible to our perceptions and stories of it.

## Conclusion

It is critical that we make linkages between the peril of the earth and the role of the artist and their practices of reflection, analysis, or activism. Our art forms can bring us closer to nature and healing and inspire us to revision the world.... We are in a time of new models, integrating commitments, practices, values and beliefs. Art is not simply a compassionate and didactic response but a complex layering of issues, metaphors and materiality and spiritual transformation.

—Amalia Mesa-Bains, "Art and Spirit across the Landscape"

Altar installations allow viewers to interact with the art in an intimate way that opens opportunities for more active and critical spectatorship. With domesticana, Mesa-Bains draws out a complex sense of belonging. Spectators are moved to see both the homely and unhomely aspects of the domestic realm, including the space of the garden. As Mesa-Bains's work recalls her own domestic spaces, viewers connect it to those places that are familiar to them, but they are called to see them differently. The memory-building, consciousness-raising potential of installation has the effect of deterritorializing spectators from their own problematic places of belonging, asking them to shift their allegiances. With the inclusion of natural effects, like moss and rocks, as well as the visible excess and accumulation of recycled materials, her autotopographies signal dual processes: (1) alienation and ecological destruction, and (2) unity across the human-made, "natural," and supernatural worlds, including care for human and more-than-human others.

As spectators walk within and around the installations, the objects that create the altars extend their own unfigured invitations to spectators even as Mesa-Bains welcomes us into her histories and landscapes. The altars may be autotopographical, telling us something about the artist's life and identity, but autobiography, too, is performative: the story of self is not a straightforward accounting of who we are, but a selection of stories meant to construct and act out a chosen self.[12] One of the reasons that Mesa-Bains's work has become so successful is precisely because her narratives are not straightforward and single-storied. Her altars multiply our understandings of history, of the artist, of the places and objects with which she works. This aesthetic of accumulation has surprising ecological implications. Rather than signaling a capitalist subject whose value lies in its ability to collect and consume, accumulation and excess—both in objects and in meanings derived from them—conjure the constructedness of gender, race, class, nation, and nature through repetition and ritual (sitting down at the altar, vanity, laboratory, or library table to create). The scenes are excessive because, traditionally, the domestic and earthly elements of human life have not belonged within the gallery or museum spaces; their "unnaturalness" highlights the strategic performance of memory-making, self-making, and nation-making both in the present by the artist and spectators, and in the past that is cited in the installations. The work of subjectification has occurred in the construction of colonialist histories through natural history museums, the double binds with which the Catholic Church has tied up women, or the circumscribed success offered to Dolores del Río, for example. The objects themselves are cleaved into subjects of the artist's making in the creation of her tableau. Domesticana relies on the excess that juxtaposes a number of different objects to tell a complex story, but it also serves as an aesthetic of excess that proudly displays items of significance among those in the working class who cannot afford much. It is a personal story (autobiography) and a communal one (autohistoria) manifested through material culture and, although it serves these purposes, it is also meant to draw in the spirit world and communicate with deities and departed loved ones. While focused on the feminine and the domestic, Mesa-Bains's art does not reinscribe women or nature within particular roles or allocate femininity or "naturalness" to certain bodies or objects. Compositionally, femininity is a drag performance, a spiritual performance, a familial performance, a performance of writing and making art, and a performance of *becoming nature*. The ecology of Mesa-Bains's altars is also performative—a ritual coming together of varied objects that pull us into these performances, transforming us as spectators as they do so, sharing with us, perhaps, what it is that nature remembers.

# Body/Landscape/Spirit Relations in *Señorita Extraviada*

## *Cinematic Deterritorializations and the Limits of Audience Literacy*

> Assemblages are interesting because A. They de-privilege the human body as a discrete organic thing. As Haraway notes, the body does not end at the skin. We leave traces of our DNA everywhere we go, we live with other bodies within us, microbes and bacteria, we are enmeshed in forces, affects, energies, we are composites of information. B. Assemblages do not privilege bodies as human, nor as residing within a human/animal binary. Along with a de-exceptionalizing of human bodies, multiple forms of matter can be bodies—bodies of water, cities, institutions, and so on. Matter is an actor.
>
> —Jasbir Puar, "'I would rather be a cyborg than a goddess'"

A number of feminist films document women's lives on the U.S.-Mexico border in the era of NAFTA's maquiladora development schemes and the femicide of the 1990s and 2000s. Among them, Vicky Funari's *Maquilapolis (City of Factories)* (2006) provides a clear analysis of the physical costs of working in factories and living in nearby rural *colonias* polluted by industrial waste. The film distinguishes the geographies of the factory and the rural landscape where workers reside as sites of danger *and* activism. *Maquilapolis* introduces the Chilpancingo neighborhood of Tijuana, which plays unwanted host to untreated sewage, a dangerous electrical network, and toxic waste runoff from a departed battery factory. Many women there have poor health, including reproductive disorders, and they care for sick and dying children as a result of these environmental harms. Nonetheless, Funari films the women as activists, including those who organized the Chilpancingo Collective for Environmental Justice. In *Maquilapolis*, the director uses an environmental justice frame to analyze the political economy of the border because gender, race, and class are obvious factors in where the women may work and build homes.

Rural *colonias* near maquiladoras have been widely studied by environmental researchers from the north—and not always in a way that does justice to the struggles of those living in the region. For example, interviews collected at the Derechos Humanos *colonia* across the Texas border near Brownsville show that families understand their home in very different ways than do northern environmentalists. Melissa Johnson and Emily Niemeyer report: "Northern visions of environmentally devastated landscapes can easily be seen as part of patterns of discursive violence. . . . Northern environmentalists see (and depict) the border as an environmental wasteland, and the people living there as victims of environmental devastation" (2008, 381). While the landscape is toxic and families do seek change, many also saw the community they built there as an improvement over the greater economic marginalization experienced while living in a more isolated region without access to factories or schools. Johnson and Niemeyer's study and Funari's documentary are careful to depict residents as agents defining their own lives and pushing for change in ways that write against the discursive and material violence that intrudes on the community. While those texts employ an environmental justice framework to consider the intersection of race, class, and gender at the border, Lourdes Portillo's documentary *Señorita Extraviada* (2001) does not consider environmentalism explicitly as it investigates murders of young women in the region. However, it does take up questions of representation, including the problem of discursive violence in the construction of women and landscapes of the borderlands.

This chapter continues this book's exploration of the power of visual and narrative cultures to bring about change in individuals, in our human communities, and in our relationships to the natural and spiritual world in and around us. In the previous chapters, Chicana feminist literature and art were considered for the ways their creators mapped varied body/landscape/spirit relationships across time and space. Chicana feminist ontologies at work in those texts suggest that naming and visualizing alternative worlds manifests them, or at least brings us closer to those more just futures. This chapter looks at just one text: *Señorita Extraviada*. The film has been skillfully reviewed by others, yet little has been written regarding its ecological cues. An ecocritical lens helps us to better see the full potential of this activism-oriented documentary and it shows the kinds of feminist and ecological consciousness the documentary may produce. Other films, such as *Maquilapolis*, may offer a clearer narrative of environmentalism as it intersects with other social justice concerns, but *Señorita Extraviada* provides a unique opportunity to consider environmental consciousness outside of the framework that has been developed by environmental justice scholars in the north who may see Ciudad Juárez and its outskirts as little more than a wasteland, factoryscape, or killing field.

## Deterritorializations

This analysis begins by asking *What can a film do?* A Deleuzian question (1986, 1989), this approach turns away from more traditional analyses that tend to focus on film and documentary in particular as a more or less distorted representation of reality. Rather, this antirepresentational philosophy reflects the strong ontological impulse in many Chicana feminist works that emphasize the power of the creative act to bring about change in oneself and in the world around us. This is particularly true for a film like *Señorita Extraviada* in which spirituality plays an explicit and central role. *Señorita Extraviada* also represents a trend of performative documentary filmmaking with the potential to deterritorialize—that is, destabilize and reorient—the subjects of the film and the film's spectators.[1] We see a clear re(w)riting of both people and the spatial relations that construct humans and the more-than-human world as the film creates room to build body/landscape/spirit intersubjectivities in ways uniquely enabled by the medium.[2] As a film, the text can circulate to a potentially wider audience than place-based murals and art that is housed in a museum for a limited period of time. In addition to wider circulation, the filmic medium can affect the viewer in a more intimate and more deeply embodied way. For instance, Deleuze's *Cinema 1: The Movement-Image* (1986) and *Cinema 2: The Time-Image* (1989) reveal how the manipulation of images and time through film editing creates the possibility in the viewer of thinking differently. Film cuts, superimpositions, the speeding up and slowing down of images, filmic dissolves—the camera's eye can see differently than the human eye and it can push us from our comfortable and routine engagement with the world around us. Thus, cinematic representations are uniquely situated as an art form that can disrupt continuous flows of time and of movement, disconnect perception from one coherent viewing subject, and play with affect in order to dislodge, disorient, and deterritorialize spectators. Ultimately, as Claire Colebrook suggests, new becomings of life may be enabled through a disruptive encounter with film: "A thing (such as the human) can transform its whole way of becoming through an encounter with what it is not, in this case the camera. But this can only be so if we encounter the camera of cinema, not as something we already know, but as something that challenges us" (2002, 37). Given the potential of film, this chapter explores the following: What sort of *becomings* does *Señorita Extraviada* enable? Can film stretch the possibilities of deterritorialization beyond the scope offered by the literature and art considered in other chapters?[3] What body/landscape/spirit intersubjectivities—or, as Puar may prefer, *assemblages*—are enabled?

Throughout this book, I elaborate on a technology often put to use by Chicana feminists that I name *performative intersubjectivity*. Following Colebrook and Puar, if cinema's potential is in its ability to create new assemblages, we can grab new language to orient ourselves to the concept.[4] Recall that ecofeminists envisioned intersubjectivity as a web of connectivity that breaks down the dichotomies between self/other, culture/nature, and human/animal (King 1989; Plumwood 1993; Plant 1997; Haraway 1991). In addition to recognizing how human social relations created a number of binaries, hierarchizing value within human communities and between humans and the natural world, scholars posited other kinds of relationships among humans and the more-than-human world, including ways to understand nonhuman agency, to recognize humans as more deeply embedded within landscapes, and to cultivate our moral commitments to the lives of others. Chicana feminists explored in this book might reach the same conclusions regarding our relationships and responsibilities to the land and to others, but arrive at them from different directions. Consider Gloria Anzaldúa's awareness that "the body is rooted in the earth, la tierra itself. You meet ensoulment in trees, in woods, in streams. The roots del árbol de la vida of all planetary beings are nature, soul, body" (Anzaldúa and Keating 2002, 560). Moreover, Chicana feminist writers and artists explored within the present text (and many others) extend these relationships into the cultural realm in ways that deconstruct culture/nature and material/discursive binaries. AnaLouise Keating reminds us, "As do indigenous practitioners, Anzaldúa grounds herself in a metaphysics and ontology positing that words, images, and material things are intimately interwoven; the performative power of specific, carefully selected words *shifts* reality. Stories and metaphors are as real as tables, chairs, lightning, doorknobs,

Kansas, the book you're holding in your hands, Catholicism, houses, rain, and rocks" (2013, 119; italics in original). In the same way, for Deleuze and Guattari (1987), as well as the scholars developing new materialist feminisms, the discursive and the material are interwoven: Intersubjectivity may be understood through assemblage theory where material objects (bodies, bushes, machines, microbes) and the social and discursive elements that bring them together form an assemblage. Assemblages come together and fall apart, and new dis/connections may be made at any time.[5] While all three bodies of literature—ecofeminism, Chicana feminism, and new materialist feminism—illuminate body/landscape/spirit intimacies, this chapter emphasizes the cinematic apparatus as a connective device. I consider how Portillo's filming strategies impact spectators, including her ability to dislocate the viewer's subjectivity and push the spectator to consider new alliances directed toward ecosocial justice. Although I highlight this film's potential, assemblages cannot be prefigured and reception is unpredictable. Is the audience prepared to understand and embrace the world made possible by the work? What audience-literacy limitations does the creator come up against? This chapter concludes with a brief reception analysis that reveals the limits of deterritorialization strategies to create coalitional and ecological intersubjectivities.

## NARRATIVE THREADS: SEARCHING FOR TRUTH, SUMMONING THE SACRED

The story of *Señorita Extraviada* moves along two lines. The first shows Portillo narrating the search for answers that might explain the hundreds of missing young women of Ciudad Juárez. Several master narratives are at work: women have fallen prey to the danger that accompanies life as a prostitute; narcotrafficking has taken the lives of the women; an American serial killer is at fault; the murders are the plot of an Egyptian national; the murders are the plot of a locally led gang controlled by the now-incarcerated Egyptian national; a police conspiracy lies behind the murders; a conspiracy between the police and the maquiladoras lies behind the murders; a conspiracy among the police, the maquiladoras, and the government lies behind the murders; and, finally, globalization writ large is responsible for the femicide. Notably, Portillo herself refuses to provide any concrete answers to her audience, although she does indicate that, at the very least, the government is at fault for failing to protect its citizens from more than two decades of continued violence. She shows less concern with finding the truth than with mapping the discursive terrain as provisional truths emerge. In this, Portillo charts not just the physical violence brought against the women of Juárez but also the discursive violence that continues to circumscribe women. With this refusal of easy answers, Amy Carroll surmises that Portillo "(re)deploys the trope of the question: How does one attempt to interpret the killing fields of Juárez? How does one attempt to interpret the sexualized and racialized sociopolitical and economic violences/violations while neither contributing to their maintenance nor choosing to ignore them?" (2006, 381).

If the first narrative line maps the discursive constructions that enfold women in the region, the second narrative line writes against the representational violence mapped in the first—including the representational violence that marks both the women *and* the land of Ciudad Juárez as degraded and exploitable. Portillo bears witness to the stories of the families of the disappeared and follows them with her camera as they reclaim symbolic and physical space in the border deserts, in the factory towns, and in the family homes. In the face of the failures of the state, its policing arm, and the media, Portillo claims, "I find myself mistrusting everything I am told and everything I read. The only reliable sources of information are from the victims and their families" (2001). While Portillo troubles given narratives and offers space for alternative stories from the victims' families, she employs another narrative strategy through the use of religious imagery that both tells and defers truths that speak against the grain of the master narratives. The funereal tone and religious symbolism are key to understanding the film's aim: The religious cues resignify the women from abject to sacred and thus demand recognition of their political subjectivity (Fregoso 2003; see also Delgadillo 2011). I elaborate on the role of spirituality, which I see as resacralizing *the land* as well as the women of Ciudad Juárez. Portillo is not only re(w)riting relations between and among humans but also addressing spatial relations in a way that recognizes an ecological element in women's struggles for justice.

## THE TIME-IMAGE: DISRUPTING TIME, DECENTERING THE SPECTATOR'S PRIVILEGE

Having drawn the broad strokes of the film's narrative structure, I focus on Portillo's cinematic strategies in more detail. The film opens with a mother of one of the disappeared telling the story of her own kidnapping and rape while pregnant with her daughter. Portillo cuts back and forth between a close-up of the woman giving testimony to the camera and a reenactment of that night eighteen years ago. As the viewer grows emotionally invested in the terror drawn out by contrasting the visual reenactment with an interview featuring the woman reciting the memory, the mother denies the viewer's sense of relief that she has survived. At the conclusion of her story, the mother reveals that "what nearly happened to me has happened to her," speaking of her daughter's kidnapping and subsequent murder (Portillo 2001). As a framing device, this opening scene shows Portillo's understanding of the complexity of time and history. Rather than show history as something that unfolds in a straightforward and linear fashion, the director employs what the works of Yreina Cervántez and Alma López have shown us in chapter 2: a sense of time as cyclical or spiral. The cyclical expression of time is repeated throughout the film as Portillo moves between the buildup of evidence and collapse of a case only to build up a new case with the same outcome—the mystery remains unresolved. Yet the sense of time as circular is compounded by the use of a Catholic Gregorian chant that crescendos at the close of each woman's narrative, the montages of news stories, and the continuous tracking of time and body counts. The effect of this time-image—what Carroll names a "circular-turned-spiraling logic"—is to disrupt the spectator's sense of time as continuous, forward-moving, and progress-oriented (2006, 385).

If subjectivity is marked by a coherent sense of self in a moment and across time, Portillo's troubling of time, indeed history, undermines any sense of the coherent self that might emerge. Further, this image of time spiraling out of control without the intervention of justice strikes a dissonant chord against the slow but crescendoing, mournful music that accompanies the melodramatic shots of a mother laying out her daughter's dress or the deliberate stroke of paint marking a cross on a telephone pole. The contradictory impulses of all too fast and the sudden stopping of time, action, and narration create anxiety in the viewer but provide no resolution. The unsettled subjectivity of the spectator caused by this play on affect can create an opportunity to undermine a sense of the bounded, autonomous self in order to invite an intersubjective positioning—a positioning that is also created by other strategies in the film and that, ultimately, is key to the film's activist orientation toward alliance-building.

Laura Marks examines the roles of time, memory, and "reality" as they are expressed in contemporary documentary filmmaking on the subject of the war in Lebanon (2000). She mobilizes Deleuze's distinctions between the virtual and the real wherein the virtual acts as "the reservoir on which thought draws in order to bring about the actual" (Flaxman 2000, 31). Accordingly, the virtual plays a potentially large role in documentary filmmaking: the role of the documentary camera might be to record and re-member history differently in order to actuate the virtual. Rather than relaying representational truths, Deleuze and Marks ask how the documentary might offer virtual images that are *more* real than reality, that might relay the unspeakable and reveal the *unvisualizable*—a question that remains particularly significant given the burden of representation on the murders of Ciudad Juárez. One of the explanations for the economic and physical violence against women in the free-trade zone is that gendered and racialized controlling images of Latinas mark women as cheap labor and as sexual objects—exploitable in both cases.[6] It is precisely these representations and the governing stories explaining away the violence that need disrupting.

This antirepresentational impulse parallels strategies that other Chicana writers and artists have used—rewriting the past outside of restricting colonialist and patriarchal frames to create grounds for a different present. That strategy is often symbolized by the re-membering of the goddess Coyolxauhqui as seen in the work of Gloria Anzaldúa, Juana Alicia, Alma López, and many other Chicana artists and writers detailed in the prior chapters. Given this, it might be said that working within the virtual also summons what Emma Pérez calls the "decolonial imaginary" or a "third space" in the gaps of status quo stories where an alternative story rooted in the invisibilized experiences of women at the margins might be formed (1999). Telling stories from the experiences and strategies of survivors can act as the fertile ground on which new subjectivities and more just modes of organizing social life might emerge.

## BECOMING COALITIONAL: SPECTATORS IN MOVEMENT

Although this strategy of re-membering works across artistic mediums, the cinematic technologies that challenge time can potentially disrupt spectators on a deeper affective level than is possible in other mediums. *Señorita Extraviada* invokes the virtual throughout the film with the effect of troubling the spectator's understanding and subjectivity. For example, Portillo cites the virtual through a series of juxtaposed images that bring the past, present, and future together through objects, such as shoes, that link multiple women. Portillo films young women window-shopping for shoes and then cuts to a close-up of the very same shoes found on the body of a murdered woman. She repeats this later in the film, showing one of the survivors slipping into her shoes before cutting to a close-up of another shoe found on another body in the desert. Shoes in this border region may remind us of other shoes—those collected at Nazi concentration camps and now displayed in Holocaust museums and memorials around the world. Collectively, many American spectators continue to recognize and mourn one genocide while failing to recognize another just on the other side of the border.

Citation of the Holocaust provides some historical and conceptual framing to understand the scope of the femicide along the border, but shoes also point in another direction: capitalism in the era of neoliberal trade agreements. The collision of present-day shoppers with the deceased bodies of the past serves two purposes. First, the deceased body implicitly raises the specter of danger in the future of the shoppers, suggesting a dire future unless an intervention is made. The conflation of women of the past, present, and future destabilizes subjectivity and pushes the spectator to take up a relational rather than indi-  vidualist perspective that recognizes continuities between people. It brings up the potential relationships among the women featured in the film, and it also creates a space for a third person: the spectator who may intervene to change the possible outcome. Second, the juxtaposition of shoe stores and women shoppers next to the factories speaks to the complicity of consumer culture and maquiladora-style trade. Portillo's camera scans the makeshift houses across the *colonias*, silently but visually documenting that free trade has not brought the promised economic security to women in the region—although it *has* brought violence. Within this moment of historical contextualization, she seems to suggest that if NAFTA brought with it a significant increase in violence against women, then perhaps the future could look different through challenging free-trade imperialism. The apparent "whodunit" narrative remains unresolved, yet Portillo's critique against gendered and racialized labor and consumption, both of which ultimately make objects of women, remains potent. Moreover, in naming the violence a *genocide*, Portillo disallows  ignorance and apathy among viewers and raises the question of our complicity.

Although disrupting time dislocates and deterritorializes spectators, there are other ways that the documentary strives to open up the self to human, nature, and spirit relationalities. The remainder of this section explores the affective potential for intersubjective relationship-building that becomes explicit when the young women return the gaze of the spectator. For instance, in the final scene, immediately after Portillo films the activist sister of one of the disappeared warning that "to be silent is to be an accomplice," she cuts to a close-up of a young woman on a bus, gazing directly back at the spectator as though she is demanding accountability. Moreover, Portillo's marketing efforts and tours with the film have consistently stressed the activist and coalition-building impulse of the work. She declares, "It is not objective journalism. It evokes compassion and *incites* action" (2003, 231; italics in original).

Portillo is not the first to deploy art's performative functions to draw spectators to coalitional subject positions. Performance artists such as the Guerilla Girls and Las Comadres are well known for their audience-challenging interactive art. Las Comadres describe themselves as a "multinational women's collective of artists, educators, and critics who studied, taught, and created art in the San Diego–Tijuana region during the years of 1988 to 1992" (Mancillas, Wallen, and Waller 1999, 107). Las Comadres, like Portillo, focus on how art can open up questions of territory, identity, and belonging. The artists use deterritorialization as a guiding idea to think about the potential for art to enable the creation of "postnational subjects" while highlighting the relationships among space, subjectivity, and privilege. For example, a border demonstration under the banner of "1,000 Points of Fear: Another Berlin Wall?" compared U.S. anti-immigrant sentiment and the militarization of the border to the divisions resulting in the construction of the Berlin Wall; with this, one of their most effective pieces of performance art, Las Comadres brought the reality of injustice home to spectators on both sides of the border. They pushed spectator-participants to think of new associations about themselves, their land, and their sense of community belonging (including dangerous nationalisms that undergird feelings of belonging). They explain, "Performance in the public sphere introduced a disordering of the status quo. In the resultant space there was an opportunity to call attention to the structure of everyday reality, to awaken the sleepwalker whose feelings and experiences are dulled by prevailing mass culture and mass information systems" (Mancillas, Wallen, and Waller 1999, 112). This seems to be Portillo's goal as well, and thus far I have shown how she achieves it through the disruption of time and historical understanding in order to push spectators into coalitional becomings; I turn now to the role of religion in the film and the ways that Portillo deploys spiritual imagery in order to deterritorialize bodies and land, disrupting understandings of space and place as Las Comadres have done.

## BECOMING SACRED: RE(W)RITING THE BODY

Portillo films with a knowledge of the representational burden she faces. To counteract negative images in the popular media, she deploys Catholic imagery to write against the overdetermining depictions of women as prostitutes and low-skill workers. Portillo also attempts to write against the portrayal of women-made-spectacle as abject corpses (Fregoso 2003). Counter to the proliferation of images in the popular press of the brutalized and decayed bodies of the victims, Portillo's filming strategies invite the ghosts of the women to reanimate their lives. This can be seen in examples of relatives of the victims telling stories of their deaths as well as of their lives. Portillo's montages of photos and letters from the deceased pass across the screen slowly for the spectator to note the details. In one important scene, the mother of one of the disappeared takes out several items of her daughter's best clothing and lays them on the bed without explanation—the sense is that this seeming altar to the daughter invites her return. The camera's lingering shot suggests that the daughter's ghost looks back from the bed, filling the screen and returning the spectator's gaze.

The construction of altars plays an important role in the film; like Portillo's other documentaries such as *La Ofrenda: The Days of the Dead* (1988), *Señorita Extraviada* is *itself* an altar and it marks the director as a *curandera* (healer) of sorts (L. Pérez 2007). Portillo deploys a camera's gaze to shift how the spectator sees; in turn, this makes a shift in cognition possible, one that centers alternative knowledges presented by the female survivors of border violence and the ghosts of those who have not survived. Not only have science and "ordered logic" failed to protect the women, but they are also partially responsible for defining such women as deviant. Adapting insights from Luis León's work on borderlands religions and the body's alternative ways of knowing, I believe that Portillo's reclamation of the gaze and use of religion to resignify the women can "challenge modern reliance on empiricism and colonial forms of knowledge" (León 2004, 248). Moreover, it does so with the charge of an *ofrenda*—Portillo's offering of the film to spectators on behalf of the victims'  families acts as a form of spiritual healing and an incitement to justice.

In addition to the altar-specific strategies to humanize the victims, Portillo makes full use of Catholic imagery, including flickering candles, refrains from mournful chants, the filming of a religious funeral, and the painting of pink-on-black crosses across the streets of Ciudad Juárez. The crosses are the primary symbol of Voces sin Eco (Voices without Echo), the organization established by the families of the disappeared to raise awareness about and find justice for the women of Juárez.[7] Fregoso (2003) notes two important points: first, the crosses underscore the fact that the murders disproportionately target racialized female bodies; thus, the intersectional nature of the activism that demands recognition of women as racialized women, pink on black, is significant. Second, the crosses insist on the sacred nature of the women and on their public visibility in the face of the state's failure to protect and its use of rhetoric that minimizes and excuses the murders.

## BECOMING SACRED: REMAPPING NATURE

While others have noted how the film writes against the abjection of the women of Ciudad Juárez, no one has taken into account the depiction of the landscape. The documentary constructs two different landscapes: the city of Ciudad Juárez with its maquiladoras, shopping districts, and clubs, and the desert outskirts. Both spaces have their own unique environmental and representational concerns. The urban geography of Ciudad Juárez finds factories closest to the center of the city. Factories have poor ventilation and, depending on the nature of production, they can subject workers to hazardous chemicals (electronics factories are among the worst offenders). Although maquiladoras are close to the center of the city where residents have access to public utilities and planned infrastructure, urban elites tend to reside in the city just outside of the environmentally hazardous zone of the factories (Grineski and Collins 2008). In the areas immediately surrounding the factories we find urban labor landscapes that are marked by gendered violence that is also environmental violence. In "Gender, Order, and Femicide," Volk and Schlotterbeck describe these areas: "Urban Juárez is pockmarked by empty lots (*lotes baldíos*) generated by the feverish land speculation that accompanied the first plants. Large parcels of urban space that never reached development stage were simply left vacant. In their movement through the city, poor women on foot traverse these *lotes baldíos*, spaces in which the bodies of murdered women are frequently found" (2010, 130).

Class, race, and gender shape women's movements through the city as well as the image of the city itself. Carroll (2006) suggests that Ciudad Juárez exists in the neocolonial imaginary as El Paso's abject other, racialized and feminized as the city of sin where prostitution and drugs reign; this colonial imagery is updated with newer NAFTA-era imagery of a neoliberal geography overdetermined by the symbol of the maquiladora and its young, racialized female workers. The conflation of border-woman-Mexico is not new. Scholars of Chicana studies have wrestled with the colonial legacy of Malinche, Cortés's translator and lover (although the consensual nature of the relationship is debated). She has been seen as the symbol on whom the primal scene of *Mexicanidad* has played out and in which the lineage of the mestiza stakes its origin. Malinche's assumed betrayal, her coding as *la chingada* (the raped or fucked one), lingers in contemporary neocolonial relations between Euro-America and Mexico. While Chicana feminists have reclaimed Malinche and have sought to resignify her (Alarcón 1994; Tafolla [1978] 1993), Portillo and Voces sin Eco aimed to wrench the women of Ciudad Juárez away from the discursive violence that claimed Malinche and that continues to figure Mexico, and particularly the border, as a feminized, racialized, and thus disposable space.

If, following Carroll, Juárez is understood as the abject other of the U.S. border towns, the desert exists in the neocolonial imaginary as the *other* other, the site against which Ciudad Juárez is defined. As is evidenced by the unsolved murders, the desert escapes surveillance. Portillo's voice-over notes that it is "full of secrets, *some* of them buried in the sand" (Portillo 2001; emphasis mine). Hundreds of bodies have been deposited there. Newspapers as well as the documentary note that the desert acts as the dumping ground for *every-thing* unwanted, including tires and other residential trash, industrial waste from factories on both sides of the border, and the victims of femicide. However, what remains mostly unnoted by film critics and theorists is that the desert is *not only* inhabited by the corpses of young women but also by the city's poor, who live there for lack of other housing options. Although the desert escapes the immediate environmental harms from factory emissions, houses are often pieced together from found elements (cardboard, scrap metal), and residents lack infrastructure, such as sewage treatment, electrical utilities, and piped-in clean water (a problem that grows worse as drought and water scarcity increase). The desert *colonias* are distant from the city center and are where the most economically marginal populations are out of sight from governing bodies. Invisibility and social marginalization masks the environmental and gendered violence that occurs there. However, not *all* of the desert's secrets are buried in the sand; the pans of the camera suggest that the desert does, or at least it *can*, stand in as something other than an abject dumping ground. In the film, the city is marked by production (maquiladoras) and consumption (bars, clubs, stores); the desert, on the other hand, is marked by the homes of the poor who are often made invisible in the production process. The film draws them into visibility as part of a larger critique against neocolonial globalization and shows the intersection of poverty with gender and race oppression as playing a role in the violence.

The resignification of the desert and the city occurs along similar lines as the resignification of the women of Juárez. Portillo takes care to characterize the families that live along the desert as impoverished but virtuous. Her camera holds on the ramshackle houses and cardboard apartments not to indict the families, but to point to the disparity between the wealthy and poor on each side of the border. Alongside these visual cues, Portillo films families talking about their daughters, highlighting the fact that they were hard workers, that they taught catechism, and so on. In one of the most important scenes in the film, the mother of a disappeared woman named Sagrario González tells the story of her daughter's disappearance. In the absence of any coherent narrative, the mother finds solace in an alternative source of knowledge. González's super/natural interpretation begins with her acknowledgment of Sagrario's disappearance and her subsequent turn to Sagrario's parakeets for answers. She recalls asking, "'Luis, do you know where Sagrario is?' And he nodded. The parakeet seemed to understand. He shook his head as if he were saying 'Yes.' The parakeet left on Tuesday ... and on Wednesday they found my daughter's body. We found out on Thursday. I felt that the parakeets knew"

(Portillo 2001). This testimony is given careful attention in the film despite the fact that this scene, including the close-up of a parakeet, does not drive the narrative forward. The scene does not contribute to any sense of the film as a "whodunit." It provides no answers. However, it does signal the role of *alternative*, oppositional knowledge systems, a sense of the supernatural that is not contained by institutionalized Catholicism, and a resacralization of the natural world that draws connections between the natural, the supernatural, and the human worlds. The parakeets double-signify as super/natural figures that connect humans to the natural and spiritual worlds and as women who are confined as birds in a cage within an oppressive network of cultures.

Significantly, the destabilizing work of that scene occurs next to, but not in tension with, Portillo's reterritorializing of both the desert and the city, providing those places with new meaning. Pans of desert expanses are cut between shots of troops of activist families combing the land for loved ones and claiming it back. In these moments, the haunting refrain of the religious chant accompanies the families as they pause in their search, scanning the acres before them. The music coinciding with this halt in the narrative marks the territory as sacred even as the visual expanses seem to cite biblical symbolism wherein the desert remains both a site of temptation as well as the setting for a journey toward greater communion with God. It is also possible that viewers will connect the desert scenes intertextually with other representations in Chicana feminist cultural production. For example, in many of her widely read works, Pat Mora envisions the desert not only as a place that is dangerous, but also as a place where women can find themselves. In *Agua Santa: Holy Water*, Mora compares La Llorona, a mother whose children have been lost to her, to "desert women / [who] know about survival" (1995, 77). The parallels between Mora's poem and Portillo's visuals of mothers and other family members asserting their agency, refusing to bend to patriarchal and neocolonial violence while searching for their disappeared daughters, is striking.

As in the desert, *Señorita Extraviada* also shows the families marching across and thus reclaiming the city of Juárez, although here they do so with protest banners. In addition, in several scenes throughout the documentary, the camera zooms in on pink-on-black crosses and pans out to streets full of crosses to show how Catholicism (and the coextensive intersectional awareness of women's sacrality) literally becomes part of the landscape of Ciudad Juárez. The tactics enacted here resignify abject landscapes as sacred as they rewrite abjected women as such, but equally important—as the scene with Sagrario's parakeets show—they also disrupt narrative flow and the spectator's sense of security and coherence by opening up the relationality of animal-human and

110

human-landscape assemblages. These two functions are important to understanding the cultural work that *Señorita Extraviada* can perform: the film not only re(w)rites our understanding of the people and geopolitical history of the region but, in concentrating on the affective potential to deterritorialize spectators, Portillo also invokes a change in relations of power by disallowing the privilege of spectators.

*not 100% clear what is meant here*

## BECOMING OTHER: SPECTATOR TRANSFORMATIONS

If Deleuze sees the viewer's relationship with film through an antirepresentational frame where film is not charged with the task of representing a certain view of reality, but with moving viewers to new associations, *Señorita Extraviada* is positioned to do the important work of enabling a becoming-other that engages with the crisis of physical and representational violence along the border. Portillo makes no explicit demands and gives no answers, but she incites a desire for change. What distinguishes this documentary is its potential for deterritorialization. To be sure, not all subjects are disrupted and made anew by this film in the same way; context is important in understanding the cultural work performed by *Señorita Extraviada.* As I have sketched throughout this chapter, the women of Ciudad Juárez are deterritorialized through sacred resignifications while the American spectators targeted by Portillo's film are deterritorialized through the destabilization of their subjectivity, including the ways they are confronted with their privilege and complicity; complicity  is marked by acceptance of the discursive frame that views Mexico and Mexican women as other and by economic violence along the border, driven by NAFTA and the consumption of cheap goods and drugs that fuel narcotrafficking.[8] Portillo's use of aural and visual religious cues to resignify the women and landscape come with their own shortcomings. Judith Butler (1997) warns that there is always a citational legacy that drags behind resignifications and here the danger is that the documentary recodes the women as sacred Catholic subjects of suffering. However, while a Deleuzian reading might describe this as a dangerous example of reterritorialization (Deleuze and Guattari 1983), the film resignifies women and landscapes outside the strict confines of institutionalized religion and, as Sagrario's story shows, it does so incompletely.

The deterritorializing impulse is not only depicted in the way the documentary unravels dominant narratives or the ways that it resignifies women's religious participation within the public realm to demand citizenship rights, but also in the ways it *defers* meaning. The crosses are provocative but do not deliver a single story that can erase or resolve the trauma enacted in the region. Rather, it is a call to envision the space for new subjects along the border, to envision the borderlands itself as a new kind of territory in which such violence is inconceivable, and to invite allies to stand in coalition to support this aim. Not only does it reconceive the land as a place where violence can no longer be brought against women's bodies, but in tying together Portillo's resignification of the land and her implicit critique of global capitalism and the maquiladora culture it engenders, the film may also combat the ecological violence of relaxed standards of environmental protection within free zones and the neoliberal commodity fetishism they support.

The portrayal of the victimized bodies and landscapes is not closed but deferred while the subjectivity of the spectators is pried wide open to force a relational positioning. That is, spectators are challenged to take up alternative knowledge systems that function outside the colonial order of things. In addition, time flows unevenly, sometimes speeding up and sometimes stopping altogether. The spectator is decentered as much by the unsettling of the traditional unitary subject position denied by the film's editing and narrative structure as by the revocation of privilege that occurs when the viewer is faced with Portillo's critiques against neocolonialism and the returning gaze of a young woman who remains vulnerable to the discursive and material violence at the border. Once moved from comfortable and easily identifiable subject positions, viewers scramble to make sense of the trauma recorded by the film and their relationship to it. Portillo's inconclusive but emotionally wrenching interrogative ending—an ending that leaves spectators with the organization Voces sin Eco marching in protest and warning us to speak out and join in protest—also leaves the spectator and the film itself in movement, striving to make new connections and to generate new solutions.

## Complications in Reception

> The question remains—who will listen and how well equipped with relevant information is that audience?
>
> —Sonia Saldívar-Hull, *Feminism on the Border*

By offering an ecocritical reading of *Señorita Extraviada* I hope to build appreciation for the complexity of the film. Despite its potential, however, the question of reception remains: does deterritorialization actually produce subjects that are affectively open to coalitional activism? In other words, does the film actually move spectators to new body/landscape/spirit relationalities? As is true for all creative works, neither writers nor artists can guarantee how their work will be received. Reception depends on many factors, including modes of the text's circulation and the cultural literacy of the audience, although in their tours with the film, Portillo and Fregoso spoke on the director's intent and the activist impulse imbedded in the work (Fregoso 2003). The remainder of this chapter investigates *Señorita Extraviada*'s reception in the United States.

*Señorita Extraviada* introduces Sagrario through her mother, who shares personal details of her daughter's life and a story of super/natural knowledge of her death; these scenes are among the longest and most poignant in the film. We also meet Sagrario's sister, who has become an activist and founder of Voces sin Eco. The scenes introducing the organization come at the end of the film and the music is surprisingly upbeat, which is in contrast to the funeral tones carried across other scenes. In these final moments Portillo cuts from footage of family members marching in protest in an effort to raise awareness to a scene of women painting the haunting pink-on-black crosses across the roads of Ciudad Juárez. Finally, as the music fades Portillo cuts back to the sister, and it is she who warns: "To be silent is to be an accomplice" (2001). As noted earlier in this chapter, this declaration is followed by a close-up of the eyes of a young woman staring back at the spectator, returning her gaze fully as if challenging spectators to speak out, to do *something*.

These scenes are recounted to emphasize the potential they bear—although strangely, they are not mentioned in any reviews of the film consulted for this chapter. Nor is the role of spatial relations or the remapping of nature mentioned in reviews and scholarly film criticism. As outlined earlier, *Señorita Extraviada* has two narrative threads: the first bears witness to the pain *and* agency of the families, including the restoration of humanity to the young women through religious resignifications; the second records the search for the causes of the femicide. However, reception of the film shows that audiences do not read evenly across both narratives. Not one popular-press review names the organization founded by the families of the disappeared. Not one reviewer consulted mentions the crosses, the dirge that weaves throughout the film, nor the altar-like quality of Portillo's juxtapositions of photos, clothes, and letters of the deceased. The first half of this chapter focused on these elements because of their power to disrupt simple, linear storytelling and the kind of colonialist knowledge frameworks that are at least partially responsible for the discursive violence that constructs the devaluation of the woman-border-Mexico assemblage named by Carroll (2006). I celebrated the interrogative force of the documentary that appears to tell two parallel stories, although one clearly interrogates and then unravels the other as it unfolds. Yet reviewers emphasized what they see as Portillo's search for answers rather than her construction of alternative knowledges. The driving questions remain: How has the reception of *Señorita Extraviada* been able to ignore entirely the interrogative force of the documentary? To what ends do spectators read the young woman's gaze as a plea for sympathy and not a challenge? I document three reception patterns that show deflection of the director's interrogative gaze while spectator assumptions regarding the nature of documentary as investigative and fact-finding erase complicity.

## PATTERN ONE: THE POLITICS OF AGENCY AND OUTRAGE

The reviews of this film that I have gathered have come to surprisingly similar conclusions, and almost all are structured the same way: they open with a murder count and a profile of the victims as young, thin, dark-skinned, and long-haired; all list the potential culprits: drug traffickers, globalization and maquiladoras, and incompetent and/or corrupt police and government officials.[9] Reviewers rehearse the master narratives reported by Portillo as though her film was solely investigative journalism. In framing the work this way—as a murder mystery where all the important players are the victims and the suspects—there is no room for extraneous characters. Indeed, families of victims and activists remain largely absent in most reviews and marginal in others. When present, they are enveloped by a sense of hopelessness and disempowerment: "There's little they can do except complain to the authorities," mourns a reviewer from the *St. Louis Post-Dispatch* (Wilson 2003). This attitude rewrites the women Portillo defines as activists, coding them as victims. Yet some reviews deny the women even this. Janice Page of the *Boston Globe* argues that the portion of the film that gives space to grieving women does not tell or show viewers enough about them. Page warns that "this is especially problematic when it comes to factual analysis. When one alleged victim of police misconduct makes some serious allegations relating to the kidnapping crimes, her credibility is impossible to judge because she's hastily sketched by the filmmaker" (2003). With the activists rewritten as either helpless or suspect and thus unworthy of empathy, what do reviewers make of the point of the film?

Thus, the first of Portillo's two aims, to resignify the women of the region as sacred and powerful social and political agents, appears to have been compromised. The success of the second aim, the potential to move spectators to new associations and new actions, is more difficult to discern. The *Boston Globe*'s headline announces "Flawed but Powerful 'Senorita' Evokes Outrage" whereas other reviews interpellate readers in more subtle ways to join the reviewer in a sense of moral outrage about the crimes. However, a closer look at the object of this outrage reveals a troubling trend. A survey of reviews offers the following:

"More disturbing than the statistics—since 1993 more than 270 young women have been raped and killed with their bodies often dumped in the Juárez desert—is the general shrug of indifference from local authorities regarding the killings" (Rechtshaffen 2002); "But, even more stunning than the number of deaths has been the failure of law enforcement officials to put a stop to the killings" (Navarro 2002); "What is even more brutal about these crimes is that they continue without anyone being positively charged with the crime" ("Reel Review" 2002); and finally, "The most incredible fact is that there have been so many victims and so very few answers" (Carreño King 2002).

In a sense, these reviewers are correct. The lack of action points to a highly complex array of factors that caused the crisis or a high degree of complicity among all parties involved. Portillo hints that it is both. Yet reviewers simplify her sketch of the causes as well as the scope of complicity she implies. In characterizing the film as a "whodunit" alongside a shallow sense of moral  outrage that decries not the murders themselves (and the loss of humanity of the victims and their advocates) but the failure of justice, reviewers suggest the solution is to find and punish the perpetrators. Of course, Portillo's aim is to create a coalitional subject position for the spectator to inhabit that "evokes compassion and incites action" (Portillo 2003, 231). In this case, the would-be heroes who might be driven to action in the face of the horror in Ciudad Juárez fail to note their complicity in the gendered neocolonialist politics that target women of the region. Without an understanding of the broader critique for  social, economic, and ecological justice, spectators fail to build coalition; at best, their activism reproduces what Uma Narayan calls the colonialist "missionary position" (1997, 46).

In some reviews even the potential action of the spectator is undermined. One reviewer resignedly states that, "unfortunately, as U.S. citizens, there's only so much we can do" (Wells 2002) and another recounts how she felt powerless and as though she were pinned down by the weight of the crimes, unable to move (Page 2003). This is particularly curious given the relatively upbeat conclusion of *Señorita Extraviada* that is both an *indictment* of complicity and an *incitement* to action. The attitude of powerlessness that inheres in these reviews displaces complicity and defers the call to action. The sense of ambivalence that emerges is reflected in Don Bain's comment in *La Voz de Colorado*: "Perhaps a wider knowledge of this injustice and the accompanying cries of outrage will cause something to be done. See this film and form your own opinion" (Bain 2003). In one swift rhetorical move, the ultimate action called for is that of spectating and armchair theorizing about the murders and possible interventions that might stop them.

*[handwritten marginalia:] Does this relate to needing greater knowledge of the Chicano/a film to be capable of understanding the other ways? to understand how/ows?*

## PATTERN TWO: GLOBALIZATION,
### THE ULTIMATE DETERRITORIALIZING MACHINE

Although the first pattern to emerge reveals the politics of agency and moral outrage in reception, the second pattern—while related to the first—explicitly considers the discourse of globalism as it works within reviews. If I left you with a sense that the activists' charge of complicity has gone completely unrecognized or ignored, in fact there is a more complex negotiation at work. Fregoso (2003) offers an expansive discourse analysis regarding the ways globalization has been called into account for its role in the murders. She focuses on the Mexican government's alibi: globalization has limited the sovereignty of the state; there is no way to intervene because the force of globalization is too great. Similarly, each review consulted underscores the compelling and unstoppable force of globalization. Some reviews do note that the majority of companies that populate the border are American and that, although some murders have been documented prior to NAFTA, the number of murders has increased dramatically post-NAFTA. Reviewers stop short of implicating American corporations, their consumers, or economies that rely on hierarchies of gender, race, and nation in which many of us participate.

While these reviews erase the political stakes, Fregoso's critique regarding the deracialization and degendering of globalism language is curiously explicit in one review: "People here are as disposable as the products they make, so is it really any wonder that drug use and sexual harassment are ingrained in the corporate culture, and that you're not safe even when your workplace is adjacent to a police station?" (Page 2003). This review yields a complex negotiation of race, gender, and national identity. Page's description of the multiple forms of vice that intersect at this site of globalization produce Ciudad Juárez as an "other" that is discrete and no longer related to conditions of its emergence. Here, U.S. complicity in the creation of the free-trade zone at Mexico's northern border is ignored. Furthermore, this review and others ignore U.S. complicity in the consumption of drugs and manufactured goods that are produced or transported through the borderlands. If we look more closely at the review quoted at the beginning of this paragraph, context-specific geopolitical analysis is undermined altogether with the conflation of *Ciudad Juárez* with *here*: "People *here* are as disposable as the products they make...." The ambiguous *people* who are disposable are without race or gender—in fact, they could be anyone. They could be *you*. This elision of the positionality of the victims, who do follow a specific gender, race, and class-based profile in that victims are reported to be young, dark-skinned with long hair, and lacking in economic security, occurs in statements that *"you're* not safe even when *your* workplace is adjacent to a police station." In implicating the spectator in the peril, Page heightens the spectator's sense of fear, but in the face of the erasure of the victims, including the characteristics that mark some as more disposable than others, readers are called to ignore their own privilege and complicity. The terror is brought home to "your" neighborhood in a way that deflects, disempowers, and further diffuses efforts of resistance so that any would-be American ally sees their work as already ineffective before they have even begun to think about it.

## PATTERN THREE: THE INVESTIGATIVE DOCUMENTARY GAZE INTERROGATED

Lastly, a third reception pattern addresses assumptions regarding the nature of the film as *investigative* (a "whodunit") rather than an *interrogative* calling of account. Reviewers are interested in the facts of the case, their truth value, and how they will lead to a break in the case and the eventual capture of the culprits. The film is seen as an investigative report; the assumption is that the documentary can give privileged, objective access to reality. Apparently caught up in the developing crime thriller unfolding before them, reviewers rarely mention the mise-en-scène, music, color filters, or the careful characterization of the women of *Señorita Extraviada.* If the film is strictly a "whodunit," what could account for Portillo's dedication of so much time and narrative space for Sagrario's mother to tell the story of her super/natural awareness of her daughter's death? Why does the spectator get called to understand the alternative knowledge systems the mother deploys through communication with the parakeets if not to interrupt the "whodunit" story line and challenge viewers to question their own confidence in neocolonialist truth narratives? This scene does not easily fit into reviewers' understanding of the investigation and, as such, it goes unmentioned in reviews. The assumptions of the investigative mode of the film allow reviewers to evade some of the more difficult impositions Portillo makes on them. In marginalizing the role of the families and activists that return the spectator's gaze, and in ignoring the careful filmic cues such as the deployment of religion to resignify the women, reviewers miss the interrogative impulse of Portillo's work.

In the single review that directly offers a filmic engagement of the text, Karen Backstein of *Cineaste* verges on offering an alternative reading, but her insight is recuperated at the conclusion. After exploring what she considers to be the strikingly personal nature of the film, including Portillo's use of family and victim testimony, close-ups, frames of personal belongings, and so on, she quotes Portillo as undertaking "an investigation into the nature of truth" (2002, 41). This telling turn of phrase speaks less about finding answers than it does about questioning how and what we know—the politics of truth-making. Yet, despite Backstein's efforts to quote the director and briefly explore this idea, she returns to familiar territory by suggesting that the film "has the fascination of any mystery story, where the 'whodunit' compels the 'reader' to sift through clues, engage deeply with the information, and try to arrive at a satisfying conclusion. Sadly, here the ending remains open and the truth is still out there, waiting to be found." Indeed, what she fails to note is that the *openness* of the film's approach *is* the key. The openness is strategic in that it continues to generate discussion and, hopefully, coalitional collaborations. Portillo purposely avoids providing any concrete answers to her audience. Rather, as the first part of this chapter shows, her aim seems to have been to chart *both* the physical *and* discursive violence brought against the women and land of Juárez. While reviewers have taken Portillo's call to action to suggest that we need to step up efforts to find the culprits and punish them, the young woman at the close of the film reminds us that the problem is less about punishment and more about calling spectators to note how relations of power distribute privilege so unevenly that the young women of Ciudad Juárez are seen as unimportant. Justice means more than catching the murderers; it needs to address the devaluation of women that is at the root of the problem and *that* requires an intervention into the racialized, classed, and gendered neocolonialist thinking that is reproduced on both sides of the border. Indeed, this line of thinking has characterized the borderlands itself as a dangerous space, a wasteland and killing field that is intricately tied to representations of women so that shifting the signification of one cannot occur without also addressing the ways it is coproduced with the other.

The filming strategies disrupt the discursive violence that figures the women and landscape of Ciudad Juárez as disposable, and Portillo asks her viewers to be self-reflexive and interrogate their own beliefs. That reviewers have missed this message so completely suggests that the project of decolonization has far to go, but what is clear is that reviewers are genuinely uncomfortable in their viewings. They may not yet have been moved to *become revolutionary* as projected earlier in this chapter, but there is evidence that *Señorita Extraviada* pushes spectators from their comfortable viewing positions while denying them an easily consumable story with stereotyped subjects. The narrative strategy of deferral and the affective potential of deterritorialization leave the viewer with many questions, which is another form of openness, although not, perhaps, the kind of radical openness that is possible. Nonetheless, the potential is present, waiting to be actualized.

## Conclusion: Recouping Deterritorialization as a Technology for the Intersubjective Self

By way of extending the insights of chapters 2 and 3 that set the groundwork for this chapter's more in-depth case-study approach, I bring together this book's three main lines of inquiry (Chicana studies, ecofeminist philosophy, and posthumanist new materialist feminism) once more. One of the most important overlaps of Chicana studies and ecofeminism is the centrality of intersubjectivity—in Chicana studies the stress on intersubjectivity emerges from multiple sites, including Gloria Anzaldúa's mestiza consciousness, Cherríe Moraga's theory in the flesh, and the coalitional impulse found in Chela Sandoval's work on differential consciousness; in ecofeminism, the ecological elements of our social worlds are foregrounded, highlighting the relationality and thus mutual reliance and responsibility of all organic and inorganic forms in the maintenance of (bio)diversity. Deleuze's antihumanism displaces the  idea of the subject (and thus also of subjectivity) wholly to privilege a shifting perception of multiple times, movements, connections. Deindividualized, we become parts of assemblages moving in many new directions in the best of cases, or stuck (territorialized) in problematic social, political, economic, and environmental patterns at other times.

*Señorita Extraviada* works to destabilize spectators and create intersubjective subject positions across all three theoretical traditions. Although this film cannot guarantee the deterritorialization of either the spectators or of the discursive violence that currently restricts the representation of women and the landscape of the border, reception analysis shows that the film does open up spectators to new and uncomfortable subject positions and it garners sympathy (if not always empathy) for women in the region and their families. As a counter to the controlling images that predominate, it defers any concrete, narrow sense of the women's subjectivities and it models an open and politicized consciousness for viewers. One of the elements that seems to get lost in the reception, however, is the film's reworking of spatial relations. Spectators are clearly made uncomfortable in their viewing and they are asked to stand in alliance with women in the borderlands, yet reviews have shown that it is  harder to recognize how centers of production and consumption, privilege and oppression are spatially segregated and socially constructed. Despite this, there is at least the possibility that these more open subjectivities can form the basis of an ecological self oriented toward coalitional activism. This chapter, along with the others, affirms the potential of cultural production to carry spectators and readers toward human/nature/spirit relationalities and, while art, literature, and film play a starring role as we transition into new subjects, so too can art, literature, and film criticism that draws an ecocritical consciousness out of those texts.

## CHAPTER 5

# Building Green Community at the Border

*Feminist and Ecological Consciousness
at the Women's Intercultural Center*

> Empowerment is the bodily feeling of being
> able to connect with inner voices/resources
> (images, symbols, beliefs, memories) during
> periods of stillness, silence, and deep listening
> or with kindred others in collective actions.
> This alchemy of connection provides the
> knowledge, strength, and energy to persist and
> be resilient in pursuing goals.
>
> —Gloria Anzaldúa, "now let us shift . . ."

In New Mexico, not far from the U.S.-Mexico border, you will find a building made of recycled tires and earth, although it has no Leadership in Energy and Environmental Design (LEED) certification. Deeply insulated, it uses little energy to heat or cool itself. The building also features rain barrels, solar panels, recycle bins, and a thrift shop for the recirculation of clothes, shoes, and furniture. The Women's Intercultural Center (WInC) in Anthony, New Mexico, is a nonprofit organization that addresses the needs of women in southern New Mexico and west Texas. WInC began in 1991 when two Anglo-American Sisters of Mercy moved to the U.S. Southwest with "a commitment to learning about multi-cultural realities and concern for women and children" ("About"). Their work was informed by *mujerista* theology, a woman-centered liberation theology developed across the United States and Latin America.[1] Informal meetings gave women in the community an opportunity to gather and talk about problems in their lives. The group grew larger each month, eventually leading to the formation of WInC and the acquisition of a building to house its programs and classes. The center's mission is to "provide a place for women to learn and work together to develop their social, spiritual, economic and political potential" ("Mission"). To this end, WInC regularly offers classes for economic self-sufficiency, such as the Small Business Academy; classes for personal empowerment, such as oil painting, sewing, ESL, and citizenship; and occasional workshops on nutrition, violence against women, and feminism.[2] Environmental programming includes classes on organic gardening, recycling, and water conservation. WInC staff do not describe the center as an environmental organization although the environment is a daily and considered part of life there. As such, their contributions toward environmentalism and green community-building do not receive the attention they deserve. I show how women at the center tie women's empowerment (in the Anzaldúan sense of the term as noted in the epigraph) to their environmental praxis; in contrast to the characteristics that opened this chapter, it may be those practices that do not seem ecological that have the most to teach us about borderlands environmentalism.

I came to WInC after studying environmental representations in Chicana feminist cultural production, such as the writings of Cherríe Moraga and Helena María Viramontes and the visual art of Juana Alicia and Amalia Mesa-Bains.[3] After learning of the center's noteworthy practices, I sought to compare ecological themes in Chicana feminist cultural production with the ways other Mexican American women understand and work toward social and ecological justice in their daily lives.[4] I employed participant observation and semistructured interviews to gather data on the participants' relationships to the center and its mission.[5] I also reviewed ten years of newspaper clippings, photos, and press releases collected by the staff, using content analysis to interpret these materials and the WInC website, brochures, and a short video of the center. Finally, I studied the poems, paintings, and crafts donated by participants and displayed in the buildings. While interviews offered insights into the lives of the women, the cultural and media artifacts allowed me to expand some of those insights through the broader historical and contemporary context they offered. I was able to see how WInC's focus evolved as it adapted to the interests of new members, the skills of new leadership, and the changing fiscal landscape for nonprofit organizations in the region.

WInC can help us theorize intersections between movements and give new insights into how ecological consciousness is developed and put to good use in different communities. As the environmental histories detailed in chapter 1 show, labor, land, and its resource use have been central geopolitical concerns in the Southwest from the colonial era onward, fueling migration throughout the region and the drawing and redrawing of national boundaries. Access to the land has had not only economic and political dimensions but environmental and spiritual ones as well. This chapter serves as a contemporary case study that is in conversation with the activist histories presented earlier; as an in-depth case study, it brings additional insight and detail into how individual actions and the personal development of ecological consciousness also mobilize a larger social body to action.

## Feminist Environmentalism in the Borderlands

Anthony, New Mexico, largely fits the mold for what Devon Peña classifies as a rural *colonia* where environmental justice struggles involve access to housing, potable water, reliable recycling and sanitation services, and health care. Other issues may include contaminated soil or groundwater (2005). Anthony is an underserved town with a population of approximately 9,000 people. According to the 2010 census, 97 percent of the population identify as Hispanic or Latino and at least 40 percent live below the poverty line. The town is located in the Mesilla Valley, which was once known for its fertile land and occasional flooding from the Rio Grande; it is now home to a large number of water-intensive alfalfa and dairy farms. Anzaldúa's *Borderlands/La Frontera* (1999) records the disastrous impact that industrial agriculture and the subsequent drying up of the Rio Grande has had on her family and the economy of her southern Texas town. Although Anthony is across the western border of Texas, it too experiences the drying of the Rio Grande and has seen drought in the past fifteen years. Drought impacts the agriculture-based economy and increases food insecurity among a population that already experiences poverty. This is a significant point given that the U.S. Department of Agriculture finds that women-headed and Hispanic-headed households experience food insecurity at the highest rates in the nation (2014). Additionally, wastewater from large-scale dairy farming has contaminated the groundwater supply, which is particularly problematic during drought years when groundwater becomes the primary source of water for farmers and public utilities ("Drought along the Rio Grande").[6]

As the population grew, residents voted to incorporate into a municipality in 2010 (town meetings were held at WInC to discuss the pros and cons of incorporation). Despite groundwater contamination, Anthony does have water and sanitation services, although its security and economic infrastructure is still formative. Nonprofit organizations (largely led by women) are playing an important role during this period of simultaneous population growth and municipal development. La Semilla, a local nonprofit organization that formed in 2010, focuses on food access and health issues such as diabetes—a food-related illness that impacts a large number of community members. Although WInC provided a community garden long before La Semilla formed, the organization has since expanded garden and education operations in the region; La Semilla offer a number of programs, including Raices (roots), a "'food systems primer' offering high school age youth hands-on experience in the nuts-and-bolts of food production, cooking and nutrition education, ancestral wellness, policy advocacy and leadership development" ("Raices"). In contrast, WInC is a multi-issue community center that fills the rural *colonia*'s other needs. For example, they provide a thrift shop and emergency food pantry, collaborate with La Piñon Sexual Assault Recovery Services and provide a safe space for survivors, offer Reiki clinics, and host needle-exchange programs. Another organization that addresses public-health needs in the area, Las Promotoras Program of La Clinica de Familia, focuses on labor and immigration concerns. Promoters "provide help to apply for medical and dental insurance to seasonal workers. Pamphlets are also given [to farm workers] with information about how to take care of their skin and disposal and managing toxic solutions" (Medina 2016).

An environmental justice framework that defines the environment as those places we live, work, and play (Adamson, Evans, and Stein 2002) and that links social and environmental needs illuminates how these features of Anthony's rural landscape shape lives in the region. However, other ecological concerns are less visible through an environmental justice lens. Earlier chapters explored the importance of place and spatial politics in Chicana feminist thought. For example, the Chicano movement activists of the 1960s and 1970s imagined a return to the Chicano homeland of Aztlán, and Moraga and Anzaldúa each updated that land-based nationalism with their own visions for a more inclusive homeland in the Southwest that is less tied to nationalist impulses and more accepting of difference and contradiction. Others, such as Pat Mora (1997) and Sandra Cisneros (1984), theorize domestic spaces in their novels. In the case of WInC, space consciousness is important for women in the region, particularly around issues of displacement, transnational migrations, and rurality. In fact, the center was born out of a primary need to overcome feelings of isolation. WInC participant Josie explains, "I live out in the country and my husband is working. I was alone most of the time and I was very depressed. . . . I tell everyone, if you come here, you won't be depressed. It's the medication that you need" ("Where It Starts").

Community-building is particularly important because the community is rural, located thirty miles from Las Cruces and El Paso, and comprised of families that leave the area after a brief stay and established immigrant families that experience an isolating life in the United States. Feelings of isolation are compounded by several factors, including gender socialization that confines women to the domestic sphere, economic marginality that limits transportation options, and fear of the border patrol and harassment. Patricia, a staff member who has been with the center for many years, explains that the interpersonal relationships are what keep women coming back:

> Because of the community we are trying to serve, especially an immigrant community . . . it's very easy to become isolated in American society. I think people feel like they belong in this community, but that they're not welcome. When you have an organization that makes *welcome* a part of what the organization is, that's part of what the Sisters of Mercy believed in . . . their "carism" and hospitality.

As the art and activism examined in prior chapters support, the theme of "belonging" is seen repeatedly in women's work for social and ecological justice across the borderlands. At WInC, several interviewees noted that the welcome begins as soon as they walk through the door and are warmly greeted by the receptionist. Staff and participants extend that greeting as they pass and the welcome is consciously enacted throughout each day. Another staff member emphasized the importance of hospitality, saying, "The idea of the welcome keeps sticking in my mind. . . . Everybody is welcome. Every person is greeted individually. . . . Even those things that are considered everyday interactions are the things that are most important." Staff members not only said that they enjoy the greeting and that they give it as part of their daily practices at the center but that they build in other practices to reward, support, and empower women. Several participants mentioned complimenting someone's painting or encouraging a woman who is having a difficult day—these seemingly small interactions are seen by staff as a way to build women's confidence so that they feel empowered to stand up for themselves and learn new skills; as director Mary Carter believes, this helps women "withstand anything that happens and start looking at options rather than barriers."[7]

Community-building represented by the welcome is important to the center's work, yet a closer look at interview themes suggests that the center offers staff and participants opportunities to transform the relationality of community belonging toward a more thoroughgoing reconstruction of the self through intersubjective *ecological* relationships. In the following sections,

125

I discuss an ecological form of community-building that reflects the kind of intersubjectivity articulated in prior chapters. Empowering skill building and education projects provide women with opportunities to learn about social and ecological justice in an instrumental fashion; however, WInC practices that performatively develop an intersubjective, ecological self are at least as important for the center's effectiveness at building a strong community. To better flesh out these practices, I borrow the idea of "ecological consciousness" from environmental studies and consider both how it manifests at WInC and how WInC participants help us see new facets of this phenomenon. This sheds light on what an environmental praxis that grows out of the social, political, economic, and bioregional characteristics of the borderlands looks like. As an in-depth case study, it adds dimension and specificity to complement the patterns already seen in the earlier history of regional activism; we also see how ecological consciousness grows in the creative work of women who are not professional writers or artists.

## Ecological Consciousness and the Ecological Self

One of WInC's goals is consciousness-raising; *consciousness* underscores the importance of reflection on our social lives and exploration of their political implications—an idea that derives from the feminist practice of consciousness-raising (i.e., making the personal political) and from Paulo Freire's "conscientization" (1970). Consciousness also incites action against these injustices. Embedded in the process of raising one's consciousness, one moves toward resistance. To raise *ecological* consciousness is to make the ecological political. First, ecological consciousness requires some understanding of the place facts for a given area or bioregion, including knowledge of regional vegetation, animal species, landscape features such as the watershed, and an understanding of how resources (e.g., water, energy, food) are managed in the region (Thayer 2003). Bioregional awareness should also account for changes to the land and its inhabitants that have occurred as a result of human interventions (Tweit 1995). Acquiring awareness is no easy task; it necessitates systems thinking to see how, for example, the consumption of bottled water may not only result in a bottle in a landfill but also in energy costs and pollutants released into the air and water at the factory site. You may become aware that the factory is likely located in an impoverished region where residents lack the power to protest its siting. You may recognize that privatized water has led to reduced access to clean water for many.[8]

In addition to establishing a sense of place, environmental scholars reflect on the kinds of subjectivity that facilitate ecological consciousness. In *Learning toward an Ecological Consciousness,* Edmund O'Sullivan and Marilyn Taylor define an *instrumental self* as a (neo)liberal subject oriented toward emotional independence from others, independence from the unpredictability of the natural world, and material dependence on the labor and goods produced by controlling the natural world (2004). As an alternative, they explore the "minimal self"—subjectivity that culls attachments to material goods and recenters "the quality of our relationships to each other and to our context, our inherent capacities to heal, renew, and evolve, and our worthiness simply to sojourn as an integral inhabitant of the earth" (11). On an intellectual level, individuals should begin to develop awareness of their place in webs of connection to activities such as goods and energy production, housing sprawl, meat consumption, environmental activism, and so on. But ecological consciousness also relies on an *affective* ability to embed ourselves in a place through what Marla Morris calls "dwelling-in-the-world" (2002, 572). Accordingly, to *dwell* is to develop bioregional knowledge and relationships to a place and its inhabitants. Yet playing on the other meaning of *dwell*, the practice also incites reflection on our thoughts and emotions, allowing us to understand the effects of place on our bodies and behavior. Dwelling is an embodied phenomenon; perception and emotions can alienate or facilitate emplacement. In her study of the production of space in Chicana literature, Mary Pat Brady emphasizes how "interactions with space are not merely schematic but also highly affective; places are felt and experienced, and the processes producing space therefore also shape feelings and experiences" (2002, 8). In sum, ecological consciousness includes both intellectual understandings of bioregionality and systems awareness *and* an emotional, perceptive, and materially embodied connection to human and nature others. Raised ecological consciousness also implies a shift from understanding to action. Although WInC does not have an explicitly environmental mission, the way it creates opportunities to develop ecological consciousness while grounding actions in a liberation theology/feminist framework of consciousness-raising and a Chicana/o framework of decolonization provides an important model for recognizing and valuing intersectional environmentalisms.

## Gendering the Ecological Self: Stretching toward Intersubjective Embodiment

Several practices at WInC encourage women to redefine their bodies in ways that are not only empowering from a decolonial feminist perspective, but that also demonstrate emplacement—an awareness of "dwelling-in-the-world." For example, staff and participants often referred to their work in terms of changes that take place within or through the body. Interviews reveal three facets of WInC life that challenge the individual to reflect on her connectedness to others and to her physical, material place within the center. These include the cultivation of strong emotionality, bodily awareness, and creative impulses that move through the body and connect us with human and nature others.

Many interviewees spoke of the center's positivity. Some suggested that, because it was a space for women, they felt safe and supported. There is an open display of emotions, and sociality is encouraged through classes and social gatherings that develop a sense of belonging among the participants. Although WInC has designated spaces for social gatherings and for popular classes such as painting, Reiki, Zumba, sewing, ESL, and citizenship, there is good flow among the spaces and a central courtyard that connects them; there are always people moving through the center who are talking and enjoying themselves. Sofía, who worked as a staff member years after joining as a participant, recalls her first experience there: Unable to pay a driving ticket, she was court-ordered to work community service hours at WInC. She approached the center with trepidation because she was a newly arrived immigrant from southern Mexico who had not felt welcome in the United States by her new neighbors with ties to northern Mexico. She said, "I came in and there was a group of women in that little building talking and laughing. It seemed to me that they were enjoying themselves . . . I felt like it was a place that I wanted to be. I didn't feel afraid or nervous anymore. . . . By the time I walked a few steps that first day I was saying, 'I want to be here! I want to be part of this!'" Sofía uses strong language to express her longing to be with others and to feel welcome.

There are affective and political aspects in efforts to belong; belonging is not just a motion toward embracing others (people, places, more-than-human others) but can also effect a change in embodiment—an idea that sutures place, affect, and embodiment. Aimee Carrillo Rowe writes, "Belonging is that movement in the direction of the other: bodies in motion, encountering their own transition, their potential to vary" (2005, 27). Through affective ties to others we rethink ourselves together into "we-ness" and the very borders of our bodies become less firm; we know ourselves through our relations through others. Similarly, Elspeth Probyn emphasizes the processual nature of becoming something new: "[Belonging] captures more accurately the desire for some sort of attachment, be it to other people, places, or modes of being, and the ways in which individuals and groups are caught within wanting to belong, wanting to become, a process that is fueled by yearning rather than the positing of identity as a stable state" (1996, 19). For Sofía, the laughter and positive sense of community caused a longing that resulted in a shift in her identity; she developed a new sense of belonging both to the center and to her new homeland—a feeling that has consolidated through her long-term commitment to WInC.

In their interviews, many staff and participants also expressed a heightened level of body awareness. First, interviewees spoke of positive changes that overcome the body when one arrives at the center. In addition to the reduction of anxiety that Sofía expressed, women who walk through the door immediately notice the moderate temperature that contrasts with the more extreme temperatures of the desert. Anna, who occasionally attended classes and served as a receptionist, explains: "When you come into the building, you see that it's cool when it needs to be cool and warm when it needs to be warm. And even that affects the way people feel when they go home because a lot of the people don't have central air so they dread going home in the summer." Others claim that making friends and developing hobbies led to a marked improvement in their health. For example, in honing her painting skills, Josie saw her depression and fibromyalgia improve—as her quote from earlier suggests, attending classes at the center is all the medicine you need! Another woman, Sandra, spoke to me of her poor eating and sleeping habits and exhaustion from the stresses of being a single mother. She had just joined the center that week, but was enthusiastic about the women she had met and the opportunity to take nutrition and Zumba classes to improve how she felt. In each case, the body is reworked as it moves through the center and, as Anna's comments suggest, that changed embodiment seeps into other relationships (to people, places)—such as into the home upon return from the classes.

For staff, they not only recognize that the female body is a site of potential for physical and emotional health and for relationship-building, but they also acknowledge the assault on women's bodies from domestic violence, sickness, and hunger as gendered, raced, and classed acts of violence. Staff members see freedom from violence as a basic human right and, as such, WInC provides opportunities for healing. Elena, a staff member and former participant, elaborates: "Basic human rights–building. . . . I think that a lot of immigrants are not empowered. They don't feel confident enough to say, 'You know what, I deserve this.' . . . We have citizenship classes that are very important. This office also used to have sexual assault counseling and resources."[9] Because staff understand women's health as a multifaceted and socially constructed arena of concern, their strategies for healing are diverse. From Reiki, labyrinth walking, organic gardening, and painting to sexual-assault awareness and the promotion of citizenship and human rights agendas, staff demonstrate systems awareness of the social and physical components of women's health in their workshop considerations. Each of these healing strategies opens up different relationalities with others, emphasizing positive connections between people and their environments and reworking negative ones, such as violence between intimate partners. Importantly, these efforts highlight women's bodies not as "natural" but contested social terrains—bodies that reveal and rework how power inscribes and subjugates. Acknowledging this gives women agency to (1) change their environments and (2) create new scripts and behaviors that are healthier for their socially, emotionally, and physically embodied selves.

In addition to emotionality and bodily awareness, WInC values women's creativity as a means to rework relationships with the world of human and nature others around them. The emphasis on tapping women's creativity is predominantly explained as an opportunity for women to find, hone, and then share their skills with others. Carter, the director, explains: "Every woman has something special to share. Women have been known to have incredible talent and creativity so the moment someone discovers a talent, then a class emerges out of that." This is how the painting and Reiki classes developed, for example. Moreover, women have the opportunity to develop not just their creativity and talent, but to potentially sell their paintings while learning important public-speaking and marketing skills.

Although the center's current focus on skill-building and economic self-sufficiency highlights the tangible rewards linked to exploring women's creativity, the intangible rewards are just as important. First, women who attend the sewing, painting, and other artistic workshops primarily come to the center to escape from social isolation. They may feel isolated because they are separated from their social network after immigration, because the rural locale makes travel difficult, and/or because they feel unwelcome in a country that does not easily accept their traditions or language. Second, classes that focus on exploring women's creativity provide opportunities for women to share ideas as well as their problems and joys. Consider Rosario, who came to WInC depressed after the death of her son. She enrolled in painting classes and eventually began to sell her work; now she teaches her own art classes. For Rosario, the center "is a support network for me. In being here, it is not only an economic support but it elevates my morale and I feel really happy particularly in sharing my knowledge" (Carter 2009). Through creative expression, some of the women are able to say things that they are not able to say otherwise; whether it is because no one was listening, no one took them seriously, or there was a language barrier, classes on dancing, singing, sewing, and quilting offer women the chance to create themselves through new relationships to each other, to the materials they work with, and to the world around them that is reimagined in their works. Creative projects allow women to speak in multiple registers while opening the possibility of inciting affective changes in the viewer. The volume of talk and laughter during class speaks, in part, to the freedom of communication along multiple trajectories that occurs in creative work.

Earlier, Sofía described her first trip to WInC and her introduction to the founders. Speaking on the potential of song, she describes how she developed a strong and immediate affiliation with the center and its participants. She recalls,

> The first [meeting] that I had, Sister Kathleen said that to end the meeting we were going sing . . . I was hiding behind others because I was embarrassed. But little by little those words changed my life. The song was "Yo Soy Mujer" and the words were "Yo so mujer en busca de igualdad. . . ." The song said that I will love myself and it was a beautiful song. . . . I learned the song and I came to the community meetings and I also sang, "Yes! Yo soy mujer!"

In addition to the feminist or woman-centered ideas that imbued the center's purpose at that time, Sofía describes creative connections facilitating community-building. However, they also act as a means by which relationality moves beyond community-building toward the potential to see ourselves as contiguous and interdependent. Women at WInC do not only share their skills and their life experiences through education and conversation; they share an affective bond that draws them together. For Sofía, the memory of that feeling is one of the most vivid she has of her early days and she continues to feel its emotional charge more than ten years later—this is evident not only through the detail in her story, but in the animated, joyously tearful way that she told it and the laughter she shared as she did so.

This section brought together themes of emotionality, body awareness, and the role of creativity to demonstrate that affect is a force with the power to change bodies in unpredictable ways. It can fundamentally rework bodily boundaries to center relationality and the creation of intersubjects. In this book's introduction, I described the idea of a transcorporeal self (Alaimo 2010), which illustrates the porous boundaries across which materials pass, creating bodies entangled with their surroundings. Teresa Brennan's studies on affect and embodiment show how emotions in the environment play a similarly constituent role in our materiality: "The transmission of affect . . . is social or psychological in origin. But the transmission is also responsible for bodily changes; some are brief changes, as in a whiff of the room's atmosphere, some longer lasting. In other words, the transmission of affect, if only for an instant, alters the biochemistry and neurology of the subject. The 'atmosphere' or the environment literally gets into the individual" (2004, 1). The literature of environmental studies advocates a maximally relational subjectivity and recognizes its ecological potential. Yet, while an essential part of building community at WInC, it does not necessarily produce ecological consciousness in terms of understanding place facts or systems awareness. Other practices at WInC *do* facilitate emplacement; I consider practices that are explicitly environmentalist as well as aspects of WInC that may be less so, but which raise ecological consciousness nonetheless. While the latter practices (such as building space consciousness) may seem less obvious in their environmentalism than a practice like gardening, they exemplify a transformation of the autonomous, instrumental self into one wherein the ties to human and nature others remain central to one's sense of self.

## En-naturing Embodiment to Build Ecological Consciousness

Although the mission statement does not reflect an environmental impulse, WInC integrates ecological awareness into daily activities. During parties, participants are reminded that all plates and cups should be recycled. When participants expressed a desire for nutrition and cooking classes, the idea to plant an organic garden sprung up and participants created a play to introduce the community to the health and flavor benefits of organic produce. Emphasizing the role many women play as household money managers, a "Go Green, Save Green" workshop taught participants how to repurpose household objects (turning plastic bottles into decorative flowers and repurposing old maps into gift bags). As Carter stated, women there regularly consider "possible activities that reduce our imprint on the environment." The fact that the center is built from tires rescued from landfills and the desert shows this. The tires are free, and tires and compacted earth insulate, keeping utility costs down and reducing natural-resource use. This reflects awareness of the place facts of the borderlands bioregion and shows an effort to enhance social and ecological health among the human and more-than-human residents.

WInC's construction was carried out as an educational activity. Participants researched methods of "green construction" and learned the skills necessary to build the center. They were responsible for everything from space planning to the finishing touches. The gallery, which is the primary entertaining space, features a partially finished segment of the wall that exposes the tires bound with compressed earth, serving as a visual aid that reminds visitors of the building process. The center also boasts solar panels, rainwater collection tanks, recycling and compost bins, and an organic garden used by the gardening and nutrition classes. Education activities raise consciousness about the social and ecological benefits of the conservation of resources and the importance of local and organically grown food. During a nutrition class I observed a discussion of the expense of fresh, organic food at the grocery store, the relative poverty of the community, and women's responsibilities for buying food and caring for their family and community. Questions arose: What are the healthiest options if you can't afford organic or fresh produce? Are frozen and canned vegetables still good choices? Why is it difficult to buy fresh vegetables when the town is surrounded by large farms? These exchanges reflect the growing systems awareness that emerges from the conditions and needs in women's lives. They also highlight how raised ecological consciousness involves an understanding of the links between class, race, gender, and environmental health.

After hearing more about the role of environmentalism in work for women's and community empowerment during my interviews, I sought to determine

12. "Window" inside the gallery exposing the tire construction of the Women's Intercultural Center. Courtesy of the author by permission of Mary Carter.

13. Rain barrel water-collection system at the Women's Intercultural Center. Courtesy of the author by permission of Mary Carter.

14. On-site organic garden at the Women's Intercultural Center. Courtesy of the author by permission of Mary Carter.

what role (if any) gender played in environmentalism at the center. In response, Elena, a staff member who had been with WInC for many years, thoughtfully replied:

> There has to be a relation. Maybe it has to do with [the fact that] most of our classes we offer to empower women; I think that learning that you could have your own garden and you could save money, you're healthier, which means that if you're healthy, you have a mind to learn, you're healthy to work, you're healthy to go to school, and you're healthy enough to be a parent . . . I think it's about empowerment in many ways.

Laura, participant turned staff member, concurs, "You see the ladies come and plant things because to them, that's helping the earth and they take that home with them. With the knowledge of how to recycle, you're going to go home and find that you don't want to throw that bottle in the trash." This comment shows how environmental education acts as a mode of healing work that spreads a spark of raised consciousness that participants bring with them into the home and other spaces in their lives. Further, environmental education at the center is not just focused on conservation, but is oriented toward the care of others. This is expressed in the care of nature others—Laura went on to say that if we can save a bird by recycling plastics, we have a responsibility to do so. It is also expressed as the care of human others—feeding yourself and your family well, being "healthy enough to be a parent," sharing your knowledge about recycling or water collection with others, building community through sharing a garden.

WInC enables women to make the most of their strategic position as social networkers, a strategy that empowers women to develop and facilitate more equitable and just relationships within their community and between their human community and the natural environment; yet no staff or participants gestured toward a "natural" or biological link between women and nature. These links were deployed through daily educational activities to empower women and teach them to change their surroundings. Some of the Chicana feminist writers and artists examined in chapters 2 and 3 have depicted women as spiritual *curanderas* that perform community healing rituals; none of the women at WInC used that language, but they do recognize the social roles women play in their communities and extend the tools that enable women to make the most of their power to create change.[10] This role may be linked to spirituality, as in the examples from the earlier chapters, but it is primarily grounded in the educational possibilities at WInC. Nonetheless, as I will show, there is also a spiritual element to the work women do at WInC that parallels and enforces the healing work performed by women's education for ecosocial justice.

In addition to gathering place facts and building systems awareness, the development of spatial and place consciousness stretches the self into body/landscape subjectivities (Davies 2000). Space consciousness is ever-present at WInC as it is in much of the art, literature, and activism seen in earlier chapters. Given its central role in borderlands environmentalism, I argue that it serves as an important expansion of the notion of place fact introduced earlier. Place-based consciousness was seen in environmental activism, such as the United Farm Workers marches introduced in chapter 1; the literature, murals, and digital art compositions analyzed in chapter 2; the domesticana displays showcased in chapter 3; and the filmic compositions discussed in chapter 4. Here, we see it in several ways: First, the center's proximity to a church facilitates a spiritual awareness despite the departure of the Sisters of Mercy several years ago. Second, the center is built on land once owned by a prominent family in Anthony and incorporates the house in which the family lived; this draws curious residents to the center. Third, WInC's location between two large metropolitan areas and near the U.S.-Mexico border contributes to its success and makes it a hub for people crossing through. This is nicely illustrated by a participant's quilting square that depicts women with arms linked as they march forward. It reads, "Across the desert came a multitude of women." In the strategic use of the word *multitude*, the artist conveys solidarity among a large number of women and references the diversity among them. While each of these examples shows how WInC took advantage of its geographic location to bring people together and strengthen community ties, other examples of space consciousness reveal a concerted effort not just to deepen communal ties, but to move toward intersubjective associations as well, which are so necessary for the building of a socially and ecologically conscious community.

The gallery is the center's most emotionally charged space. It is the gathering place for events and features a labyrinth that was researched, designed, and tiled by the participants. The gallery also displays an internal "window" that exposes the tire construction and it houses participants' artwork, including a quilt that stitches together messages of gratitude to WInC. Several interviewees believed that there was something social, positive, and peaceful about the gallery despite its nearness to the reception area that occasionally becomes congested and hectic. This may be, as geographers note, because creative activity within a space shapes how we think of ourselves within a particular environment (Bingley 2003; Davies 2000). These findings mirror my own: creative practices and behaviors that prod us to rethink our relations with others and the landscape produced a change in the embodiment of the subjects—interviewees became more animated, more likely to speak of themselves in relation

15. Labyrinth at the Women's Intercultural Center. Courtesy of the author
by permission of Mary Carter.

16. Square from a participant-made quilt of good wishes hanging in the gallery at the
Women's Intercultural Center. Courtesy of the author by permission of Mary Carter.

to particular places and spaces, more likely to see *relationships* in general as constitutive of their subjectivity. The gallery, which displays art, exposed construction efforts, and a labyrinth, is a space marked by women's creativity, prayer, and reflection; as such, it brought out emotional reactions among WInC participants.

While the social and creative purposes for which the gallery is used contribute to its calm, positive feeling, there is also an important piece of folklore that marks the center and the gallery in particular. The director describes the construction process:

> Whenever they would get really stressed through the construction of the building . . . they had this ceremony. They would get a couple of pens out and they would start thinking and really try to connect with the idea behind the center. On little pieces of paper they would write their dreams and wishes for themselves and for the center. Then they would dump all the little pieces of paper within the dirt and within the tires. . . . I always laugh when somebody tells me that as soon as you come in, you have this sense of peace even if you're having problems at home. I really think it has to do with all the beautiful well wishes that are located in the different sections of the center because there's so much positivity that was given to it and that's how they were able to connect to the vision and the mission of the center and they were able to refocus.

In this ritualized enactment of the mission, participants forge a connection to each other as well as to future generations of staff and participants through the sharing of hopes, dreams, and contagious positivity. Through affective communion, the women energize themselves in the wake of their physically and emotionally exhausting labor, and they do so by focusing on their shared strength and shared futures. It is a conscious performance of intersubjective relationality wherein women redraw their ties with each other and, in putting parts of themselves (i.e., their dreams and wishes) into the soil and tires, they become coextensive with the center and more deeply invested in its success. The reiteration of this story to new participants bolsters the effect of space consciousness on the women and embeds them in their environment; they refigure their sense of self as contiguous with the human and nature others that comprise their environment both in the present and the past as a result. Capitalizing on this knowledge, Carter hopes to introduce additional spaces that draw community together, what she calls "a gathering space that is really open to all." Modeled after el Zócalo, the main public square in Mexico City, she envisions a large concrete patio that could host dances, farmers' and craft markets, and forums on community development. Carter explains, "That attracts me, that something so simple as an area of cement would provide so much to a community. Creating those types of community spaces that are spearheaded not only by the center, but by community members, that we can combine those types of events to bring different people together to share—that's what we need."

These examples show WInC's broader sense of the environment that includes not just the natural world, but also an individual's relationship to natural and built environments. This expands the narrow ideas of ecological belonging that can be found in some environmentalist and ecofeminist work. The gallery and other communal spaces facilitate intersubjective selves that are oriented toward community-building and education for consciousness-raising, but they are also working toward more thoroughgoing connections between humans, nature, and the built world that surrounds them. As the interviews show, the staff and participants develop identities that are directly linked to these relationships and, maintained through the affective ties and sense of responsibility for ecosocial justice, these identities are solidified through constant performance of WInC's mission. This is visible in the examples given previously, from the ritualized construction of the center to the ritualized daily welcomes to the constant reminders about the importance of recycling.

## Embracing the Spirit of Ecological Consciousness

In the previous section, we saw the center's explicit and institutionalized commitment to environmentalism alongside more subtle ecological work (e.g., practices of dwelling); the two move in tandem toward the development of a borderlands environmental subjectivity. Similarly, there is a more overt spiritual presence that coexists with a subtler and more diffuse spirituality—interviews show that the narrative of spiritualty emerging at the center is one that stretches human ties into the nature and spirit realm, facilitating new body/landscape/spirit intersubjectivities. Overtly, the Sisters of Mercy founded the center, and its location across from a church links it with a religious community in the area. In fact, some continue to confuse WInC for a Catholic community center despite its nondenominational status. A multicultural approach to spirituality can be seen in the different traditions celebrated at the center, including Reiki and meditation, healing arts associated with Eastern practices such as Buddhism; the labyrinth, which can be found in indigenous cultures around the world; and prayer, which interviewees described as a reflection and appreciation of life rather than a narrowly Catholic focus on sin and forgive-ness. There is also a dedicated celebration of the Virgin of Guadalupe. One employee, Elena, noted that this celebration is one of the biggest community-building events, drawing those who do not regularly visit the center and intro-ducing it to them for the first time. She explained, "We celebrate the Dia de la Virgen de Guadalupe. . . . We've been doing the celebration for the longest time and we bring the chiles, the Danza Azteca, we have an altar for her, we bring flowers. . . . And we do the *ofrendas*. At least in Anthony, we're the only not-church that celebrates the Dia de la Virgen de Guadalupe."

While Elena happily recalled her favorite parts of the celebration and emphasized its contribution to the multicultural aspects of the center's prac-tice, explaining that "it's very Catholic, it's very Mexican," others struggled to articulate the role that spirituality plays at WInC. Perhaps because of the center's efforts to be spiritually open without imposing any particular belief system on staff and participants, there was no single driving narrative about religion in place at WInC to shape interviewees' responses. One person char-acterized the spirituality cited in the mission as less about religion and more about the Golden Rule—doing unto others as you would have them do unto you. Another spoke of it as a feeling that overcomes you: "If you don't want to go to church, it's okay. . . . It's not so much a 'doing'; it's not a verb, it's a *feel-ing*. It's something like a feeling of calm; you have peace." As seen earlier with respect to issues of intersubjective embodiment and human-nature relation-ality, mobilizing affect seems key to creating intersubjective identities—espe-cially in prayer and group reflection. Angelle, one of the younger participants, explicitly named the relationship between affect and prayer and their ability to build strong ties to others: "I think it [group prayer] is important because you get to understand what they're feeling and the prayers connect you more to everyone else. For me, when I pray with my family, it connects us more."

Amanda, a staff member, focused on the practice of hospitality within the belief system of the Sisters of Mercy, but she emphasized that what is impor-tant about hospitality is not its link to religion, but that it offers "a welcome." Although the interviewee was careful to note that she believes this ritual to be independent of religion, the feeling it generates is comparable to the feeling expressed by the participants and staff mentioned earlier. While the focus on hospitality and the ritualized welcome may appear on the surface to be a non-religious phenomenon, some have simply defined religious activities as those that generate what Emile Durkheim calls "collective effervescence" ([1965] 1995, 218–31). For Durkheim, religion is seen as a primarily social phenom-enon wherein the collective energy from a gathering of individuals takes on a character of its own, a social euphoria that can sometimes be seen in political rallies, for example. Religion builds community, but more than that, with the generation of great emotional or affective energy, individuals deindividu- ✾ ate and come to collectivize themselves. Recalling Carter's description of the ritualized writing of positive notes that were placed into the tires, the energy at WInC during the highly social event of the building's construction exemplifies this phenomenon. The rituals that propel affect through individuals and the social body—the welcome, the consecration of the building with positive messages, the labyrinth walks and morning meditations held for years at the center—are responsible for WInC's success in building ecological consciousness through performatively intersubjective associations.

Victor Turner theorized ritual as a socially significant performance that creates meaning from the ambiguity of cultural liminality (1995). Understanding ✾ ritual as a mechanism of social cohesion may be particularly important for the study of a community that is largely comprised of immigrants striving to build a new home on the unwelcoming northern side of the border; indeed, his description of liminality shares much in common with what Gloria Anzaldúa describes as the borderlands. At one point, the center's website bore out this parallel, citing Anzaldúa's claim that "the U.S.-Mexican border *es una herida abierta* where the Third World grates against the first and bleeds" (1999, 25). Anzaldúa saw the border as a third space, an in-between space populated by outsiders and from which residents can develop a critical consciousness—*la conciencia de la mestiza*—that draws on experiences of outsiderness to forge a new kind of belonging. In this case, the ritualized welcome and construction efforts act as place-making practices that invite participants to belong to the center, to the community, and to the land in Anthony. Reclamation of this ✾ land, as earlier activists sought to reclaim the Chicana/o homeland of Aztlán and as Anzaldúa sought to create a new borderlands home, is a strategy for ecological justice.

Although I have been writing about a link between spirituality and ecological consciousness that uses affect to connect people to each other and to place as a means of belonging, spirituality is also *en-natured* at the center. A participant who has been with the center since its early days explains that, before she joined, "I was used to staying at home with my family, praying in front of an image or something. Now, we do it in nature, giving thanks to God for the day, for what we see, and to appreciate what we see because sometimes we are walking through the desert or the street and you don't appreciate what you are seeing, what nature is showing to you." She describes religious practice at the center as en-natured, as an appreciation that joins us with nature

*Does this create an opening for men? coalition?*

and spirit others in a web of connectivity. For her, nature lives as much in the street as it does in the desert. Importantly, she does not claim that women are essentially linked to the natural world or that they share a unique connection to the spiritual world—be it socially constructed or otherwise. Rather, this appreciation needs to be taught and what is most important, as the others discussed earlier have said, is the *feeling* that connects minds, bodies, spaces, and spirits. This is not an easy task, as this participant went on to say: "We can talk about spirituality, but I cannot move your feelings inside." Here, she is referencing the fact that some activities, such as the sing-along to "Yo Soy Mujer" and morning meditations—spiritual activities that have affective import—have disappeared with the departure of the Sisters of Mercy; in their place the center moved toward an increasing focus on personal and economic self-sufficiency. There does not have to be a discrepancy between practices that use affect to build social cohesion and those practices that instrumentally emphasize skill-building, as many of the prior examples have shown. However, this example makes a case for diverse programming that includes a celebration of en-natured spirituality as part of individual and community healing.

## Conclusion: Lessons on Affect and Bioregionality in Building Green Community

The shift from an overt spiritual presence to a more latent one coincides with a larger shift from more affective modes of gathering to combat social isolation toward gatherings explicitly aimed at education, skill-building, and economic self-sufficiency. Examples of these programs include the Small Business Academy and workshops on how to market one's paintings, food, jewelry, and clothes; workshops on how to fill out a job application and practice for an interview; and classes on how to study for and successfully complete the citizenship exam. This programming is important to women and makes a real difference in their lives and those of their families. While there is a critique of this model for the ways it fits within a neoliberal economic agenda that measures women's empowerment by their ability to participate in traditional economic and state-making practices, here I note that the model of self-sufficiency is essential to disenfranchised women in an underserved rural town in New Mexico.[11] Furthermore—and this is a point that grows more important as the center gains visibility—a focus on economic self-sufficiency programming is more legible to national and regional funding agencies that can provide financial support for the center's expansion of programming as well as its expansion into additional satellite offices in neighboring rural communities, which remains crucial for those who lack transportation. This point cannot be emphasized enough since, between my first visit in 2009 and a second one in 2012, the impact of the financial downturn of 2008 led to staff reductions and the need for more creative partnership opportunities with regional service providers.

However, by shifting away from programming that provides less visibly tangible rewards, the center may lose that element of affective cohesion that was so important during its founding years. Longtime staff say that participants continue to find the sociality the best part of their experience, although women who have seen the evolution of WInC remark that the feeling is not as strong as it once was. This chapter argues that the ability to draw affective connections between human, nature, and spirit others is what deterritorial-izes participants, pushing them from instrumental education and community-building toward the long-standing and deeper connections that have enabled the center to become as strong as it has and to form a base for wider community change. This move meshes well with the center's mission, which is not just about education and personal development for economic self-sufficiency but also about consciousness-raising for change where so much of the difficult change work requires affective connections to sustain it.

WInC's performative strategies to rework subjectivity in relation to one's body, to the natural world, and to the spirit world can create social, political, and environmental healing; they can be the basis on which to build community that is inclusive of both human and nature others. The ecological consciousness that emerges at WInC conceptualizes human/nature/spirit co-being, which recognizes more agency in the more-than-human world than much of the literature on environmental justice allows because the focus is often on the effects that toxicity and dislocation have on particular human communities rather than the human-nature relation itself. It adds to ecofeminist models for green community because it recognizes the specific needs of working-class and recently immigrated Mexican American women, including the importance of developing a sense of belonging to the land, region, and nation. Moreover, while skill-building is extremely important in enfranchising women in the region, it is only part of the work that occurs at the center. Efforts to produce affective connections between human, nature, and spirit others are extremely important in drawing women back to WInC day after day, in bringing their friends and family to the center, and in bringing the work and values of WInC into other spaces in their lives, including their homes.

WInC teaches us important lessons by demonstrating the connection between raised consciousness and action from feminist and critical pedagogy studies (e.g., learning about nutrition led to action—planting an organic garden); it also shows how place facts and systems awareness can grow organically from roles the participants take on (e.g., recycled tires provide an environmental good—a well-insulated center—and a social good—happier, more comfortable participants). Scholars of environmental studies have argued for the importance of developing an emplaced sense of self, a point this chapter has discussed at length by offering concrete evidence of how to facilitate emplacement through performative expansions of embodiment, self-landscape, and self-spirit relations; this strategy adds to current discussions of ecological consciousness in environmental studies while reframing theories of (inter)subjectivity in Chicana and Latina studies to emphasize their ecological relevance. For scholars, activists, and funding agencies, perhaps the most important point to take from this chapter is the imperative of supporting (monetarily and otherwise) programming to develop the kinds of affective practices that create intersubjective emplacement, focusing on the three levels on which the self can be reworked: bodies, physical and social landscapes, and spirits. At the very least, there is a need to cast a wider net when determining what kinds of projects to support when designing programs for justice.

# CONCLUSION

# Bridging Movements with Technologies for the Ecological Self

> Oppositional thinking erodes our alliances and communities. As the histories of numerous social movements have demonstrated, all too often oppositional politics fragment from within, damaging the individual and the group.
>
> —AnaLouise Keating, *Transformation Now!*

I began this book wondering how ecofeminism and its relative, new materialist feminisms, differed from Chicana feminist and borderlands environmentalisms. As a field of theory and activism concerned with the related ways human and environmental oppressions are naturalized, ecofeminism has been marginalized by feminist scholars for several reasons. Primarily, ecofeminism has been seen to be too universalizing and Western-focused, and it has been accused of essentializing "woman" and "nature" as well as any supposed links between them. Secondarily but of equal importance, there remain disciplinary and geographical divides in the canon of ecofeminist literature. Scholars who approach ecological feminism from humanistic and social scientific backgrounds have not often been in dialogue with each other and may not recognize or appreciate the benefits of an interdisciplinary standpoint. Further, borderlands studies have not received much attention from ecofeminist scholars, and the activism and cultural production of Chicanas and Mexican American women is either overlooked or fit within an environmental justice frame that misrecognizes or squeezes out some of the nuances of that work. This is a particularly significant omission because of the strong sense of bioregion present in feminist borderlands studies and activism wherein the politics of place (including spatial relations and land, water, and biodiversity politics) plays a large role in how efforts for justice are conceptualized.

Despite the marginalization of ecofeminism by feminist scholars, our relationships with the environment remain important, and feminist scholars should not avoid theorizing our responsibilities to human and nature-others. Our work on social justice should include concerns about ecological justice. My contention is that feminist thought about the environment needs to be set into new motions by putting it into conversation with that which it excludes. New materialist feminisms are garnering so much interest in part because theorists are twining scientific, humanistic, and social science studies of the environment and our place in it to create new and productive ways of thinking. Yet so much of that thought traces its foundations to Western philosophers (e.g., Spinoza, Deleuze, Heidegger, Kant) rather than engaging with materialist threads in other worldviews; Gloria Anzaldúa's study of Mesoamerican thought provides just one example of where else we may look. Chicana feminisms and border studies exist in an ethnic studies enclave within the academy—even in feminist spaces—and audiences have much to gain from looking at ecological consciousness from the standpoint of the Chicana artists, writers, and activists explored here. With a focus on performative intersubjectivity and an emphasis on building place-specificity (but not place-exclusivity as is sometimes seen in bioregionalism), the works under consideration in this book respond to the universalizing and essentializing tendencies of which ecofeminist literature has been accused. I hope this book also offers readers new ways to think about key debates in the field of ecofeminism, which include the role of the body, the role of spirituality, and the connections (if any) that are staged between "woman" and "nature" in ecological theory and activism. For those who work in the fields of Chicana feminisms and border studies, I hope this book illuminates the ecological elements of familiar works and contributes to a growing body of ecocriticism. My aim, in other words, is to enact a postoppositional politics that bridges disjointed movements and research methodologies (Keating 2013).

The introduction interrogated the given genealogies of ecofeminism, including its exclusions and "stuck places" as well as its points of intersection with Chicana and new materialist feminisms; the remaining chapters of this book explored ecological narratives expressed in the work of Chicanas and Mexican American women living and working in the borderlands. Addressing both the geographical and disciplinary divides that have plagued ecofeminism, I employed interdisciplinary historical and regional analysis of Chicana and

Mexican American women's participation in movements in chapter 1; textual, iconographic, and intertextual analysis of Chicana feminist cultural production in chapters 2 and 3; film analysis, including visual and aural analysis and the study of the film's reception in chapter 4; and interviews, participant observation, and textual analysis of media data of a women's direct-action organization in chapter 5. In the case of the chapters on cultural production and the final chapter that employs ethnographic methods, my examples were chosen because of key similarities shared across them: the founding of WInC and the production of much of this art and literature coincided with a peak of interest in ecofeminism in the American academy (some believed ecofeminism would define the third wave), although there appears to be little communication among scholars; the gulf between environmental and Chicana/o studies scholars persists today. WInC is not seen as an environmental organization, and very few of the cultural productions highlighted here are valued for their environmental contributions. The ecological themes in the works and at WInC are misrecognized and seem only to be noteworthy for the social justice work that they do. In centering work that emerges from the border bioregions that is ecological in both obvious and subtle ways, we can learn new things about feminist ecological praxis and contribute to the environmental goals that many of the artists, writers, and activists share, though they get little attention from critics, scholars, and funders.

Taken together, these chapters reveal a major finding: borderlands environmentalisms display a politics of deterritorialization aimed at decolonization. By now, arguments detailing the deterritorializations of the self should be familiar. Throughout this book, I argued that the politics of the body, of spirituality, and of the connections between women and their "natural" and built environments could be usefully explored with a focus on the performative practices that create selves-in-community or performative intersubjectivities. These intersubjectivities are also ecological ones that draw selves into broader landscape and spirit relations that extend one's sense of self and one's obligation to the human and nature-others with which one becomes coextensive. Counter to criticisms that have rendered ecofeminist representations of women and nature as essentialist, a focus on the ways women strategically hail discourses of the body, woman-nature links, and spirituality in order to contest and rework hegemonic notions of culture, nature, and history has served the artists and activists studied here well. As chapters 2, 3, and 4 show, in staging cultural productions that point to a legacy of the oppressive social construction of Mexican Americans while at the same time forging decolonial images of women in coalition with human, nature, and spirit others, artists expose the

performativity of identity and enact a self-in-community with allied spectators.[1] This is especially clear with respect to Juana Alicia's *La Llorona's Sacred
Waters* (2004) and Lourdes Portillo's *Señorita Extraviada* (2001), which extend
open invitations to spectators to join in a shared struggle. Similarly, chapters 1
and 5 explore how Chicana and Mexican American activists use ritualized performances to critique social and ecological injustices and to form coalitional
bonds with the human and more-than-human others in their environments.
The United Farm Workers demonstrated this well in the activisms I discuss in
chapter 1, including their pilgrimages and fasts. In chapter 5, we also witness
many rituals of performative intersubjectivity that are ecological, including
the participants of the Women's Intercultural Center sacralizing their "green"
building with notes of their hopes and dreams for themselves and future participants. In all the examples across this book, the development of a performative ecological intersubjectivity both reworks colonialist representations of
identity and creates new, open, and counterhegemonic subject positions for
writers, spectators, audience members, activists, and their allies. These subject
positions are deterritorializing in that they ask artist and activist, spectator and
ally, to rethink their relationships and to see themselves as interconnected.
Recalling Chela Sandoval's study of the "inner and outer technologies that
construct and enable the differential mode of social movement and consciousness" (2000, 3), I name the specific means by which this occurs a *technology for
the intersubjective or ecological self* wherein the ecological self is conceptualized
within the landscape of human, nature, and spirit entanglements in which it
lives; as the introduction notes, this theory amends Sandoval's work by noting how the inner and outer technologies, self/subject and other/object, are
themselves entwined.[2]

Technologies of intersubjectivity capable of deterritorializing spectators
have differed somewhat throughout the chapters and have depended on the
site of research and the method used by the participants. Writers like Anzaldúa
(1999) and Sánchez (2003) disrupt their sense of self as autonomous and independent by writing a personal narrative that is also meant to be collective in
that it speaks for others in the writer's community and it speaks through the
reader. This has the effect of calling the reader to identify with the author and
to stretch herself into the shared consciousness and landscapes presented in
the texts. Visual texts, from murals to installations, have used technologies of
intersubjectivity that challenge viewers' sense of history, or at least the colonial
narrative that predominates in histories of Mexican Americans in the United
States, and to see themselves as implicated in hegemonies as well as potentially implicated in resistances. Thus, in many of the examples explored in the

chapters on cultural production and those concerned with activist organizing, rewriting history can become a technology of intersubjectivity.

Spirituality is another technology for the ecological self that can be seen throughout many of the examples. In her documentary *Señorita Extraviada*, Lourdes Portillo deterritorializes the subjectivity of her spectators in a variety of ways. She uses the camera and editing to disrupt a sense of time and historical "progress." She reads contradictory news stories to disrupt the spectators' sense of justice and their understanding of the causes of the border violence. Finally, she presents spiritual elements such as altar building, the ritualized painting of crosses, and stories of the victims' lives as sacred to create a relationship between spectators and border activists fighting for justice. With *The Curandera's Botanica* (2008), Amalia Mesa-Bains uses an altar to draw out the sacred power of scientific and natural objects to bring about personal and social healing; with *Private Landscapes/Public Territories* (1996) and other exhibits, she has also used altars to strengthen her relationships to land, to family members, and to feminist icons, marking these people and places as sacred.

Place-centeredness is another common technology of intersubjectivity in borderlands environmental praxis. Place-centeredness addresses how activists and artists conjure a sense of belonging while also highlighting the negotiation of power in the construction of spaces and those who do or do not belong in those spaces. For example, in chapter 2, Cherríe Moraga's queering of Aztlán (1993) claims and troubles place-based subjectivities in the Southwest. Similarly, chapter 1 showed how Chicana and Mexican American women participate in movements for social and ecological justice that are rooted in a particular ecoregion but must extend transnationally (or translocally) to shift their allies' thinking beyond the "not in my back yard" syndrome. Place-based consciousness exists in balance with transnational analysis of the politics of production and consumption that figure some people and some environments as exploitable.

Behind each of these technologies that can potentially deterritorialize artists, activists, and allies is the fact that they are motivated by an affective push that destabilizes the subjectivities of participants. Affect is particularly important because it shifts us from intellectual engagements to a deeper, more wholly physical and emotional embodied sense of ourselves and our surroundings. Affective connections can be inspired by fear, sadness, terror, or hope—emotions at the heart of Portillo's documentary. They may also be inspired by joy, a deep desire to belong, or the sense of freedom and accomplishment that comes with moving your body in a new way or learning a new skill, as participants at the women's center demonstrated. The careful negotiation of affect in cultural production and movement politics can have a profound effect on individuals *and* social movements. Though affect can certainly be deployed to motivate organizing along hegemonic lines, the focus on intersubjective and counterhegemonic relations of belonging that were witnessed across the chapters of this book shows that deterritorializing social movements creates possibilities in those movements; movements may gain resiliency and become more open to alliance-building. In this, borderlands environmentalisms differ from mainstream environmental and conservation movements, ecofeminism, and environmental justice movements. Not only do borderlands environmentalisms show women bringing together cultural production and direct-action approaches to activism, but they strive to be broadly inclusive and coalitional as well: they include attention to the role of spirituality, social and economic justice, indigenous rights, ethnic and intercultural community-building, and support for women among concerns that are entwined with concern for the environment. As such, borderlands environmentalisms challenge the insularity of movements and they require a research methodology that can see activism at the intersections of movements and disciplines. Thus, deterritorialization, or keeping subjectivity and movements *in movement*, is a common practice here that deserves more attention for the importance it plays toward efforts at decolonization. Decolonization is, after all, an ultimate deterritorialization from hegemonic logics. Placing interconnection and a deterritorialized sense of belonging at the center of work toward ecosocial justice counters ruling logics that rely on isolation, objectification of humans and nature, and the hierarchicalization of differentiated human and nature bodies for exploitation.

Given these findings, I hope this book offers readers some new theoretical and methodological tools. The concept of performative intersubjectivity expands Judith Butler's important work in feminist theory by looking to the ways (inter)subjectivity is staged through practices that construct body/nature/spirit relationalities. By extension, this concept also highlights the importance of place and spatial relations in constructing (inter)subjectivity performatively. This bridges the social construction impulse in Butler's work with recent approaches in new materialist feminisms that highlight the materiality and coextension of bodies and their environments. Indeed, to important works such as Stacy Alaimo's *Bodily Natures* (2010) and its theorization of the "transcorporeal body," I introduce spirituality into the human-nature dyad. I illustrate the role it plays in healing bodies and natures and show how spirituality gets us beyond the social and biological dualism that also governs so much writing in environmental and feminist studies. In addition to the conceptual framework offered by "performative intersubjectivity," this book reclaims deterritorialization as a subversive politics for decolonization. As shown in the introduction, critics have argued that "deterritorialization" evacuates the politics of privilege and place. However, as many examples illustrated here reveal, Deleuze and Guattari's work on deterritorialization parallels what many Chicana feminists, including Gloria Anzaldúa and Cherríe Moraga, have found in Chicana writing and activism: that deterritorialization is a multifaceted process of sometimes forced and sometimes chosen displacement, of physical and discursive dislocation, and of a search to belong somewhere else and become something new.

In drawing together different movements, such as the environmental justice movement, ecofeminist activism, Chicano nationalism, workers' movements, and women's antiviolence and ecological protests, *Ecological Borderlands* elucidates the interconnectedness of movements. We need interdisciplinary research approaches that can read across disciplines and their theory production. In line with this, I offer a methodological innovation by reading cultural production, historical and intellectual genealogies, and activism together using research methods from the social sciences and humanities to understand how complex subjectivities and movement politics are negotiated when they do not fit easily into any singular disciplinary or social movement framework. This counteracts one of the more striking limitations of environmental literature—whether it is mainstream, ecofeminist, or environmental justice literature. Thus, in addition to the deterritorializations mentioned earlier that have included the deterritorialization of subjectivity and of movements, this book attempts one further deterritorialization—that of the academy and the ways it is disciplined to limit thought and erase the complex experiences and resistance strategies of those it continues to marginalize.

151

# Notes

Introduction. Ecological Borderlands:
Connecting Movements, Theories, Selves

1. I distinguish the chosen political identity *Chicana/o* that emerged during the protest movements of the 1960s from the ethnic identity *Mexican American.* The writers and artists discussed in chapters 2, 3, and 4 self-describe as *Chicana* feminists. Some of the activists reviewed in chapter 1 and interviewed in chapter 5 self-identify as *Mexican American* and/ or *Hispanic*. Regional differences, class status, political views, and im/migration history contribute to identity development. For this book, I follow the research subjects' self-naming practices where known.

2. See Bina Agarwal's (1997) critique that, even among socialist ecofeminists who claim a constructed relationship between women and the environment based on gender-role expectations, the assumed connection between women and nature merely sets women up to perform more labor; especially in development schemes and ecotourism, women can be exploited because programs burden them with the additional task of environmental conservation.

3. In addition to Sandilands's work, a number of good ecofeminism genealogies have been published, including works by Moore (2015), Gaard (2011), Thompson (2006), Cudworth (2005), and Sturgeon (1997).

4. Not all spiritually or religiously grounded versions of ecofeminism were based on pagan or earth goddess traditions. See, for example, Ruether (2005), Gebara (1996), Eaton and Lorentzen (2003), Low and Tremayne (2001), and Shiva (1997).

5. Chris Cuomo offers a similar critique of Sandilands—she advocates for a contextual understanding of when and why identity politics may be important rather than relying on the narrower notion of identity that comes out of Marxist analysis of workers' movements. She writes, "Sandilands fails to get curious about the many shapes of feminist identity politics and feminist female subjectivities—and of the fascinating convergence in ecofeminism of these subjectivities and ethical regard for the more-than-human world" (2001, 154).

6. Rosemarie Tong's (1998) taxonomy of Western feminist theories is a useful guide for understanding how liberal feminism, radical cultural feminism, socialist feminism, poststructural feminism, and other forms have been defined in the field.

7. These works aim to take seriously critiques from Chicana studies scholars such as Saldívar-Hull (2000), who warns of the ways Chicana works may be subsumed by cultural outsiders in the academy: "Even in the face of our active struggle with unreconstructed Chicanos and Eurofeminists who footnote our work but have yet to discover or use our theories *as* theory, we acknowledge the influence of U.S. White feminists in academia" (35; emphasis in original).

8. *Environmental* denotes the physical environment and often implies a normative orientation to human impacts on the environment—are our behaviors "environmentally friendly"? *Ecology* is the study of the relationships among organisms and between them and their physical environment; as in the term *ecosystem*, relationships take center stage and humans are seen within an assemblage of organisms and the physical environment, just one player among many. Many ecofeminists and queer ecologists also note their preference for the term *ecological* because of its derivation from the ancient Greek for *house*. This play between house and physical environment signified by *ecological* resonates closely with the texts and activists surveyed here who focus so much on questions of home and belonging.

9. For examples of texts concerned with representations of the landscape and symbolic as well as material reclamations of space, see Anzaldúa (1999), Brady (2002), Moraga (1993), Oliver-Rotger (2003), and E. Pérez (1999).

10. Interconnectivity is a dominant theme in ecofeminist writing and can be seen in many texts. To name just a few writers, see Plumwood (2002), Warren (2000), Starhawk (1999), King (1995), and Mies and Shiva (1993).

11. My work on performative intersubjectivity is indebted not only to Butler but also to Catriona Sandilands, who sketched the value of performativity theory to ecofeminism in "Mother Earth, the Cyborg, and the Queer: Ecofeminism and (More) Questions of Identity" (1997). Sandilands draws from Donna Haraway's cyborg and coyote as queer figures that disrupt notions of "human" and "nature" and reveal the unnaturalness of each and thus their coconstruction and their possible disruption of each other. She writes, "The 'woman-nature' affinity becomes a statement in which the one set of constructions is constantly held up to the other to show the contingent, fictitious character of each. This stance is a playful one, marking a world full of imaginative women-nature boundary breaching, at the same time as it is a political one, causing us to make strange, to queer

the discourses in which feminist environmental politics are constituted and negotiated" (34).

12. See Suzanne Bost's *Encarnación: Illness and Body Politics in Chicana Feminist Literature* (2010) for a study on embodiment, troubled materialities, and dis/ability in literature by Anzaldúa, Moraga, and others.

13. For a critique of Anzaldúa's appropriation of indigenous mythology, see Saldaña-Portillo (2001). Anzaldúa responds in "Speaking across the Divide," an e-mail dialogue with Inés Hernández-Ávila published in *The Gloria Anzaldúa Reader* (2009b).

## Chapter 1. Borderlands Environmentalism: Historiography in the Midst of Category Confusion

1. See Alarcón (1999); Castañeda (1990, 2001); Chabram-Dernersesian (1999, 1993); and Vásquez and Torres (2003) for more on how to tell decolonizing histories while respecting the numerous differences among Chicana/os.

2. In the past few years, we are beginning to see more ecocritical readings of fiction that engages with an environmental justice framework. *The Environmental Justice Reader: Politics, Poetics, and Pedagogy*, edited by Joni Adamson, Mei Mei Evans, and Rachel Stein (2002) was one of the first texts to call for an expansion of the environmental justice movement into "poetics and pedagogy," broadening the disciplinary reach of the field.

3. For histories of the environmental movement in the United States, see Dunlap and Mertig (1992) and Visgilio and Whitelaw (2003). I also note that this historiography is in no way comprehensive, not even of the borderlands region on which I focus. For other examples of American environmental historiography, see Dorceta Taylor's works, especially *The Environment and the People in American Cities, 1600s–1900s: Disorder, Inequality, and Social Change* (2009), which traces environmentalism back to urban communities rather than wilderness and conservation movements.

4. According to findings from the U.S. Department of Labor's National Agricultural Workers Survey (NAWS) conducted in 2001 and 2002, approximately 75 percent of farmworkers in the United States are Mexican and 8 percent identify as Mexican American or Chicano (NAWS does not include information on the dairy industry, which has a similarly large proportion of Mexican and Mexican American workers) (U.S. Department of Labor 2005).

5. For a good analysis of the Mothers of East Los Angeles, see Mary Pardo's "Mexican-American Women Grassroots Community Activists: 'Mothers of East Los Angeles'" (1990).

6. The documentary *Homeland: Four Portraits of Native Action* (Grossman 2005) includes a segment on a Navajo community's activism in New Mexico against mined uranium leeching into the water system.

7. Research on acequia farmers prior to American development in the region suggests that women in the Southwest served as water managers and had voting rights for water and land use while women in the East were struggling to have their legal rights recognized. Feminist scholars have remarked that development schemes that import Western gender

binaries and their associated role expectations into communities to bring about techno-logical and economic "advancement" often have negative impacts on women. This seems to be the case with American westward expansion as well. Peña concludes, "Conquest and colonialism for most Mexican women meant degradation of their status, privileges, and rights. It brought the loss of their property and their land and water rights" (2012).

8. See Enloe (2000), Abell (1999), and Wright (2003) on the treatment of women in maquiladoras.

9. For an overview of rhizomal politics within movements, see Deleuze and Guattari's *A Thousand Plateaus* (1987) and Hardt and Negri's *Multitude* (2004).

10. Nira Yuval-Davis's transversal politics is an epistemological framework based in standpoint theory; it provides insight for relating across different kinds of standpoints in a coalitional engagement: "The idea is that each 'messenger,' each participant in a politi-cal dialogue, would bring with them the reflexive knowledge of their own positioning and identity. This is the 'rooting.' At the same time, they should also try to 'shift'—to put themselves in the situation of those with whom they are in dialogue and who are differ-ent" (1999, 96).

11. Ursula Heise, in her book *Sense of Place and Sense of Planet: The Environmental Imagi-nation of the Global* (2008), reflects on the limits of localist thinking as we face problems that exist on a global scale, such as climate change and its associated temperature, storm, and drought shifts.

## Chapter 2. Misrecognition, Metamorphosis, and Maps in Chicana Feminist Cultural Production

1. For more on social ecofeminism, see Warren (2000), Plumwood (1993), and King (1995).

2. Here and elsewhere I use the terms *co-being* and *co-arising* strategically to link Anzaldúa's theories on borderlands subjectivity with Buddhist philosophies that also informed her ecological thinking. Theresa Delgadillo's *Spiritual Mestizaje: Religion, Gen-der, Race, and Nation in Contemporary Chicana Narrative* (2011) considers the relationship between Buddhism and other spiritual influences in Anzaldúa's *Borderlands/La Frontera*. For more on Buddhist ecofeminist praxis, see Wan-Li Ho's "Environmental Protection as Religious Action: The Case of Taiwanese Buddhist Women" (2003).

3. For an ecocritical analysis of Moraga's other works, see Priscilla Solis Ybarra's "'Lo que quiero es tierra': Longing and Belonging in Cherríe Moraga's Ecological Vision" (2004).

4. The North American Free Trade Agreement (NAFTA) was initiated in 1994 to facili-tate trade among North American nations and bring jobs and wealth to Mexico. Despite these aims, Mexico has not seen the promised economic benefits and many consider NAFTA to be an example of free-trade neocolonialism (see, e.g., Bigelow [2006]).

5. Similar to the actions of Toni Morrison's character Sethe in *Beloved*, an anticolonial reading of La Llorona describes her as sacrificing her children to free them from the horrors of colonial violence. For varied interpretations of La Llorona, see Debra Blake's

*Chicana Sexuality and Gender: Cultural Refiguring in Literature, Oral History, and Art* (2008) and Domino Renee Perez's *There Was a Woman: La Llorona from Popular Folklore to Popular Culture* (2008).

6. For a Chicana and ecofeminist reading of Pat Mora's *House of Houses* (1997), see Imelda Martín-Junquera's "Healing Family History/(Her) Story: Writing and Gardening in Pat Mora's *House of Houses*" (2014).

7. For more on Aztec metaphysics, including the ways paired terms such as *life* and *death* and *male* and *female* function as cyclical and dynamic facets of the same material force rather than opposing and separate binaries as in Western philosophical traditions, see James Maffie's *Aztec Philosophy: Understanding a World in Motion* (2013) and Miguel León-Portilla's *Aztec Thought and Culture: A Study of the Ancient Nahuatl Mind* (1963).

8. Michel Foucault's theories of embodiment and subjectification can be found in a number of texts. In particular, see *Discipline and Punish: The Birth of the Prison* (1977) and *The History of Sexuality: An Introduction, Volume 1* (1990).

9. Although I do not have the space to discuss them here, the other works in the *1848: Chicanos in the U.S. Landscape after the Treaty of Guadalupe Hidalgo* series (e.g., *Juan Soldado* and *Santa Niña de Mochis*) also map relations of power from 1848 onward, especially with respect to the theme of migration.

## Chapter 3. Allegory, Materiality, and Agency in Amalia Mesa-Bains's Altar Environments

1. See Anzaldúa's essay "now let us shift . . ." in Anzaldúa and Keating's *this bridge we call home: radical visions for transformation* (2002).

2. In this paragraph, I use *entanglement* and *intra-acting* to describe states of being and becoming to recall Karen Barad's theory of agential realism. Objects (including humans) are not separate, distinct from each other, but are the effects of ongoing processes— inter- and intra-actions—that enable their materializations. She explains, "Bodies are not objects with inherent boundaries and properties; they are material-discursive phenomena. 'Human' bodies are not inherently different from 'nonhuman' ones" (2003, 823).

3. See, for example, Anzaldúa (1999), Delgadillo (2011), and Facio and Lara (2014).

4. Alicia Gaspar de Alba (1998) discusses the Chicano Art: Resistance and Affirmation exhibition (CARA) and its importance to the development of an emerging Chicana/o aesthetic. Mesa-Bains describes her own sense of responsibility toward the Chicana/o artist-activist community; see, for example, "Spiritual Geographies" (Mesa-Bains 2001b) and *Amalia Mesa-Bains: Cihuatlampa, the Place of the Giant Women*, an interview with the artist and video recording of the opening of her *Venus Envy Chapter III* exhibit (Steinbaum Krauss Gallery 1997).

5. See Mesa-Bains's conversations with bell hooks in *Homegrown: Engaged Cultural Criticism* (2006) for more background on the artist's parents and her upbringing.

6. According to the museum that houses *The Little Garden of Paradise*, "Nineteen plants and twelve types of birds, fish, butterflies and dragonflies have been reproduced with the utmost botanical and zoological precision." For more information, visit the Städel

Museum web page, http://www.staedelmuseum.de/en/collection/little-garden-paradise -ca-1410-20.

7. Mesa-Bains describes mapping her family's human geography in *Private Landscapes/ Public Territories* in her essay "Nature and Spirit" (2011).

8. For an alternative reading of *Venus Envy Chapter III*, see Laura Pérez's *Chicana Art: The Politics of Spiritual and Aesthetic Altarities* (2007). Pérez argues that the citation of the spiritual symbolizes "the transcendence of social gender, and indeed their [the feathered, branched vestiture figures'] styling would appear to confirm this" (67). Placed next to the large moss-covered female body and surrounded by images of famous feminists, I contend that the installation does not seek to transcend gender altogether, but poses a less anthropocentric reflection of gender performance, one that moves us from rigid gender (and human) identities toward *becoming-nature* and *becoming-spirit*.

9. For more on Mendieta's earthworks, see Blocker (1999) and Boetzkes (2010).

10. See the 2013 installation *New World Wunderkammer* at UCLA's Fowler Museum for a recent example of Mesa-Bains's curiosity cabinets and read her discussion of the cabinets as an art form in "A Latino Cabinet of Curiosities: A Postcolonial Reopening" (Mesa-Bains 2013).

11. Elizabeth de la Portilla explains the role of deer antlers in healing rituals in her book *They All Want Magic: Curanderas and Folk Healing* (2009).

12. See Smith and Watson's *Getting a Life: Everyday Uses of Autobiography* (1996) and the second edition of their *Reading Autobiography: A Guide for Interpreting Life Narratives* (2010) for a complete overview of theoretical frameworks for interpreting life writing and, to a lesser extent, self-representation in other forms.

## Chapter 4. Body/Landscape/Spirit Relations in *Señorita Extraviada*: Cinematic Deterritorializations and the Limits of Audience Literacy

1. According to Bill Nichols, a performative documentary constructs a world for its audience that is interrogative in that it questions the world around us and our meaning-making process. The filmmaker strives to draw the audience into the meaning-making process rather than to relay a single, coherent truth about the world. As such, the performative mode of documentary "addresses the fundamental question of social subjectivity, of those linkages between self and other that are affective as fully as they are conceptual" (1994, 104). See also Nichols's *Introduction to Documentary* (2001).

2. As in other chapters, I rely on Bronwyn Davies's notion of "body/landscape" inscriptions (2000) to develop my discussion of body/landscape/spirit interconnections.

3. I use the term *deterritorialization* to draw on Deleuze and Guattari's (1983, 1987) efforts to move from a molar to a molecular politics; molar politics congeal into fixed identities and bounded movements that assume a stasis or fixed end point. Deterritorialization can unfix a molar politics and push it toward a molecular model—movements and identities that are mobile, without clear direction, open to new and changing assemblages. Molar politics is to "states of being" as molecular politics is to "states of becoming." A number

158

of post- and decolonial scholars have taken up and troubled "deterritorialization" as a potentially context-free celebration of postidentitarianism in an age in which identities and identity-based movement continue to matter greatly to the disempowered and in which forced displacement characterizes the kinds of deterritorializations faced by many. My use of the term is inflected with these critical understandings, reflecting both forced displacements in a very real, material sense, and the need to open up discursive sedimentations that materialize unjust conditions. The collection *Uprootings/Regroundings: Questions of Home and Migration*, edited by Ahmed, Castañeda, and Fortie (2003), grapples with a similar set of concerns.

4. In "'I would rather be a cyborg than a goddess': Becoming Intersectional in Assemblage Theory" (2012), Jasbir Puar takes on Sandoval's (2000) critique that assemblage theory, and Donna Haraway's (1991) celebration of the cyborg in particular, reifies women of color (especially the many Chicanas who work in maquiladoras) as machines at the cost of recognizing their humanity.

5. For more on assemblage theory, see Deleuze and Guattari's *A Thousand Plateaus: Capitalism and Schizophrenia* (1987) and Manuel De Landa's *A New Philosophy of Society: Assemblage Theory and Social Complexity* (2006).

6. For an ethnographic study detailing this logic at work in the factories, see Melissa Wright's "The Politics of Relocation: Gender, Nationality, and Value in a Mexican Maquiladora" (2003).

7. Voces sin Eco disbanded in 2001; members of the group explain that people in the media and other nongovernmental organizations (NGOs) were financially profiting from the group. Family members were exploited with numerous interview requests, and earnings from the many news stories and documentaries women participated in were never returned to the organization. For more information, see "No Echo: Juárez Murdered Women's Group Disbands."

8. Since the release of *Señorita Extraviada* in 2001, drug cartels have played an increasingly obvious role in perpetuating violence in the region and all across Mexico in their effort to supply drugs to a largely American market.

9. I surveyed all reviews that were available on the Internet without a newspaper or magazine subscription. They include: Adams, "Missing Young Woman" (2002); Backstein, "*Señorita Extraviada*" (Winter 2002); Bain, "Murders in Juárez Remain Unsolved, Unabated" (2003); Baumgarten, "*Señorita Extraviada*" (2002); Boshra, "Justice Is Missing for Murdered Women" (2002); Broeske, "400 Dead Women: Now Hollywood Is Intrigued" (2006); Carreño King, "City of Lost Souls" (2002); Ibarra, "*Señorita Extraviada*" (2003); Lowerison, "'*Señorita Extraviada* (Young Woman Missing)': The Politics of Murder Investigation" (2003); Navarro, "A Filmmaker Seeks Answers about Killings in Mexico" (2002); Page, "Flawed but Powerful 'Senorita' Evokes Outrage" (2003); Rechtshaffen, "Review from the Los Angeles Latino International Film Festival" (2002); "Reel Review: *Señorita Extraviada*" (2002); Thomas, "*Señorita Extraviada*" (2003); Wells, "*Señorita Extraviada*" (2002); and Wilson, "*Señorita Extraviada*" (2003).

Chapter 5. Building Green Community at the Border:
Feminist and Ecological Consciousness at the Women's Intercultural Center

1. For more on *mujerista* theology, see Ada María Isasi-Díaz's works, including *Mujerista Theology: A Theology for the Twenty-First Century* (1996).

2. Although the center primarily serves local women who self-identify as Hispanic, it also hosts a Border Awareness Experience (BAE) that brings college students and church groups from across the United States to WInC to raise consciousness about contemporary border issues such as immigration and law enforcement, the loss of manufacturing jobs on the northern side of the border after NAFTA, and ecological degradation across the region. As such, WInC presents a multifaceted approach to social and ecological justice for women in the region, and it is also a coalitional (and intercultural) site that openly welcomes others to visit, learn, and stand in alliance with the community. There were no BAE trips scheduled during my visits to the center. For more information on the program, visit http://www.womensinterculturalcenter.org/68-border-awareness-experience.

3. This project heeds the methodological concerns raised by Debra Blake, whose book *Chicana Sexuality and Gender: Cultural Refiguring in Literature, Oral History, and Art* (2008) compares the differences in how noted Chicana artists and writers depict cultural icons (e.g., La Llorona, Aztec deities, The Virgin of Guadalupe) with interpretations of those figures by Mexican American women who may share different class, education, migration, and political backgrounds.

4. Whereas the artists and writers of prior chapters largely name themselves with the political and self-chosen identity *Chicana*, the women interviewed for this chapter described themselves as *Hispanic* (although not all interviewees were fluent in Spanish) or *Mexican American*.

5. In 2009, I visited the center and conducted ten interviews with staff and participants; during a follow-up trip in 2012, I conducted five new interviews. I follow the naming preferences given by each of the interviewees—most names provided in this chapter are pseudonyms. The director, Mary Carter, elected to use her name in all quotes. Based on initial research of website materials and conversations with the director, the interview schedule included questions about the role of the individual within the organization, the participant's understanding of the organization's mission, beliefs about personal growth and empowerment, social issues that are important to the individual, WInC's role in the community, and the participant's understanding of spirituality and environmentalism at the center. Interviews were loose enough to allow individuals to redirect the conversation in ways that were most meaningful for them.

6. The issue of water contamination came to light during the time between my two visits to Anthony. None of the participants seemed aware of the problem in 2009 and spoke more of issues impacting nearby El Paso, such as poor air quality from the manufacturing industry. The New Mexico Environmental Department has ordered abatement measures.

7. Rosemary Hennessy's "Open Secrets: The Affective Cultures of Organizing on Mexico's Northern Border" (2009) lays bare what is at stake in organizing in the borderlands:

"Bonds of loyalty, camaraderie, and friendship, of competition, jealousy, and betrayal are seething presences that act on and meddle with the processes whereby the collective bonds are formed that enable people to take action" (310). Because community-building and ending social isolation are so important to WInC's work, moments of exclusion and failures to build connections may be all the more painful a betrayal to some women at WInC. This study mostly focuses on the positive connections created at WInC—and most of the interactions I witnessed and that came up in interviews were positive—but there were some points of rupture. One woman spoke of a classist incident and two others told stories that exposed a sexual politics of respectability at work. Moreover, most interviewees spoke of the center as an extension of the heterosexual family unit and  described their work at WInC as a form of caregiving or mothering. There seemed to be little space for nonnormative sexual expression within this model of social organizing.

8. For a full explanation of "systems thinking," see Jim Dodge's "Living by Life: Some Bioregional Theory and Practice" (1990).

9. At the time of writing, WInC has been able to expand its offerings by establishing joint programs with other organizations in the region. They partner with La Piñon Sexual Assault Recovery Services of Southern New Mexico and offer counseling services through the New Mexico State University Counseling and Educational Psychology Training and Research Program.

10. For other studies that show women developing as environmental justice activists and community leaders by mobilizing their skills as community networkers, see Pardo (1990) and Prindeville (2003).

11. This argument deserves more attention than I can give it in this chapter; however, rather than see this component of the center's work as complicit in neoliberal politics in the borderlands, Chela Sandoval (2000) reminds us of the uses of differential consciousness that may employ equal rights strategies and more revolutionary tactics in tandem. We saw this in other chapters, such as in the discussion of land rights in chapter 1.

## Conclusion. Bridging Movements with Technologies for the Ecological Self

1. Many have used the term *self-in-community* to theorize selves that are relational rather than autonomous. For examples, see Sarah Hoagland's *Lesbian Ethics: Toward New Value* (1988) and Paula Moya's "Postmodernism, 'Realism' and the Politics of Identity: Cherríe Moraga and Chicana Feminism" (1997).

2. In addition to Chela Sandoval's *Methodology of the Oppressed* (2000), my use of the term *technologies for the intersubjective or ecological self* is also informed by Michel Foucault's *Technologies of the Self* (1988), in which he details not just technologies of the self, but also technologies of production, technologies of sign systems, and technologies of power (as Sandoval notes, Foucault informs much of her own work as well).

# Bibliography

Abell, Hilary. 1999. "Endangering Women's Health for Profit: Health and Safety in Mexico's Maquiladoras." *Development in Practice* 9 (5): 595–600.

"About." 2016. Women's Intercultural Center. Accessed January 26. http://www.womens interculturalcenter.org/about.

"About Us." 2016. Southwest Network for Environmental and Economic Justice. March 13. http://www.supergreenme.com/SouthwestNetworkforEnvironmentaland EconomicJustice.

Adams, Carol. 1993. "The Feminist Traffic in Animals." In *Ecofeminism: Women, Animals, Nature*, edited by Greta Gaard, 195–218. Philadelphia: Temple University Press.

Adams, Derek. 2002. "Missing Young Woman." *Time Out Film Guide*. Accessed January 26, 2016. http://www.timeout.com/film/reviews/73279/missing_young_woman.html.

Adamson, Joni. 2002. "Throwing Rocks at the Sun: An Interview with Teresa Leal." In *The Environmental Justice Reader: Politics, Poetics, and Pedagogy*, edited by Joni Adamson, Mei Mei Evans, and Rachel Stein, 44–57. Tucson: University of Arizona Press.

Adamson, Joni, Mei Mei Evans, and Rachel Stein, eds. 2002. *The Environmental Justice Reader: Politics, Poetics, and Pedagogy*. Tucson: University of Arizona Press.

Adamson, Joni, and Rachel Stein. 2002. "Environmental Justice: A Roundtable Discussion with Simon Ortiz, Teresa Leal, Devon Peña, and Terrell Dixon." In *The Environmental Justice Reader: Politics, Poetics, and Pedagogy*, edited by Joni Adamson, Mei Mei Evans, and Rachel Stein, 15–26. Tucson: University of Arizona Press.

Agarwal, Bina. 1997. "The Gender and Environment Debate: Lessons from India." In *The Women, Gender and Development Reader*, edited by Nalini Visvanathan, Lynn Duggan, Laurie Nisonoff, and Nan Wiegersma, 68–75. London: Zed Books.

Ahmed, Sara, Claudia Castañeda, and Anne-Marie Fortie, eds. 2003. *Uprootings/Regroundings: Questions of Home and Migration.* Oxford: Berg Press.

Alaimo, Stacy. 2010. *Bodily Natures: Science, the Environment, and the Material Self.* Bloomington: Indiana University Press.

Alaimo, Stacy, and Susan Hekman, eds. 2008. *Material Feminisms.* Bloomington: Indiana University Press.

Alarcón, Norma. 1994. "Traddutora, Traditora: A Paradigmatic Figure of Chicana Feminism." In *Scattered Hegemonies: Postmodernity and Transnational Feminist Practices,* edited by Inderpal Grewal and Caren Kaplan, 110–33. Minneapolis: University of Minnesota Press.

———. 1995. "Cognitive Desires: An Allegory of/for Chicana Critics." In *Chicana (W)rites on Word and Film,* edited by María Herrera-Sobek and Helena María Viramontes, 185–200. Berkeley: Third Woman Press.

———. 1999. "Chicana Feminism: In the Tracks of 'The' Native Woman." In *Between Woman and Nation: Nationalisms, Transnational Feminisms, and the State,* edited by Caren Kaplan, Norma Alarcón, and Minoo Moallem, 63–71. Durham, NC: Duke University Press.

Aldama, Arturo J. 2001. *Disrupting Savagism: Intersecting Chicana/o, Mexican Immigrant, and Native American Struggles for Self-Representation.* Durham, NC: Duke University Press.

Aldama, Arturo, and Naomi Quiñonez, eds. 2002. *Decolonial Voices: Chicana and Chicano Cultural Studies in the 21st Century.* Bloomington: Indiana University Press.

Aldama, Arturo, Chela Sandoval, and Peter García. 2012. *Performing the US Latina and Latino Borderlands.* Bloomington: Indiana University Press.

Alexander, M. Jacqui. 2005. *Pedagogies of Crossing: Meditations on Feminism, Sexual Politics, Memory, and the Sacred.* Durham, NC: Duke University Press.

Alicia, Juana. 2016. "Narrative for Murals at El Centro Chicano de Estánfor" (blog). Accessed January 27. https://juanaaliciaatcentro.wordpress.com/narrative-for-murals-at-el-centro-chicano-de-estanfor/.

Anzaldúa, Gloria. 1999. *Borderlands/La Frontera: The New Mestiza,* 2nd ed. San Francisco: Aunt Lute Books.

———. 2000. "Doing Gigs: Speaking, Writing, and Change—An Interview with Debbie Blake and Carmen Abrego (1994)." In *Interviews/Entrevistas,* edited by AnaLouise Keating, 212–34. New York: Routledge.

———. 2002. "now let us shift . . . the path of conocimiento . . . inner work, public acts." In *this bridge we call home: radical visions for transformation,* edited by Gloria Anzaldúa and AnaLouise Keating, 540–78. New York: Routledge.

———. 2009a. "Let us be the healing of the wound: The Coyolxauhqui imperative—la sombra y el sueño." In *The Gloria Anzaldúa Reader,* edited by AnaLouise Keating, 303–17. Durham, NC: Duke University Press.

———. 2009b. "Speaking across the Divide." In *The Gloria Anzaldúa Reader,* edited by AnaLouise Keating, 282–94. Durham, NC: Duke University Press.

Carson, Rachel. 1962. *Silent Spring*. Boston: Houghton Mifflin.

Carter, Mary. 2009. "Reflections: Women's Intercultural Center First Annual Report to the Community." Anthony, NM: Women's Intercultural Center.

Castañeda, Antonia. 1990. "Gender, Race, and Culture: Spanish-Mexican Women in the Historiography of Frontier California." *Frontiers* 11 (1): 8–16.

———. 2001. "'Que Se Pudiera Defender (So You Could Defend Yourselves)': Chicanas, Regional History, and National Discourses." *Frontiers* 22 (3): 116–40.

Chabram-Dernersesian, Angie. 1993. "And, Yes . . . The Earth Did Part: On the Splitting of Chicana/o Subjectivity." In *Building with Our Hands: New Directions in Chicana Studies*, edited by Adela de la Torre and Beatríz Pesquera, 34–56. Berkeley: University of California Press.

———. 1999. "'Chicana! Rican? No, Chicana Riqueña!' Refashioning the Transnational Connection." In *Between Woman and Nation: Nationalisms, Transnational Feminisms, and the State*, edited by Caren Kaplan, Norma Alarcón, and Minoo Moallem, 264–95. Durham, NC: Duke University Press.

Christ, Carol, and Judith Plaskow, eds. 1992. *Womanspirit Rising: A Feminist Reader in Religion*. San Francisco: Harper and Row.

Christensen, Linda. 2006. "Reading Chilpancingo." In *The Line between Us: Teaching about the Border and Mexican Immigration*, edited by Bill Bigelow, 97–101. Milwaukee: Rethinking Schools.

Cisneros, Sandra. 1984. *The House on Mango Street*. Houston: Arte Público Press.

———. 1991. *Woman Hollering Creek and Other Stories*. New York: Random House.

Colebrook, Claire. 2002. *Gilles Deleuze*. London: Routledge.

Commission for Racial Justice. 1987. *Toxic Wastes and Race: A National Report on the Racial and Socioeconomic Characteristics of Communities with Hazardous Waste Sites*. New York: United Church of Christ.

Conradson, David, and Deirdre McKay. 2007. "Translocal Subjectivities: Mobility, Connection, Emotion." *Mobilities* 2 (2): 167–74.

Coole, Diana, and Samantha Frost, eds. 2010. *New Materialisms: Ontology, Agency, and Politics*. Durham, NC: Duke University Press.

Córdova, Teresa. 1998. "Anti-Colonial Chicana Feminism." *New Political Science* 20 (4): 379–97.

Cudworth, Erika. 2005. *Developing Ecofeminist Theory: The Complexity of Difference*. New York: Palgrave Macmillan.

Cuomo, Chris. 1998. *Feminism and Ecological Communities: An Ethic of Flourishing*. New York: Routledge.

———. 2001. "Still Fooling with Mother Nature." *Hypatia* 16 (3): 149–56.

Daly, Mary. 1978. *Gyn/Ecology: The Metaethics of Radical Feminism*. Boston: Beacon Press.

Davidson, Joyce, Liz Bondi, and Mick Smith, eds. 2005. *Emotional Geographies*. Hampshire, UK: Ashgate.

Davidson, Joyce, and Christine Milligan. 2004. "Embodying Emotion, Sensing Space: Introducing Emotional Geographies." *Social and Cultural Geography* 5:523–32.

Davies, Bronwyn. 2000. *(In)Scribing Body/Landscape Relations*. Walnut Creek, CA: AltaMira Press.

Davis, Malia. 1998. "Philosophy Meets Practice: A Critique of Ecofeminism through the Voices of Three Chicana Activists." In *Chicano Culture, Ecology, Politics: Subversive Kin*, edited by Devon Peña, 201–31. Tucson: University of Arizona Press.

De Landa, Manuel. 2006. *A New Philosophy of Society: Assemblage Theory and Social Complexity*. New York: Continuum.

Deleuze, Gilles. 1986. *Cinema 1: The Movement-Image*. Translated by Hugh Tomlinson and Barbara Habberjam. Minneapolis: University of Minnesota Press.

———. 1989. *Cinema 2: The Time-Image*. Translated by Hugh Tomlinson and Robert Galeta. Minneapolis: University of Minnesota Press.

Deleuze, Gilles, and Félix Guattari. 1983. *Anti-Oedipus: Capitalism and Schizophrenia*. Translated by Robert Hurley. Minneapolis: University of Minnesota.

———. 1987. *A Thousand Plateaus: Capitalism and Schizophrenia*. Translated by Brian Massumi. Minneapolis: University of Minnesota.

Delgadillo, Theresa. 2011. *Spiritual Mestizaje: Religion, Gender, Race, and Nation in Contemporary Chicana Narrative*. Durham, NC: Duke University Press.

Dodge, Jim. 1990. "Living by Life: Some Bioregional Theory and Practice." In *Home! A Bioregional Reader*, edited by Van Andruss, Christopher Plant, Judith Plant, and Eleanor Wright, 5–12. Philadelphia: New Society.

Driver, Alice. 2012. "Ciudad Juárez as Palimpsest." In *Pushing the Boundaries of Latin American Testimony*, edited by Louise Detwiler and Janis Breckenridge, 181–200. New York: Palgrave Macmillan.

"Drought along the Rio Grande Highlights Water Management Complexities." 2013. New Mexico Water Dialogue. Accessed January 27, 2016. http://allaboutwatersheds.org/new-mexico-water-dialogue/news/drought-along-the-rio-grande-highlights-water-management-complexities.

Dunlap, Riley, and Angela Mertig, eds. 1992. *American Environmentalism: The U.S. Environmental Movement, 1970–1990*. Washington, DC: Taylor and Francis.

Durkheim, Emile. (1965) 1995. *The Elementary Forms of the Religious Life*. Translated by Karen Fields. New York: Free Press.

Eaton, Heather, and Lois Ann Lorentzen, eds. 2003. *Ecofeminism and Globalization: Exploring Culture, Context, and Religion*. New York: Rowman and Littlefield.

*El Plan Espiritual de Aztlán*. 1969. Accessed March 16, 2016. http://www.umich.edu/~mechaum/Aztlan.html.

Enloe, Cynthia. 2000. *Bananas, Beaches, and Bases: Making Feminist Sense of International Politics*. Berkeley: University of California Press.

Facio, Elisa, and Irene Lara, eds. 2014. *Fleshing the Spirit: Spirituality and Activism in Chicana, Latina, and Indigenous Women's Lives*. Tucson: University of Arizona Press.

Farley, Lisa. 2004. "Useless Suffering: Learning from the Unintelligible and the Re-Formation of Community." *Interchange* 35 (3): 325–36.

Feiner, Susan, and Drucilla Barker. 2007. "The Dickensian World of Micro-Finance: Grameen May Not Be So Good for Women After All." *Women's Review of Books* 24 (3): 23–25.

Fernández-Kelly, Patricia. 1986. "International Development and Women's Employment: Issues for a Feminist Agenda." *Women's Studies Quarterly* 14 (3/4): 2–6.

Fielding, Helen. 2000. "'The Sum of What She Is Saying': Bringing Essentials Back to the Body." In *Resistance, Flight, Creation: Feminist Enactments of French Philosophy*, edited by Dorothea Olkowski, 124–37. Ithaca, NY: Cornell University Press.

Firestone, Shulamith. 1970. *The Dialectic of Sex: The Case for Feminist Revolution*. New York: Farrar, Straus and Giroux.

Flaxman, Gregory. 2000. "Introduction." In *The Brain Is the Screen: Deleuze and the Philosophy of Cinema*, edited by Gregory Flaxman, 1–57. Minneapolis: University of Minnesota Press.

Flieger, Jerry Aline. 2000. "Becoming-Woman: Deleuze, Scheber and Molecular Identification." In *Deleuze and Feminist Theory*, edited by Ian Buchanan and Claire Colebrook, 38–63. Edinburgh: Edinburgh University Press.

Foucault, Michel. 1977. *Discipline and Punish: The Birth of the Prison*. Translated by Alan Sheridan. New York: Pantheon.

———. 1984. "Nietzsche, Genealogy, History." In *The Foucault Reader*, edited by Paul Rabinow. New York: Pantheon.

———. 1988. *Technologies of the Self: A Seminar with Michel Foucault*. Edited by Luther H. Martin, Huck Gutman, and Patrick H. Hutton. Amherst: University of Massachusetts Press.

———. 1990. *The History of Sexuality: An Introduction, Volume 1*. Translated by Robert Hurley. New York: Vintage Books.

Fowlkes, Diane. 1997. "Moving from Feminist Identity Politics to Coalition Politics through a Feminist Materialist Standpoint of Intersubjectivity in Gloria Anzaldúa's *Borderlands/La Frontera: The New Mestiza*." *Hypatia* 12 (2): 105–24.

Fregoso, Rosa Linda. 1995. "Chicana Film Practices: Confronting the 'Many-Headed Demon of Oppression.'" In *Chicana (W)rites on Word and Film*, edited by María Herrera-Sobek and Helena María Viramontes, 259–73. Berkeley: Third Woman Press.

———. 2003. *MeXicana Encounters: The Making of Social Identities on the Borderlands*. Berkeley: University of California Press.

Freire, Paulo. 1970. *Pedagogy of the Oppressed*. Translated by Myra Ramos. New York: Continuum.

Freudenberg, Nicholas, and Carol Steinsapir. 1992. "Not in Our Backyards: The Grassroots Environmental Movement." In *American Environmentalism: The U.S. Environmental Movement, 1970–1990*, edited by Riley Dunlap and Angela Mertig, 27–37. Washington, DC: Taylor and Francis.

Funari, Vicky. 2006. *Maquilapolis (City of Factories)*. DVD. San Francisco: California Newsreel.

Gaard, Greta. 2011. "Ecofeminism Revisited: Rejecting Essentialism and Re-Placing Species in a Material Feminist Environmentalism." *Feminist Formations* 23 (2): 26–53.

Gaspar de Alba, Alicia. 1998. *Chicano Art inside/outside the Master's House: Cultural Politics and the CARA Exhibition*. Austin: University of Texas Press.

Gates, Barbara. 1998. "A Root of Ecofeminism: *Ecoféminisme.*" In *Ecofeminist Literary Criticism: Theory, Interpretation, Pedagogy,* edited by Greta Gaard and Patrick Murphy, 15–22. Urbana: University of Illinois Press.

Gebara, Ivone. 1996. "The Trinity and Human Experience." In *Women Healing Earth: Third World Women on Ecology, Feminism, and Religion,* edited by Rosemary Radford Ruether, 13–23. Maryknoll, NY: Orbis Books.

González, Jennifer. 1999. "Archaeological Devotion." In *With Other Eyes: Looking at Race and Gender in Visual Culture,* edited by Lisa Bloom, 184–212. Minneapolis: University of Minnesota Press.

———. 2008. *Subject to Display: Reframing Race in Contemporary Installation Art.* Cambridge, MA: MIT Press.

González, Rita. 2003. "The Said and the Unsaid: Lourdes Portillo Tracks Down Ghosts in *Señorita Extraviada.*" *Aztlán* 28 (2): 235–40.

Gorton, Kristyn. 2007. "Theorizing Emotion and Affect: Feminist Engagements." *Feminist Theory* 8 (3): 333–48.

Griffin, Susan. 1978. *Woman and Nature: The Roaring inside Her.* San Francisco: Harper and Row.

Griffith, Emily. 2002. "Three Women's Formative Experiences in Art: Amalia Mesa-Bains, Miriam Schapiro and Jaune Quick-to-See Smith." Master's thesis, Concordia University, Montreal, Canada.

Grineski, Sara, and Timothy Collins. 2008. "Exploring Patterns of Environmental Injustice in the Global South: Maquiladoras in Ciudad Juárez, Mexico." *Population and Environment* 29 (6): 247–70.

Grossman, Roberta, dir. 2005. *Homeland: Four Portraits of Native Action.* DVD. Reading, PA: Bullfrog Films.

Grosz, Elizabeth. 1994. *Volatile Bodies: Toward a Corporeal Feminism.* Bloomington: Indiana University Press.

Haraway, Donna. 1991. *Simians, Cyborgs, and Women: The Reinvention of Nature.* New York: Routledge.

Harding, Vincent. 2016. "An Interview with Delores Huerta." Veterans of Hope Project. Accessed January 27. http://www.veteransofhope.org/veteran/delores-huerta/.

Hardt, Michael, and Antonio Negri. 2004. *Multitude: War and Democracy in the Age of Empire.* New York: Penguin Press.

Harper, A. Breeze. 2011. "Connections: Speciesism, Racism, and Whiteness as the Norm." In *Sister Species: Women, Animals, and Social Justice,* edited by Lisa Kemmerer, 72–78. Urbana: University of Illinois Press.

Hawthorne, Susan. 2002. *Wild Politics: Feminism, Globalization, Bio/Diversity.* North Melbourne, Australia: Spinifex Press.

Heise, Ursula. 2008. *Sense of Place and Sense of Planet: The Environmental Imagination of the Global.* Oxford: Oxford University Press.

Hemmings, Clare. 2005. "Telling Feminist Stories." *Feminist Theory* 6 (2): 115–39.

Hennessy, Rosemary. 2009. "Open Secrets: The Affective Cultures of Organizing on Mexico's Northern Border." *Feminist Theory* 10 (3): 309–22.

Hernández, Leticia, with Juana Alicia. 2003. "Juana Alicia: An Artist Takes a Global Look at the Spirit of Women" (blog). October 6. Accessed January 27, 2016. http://www .juanaalicia.com/content/57/.

Herrera-Sobek, María, and Helena María Viramontes, eds. 1995. *Chicana (W)rites on Word and Film*. Berkeley: Third Woman Press.

Hoagland, Sarah. 1988. *Lesbian Ethics: Toward New Value*. Palo Alto, CA: Institute of Lesbian Studies.

hooks, bell, and Amalia Mesa-Bains. 2006. *Homegrown: Engaged Cultural Criticism*. Boston: South End Press.

Houston, Donna, and Laura Pulido. 2005. "The Work of Performativity: Staging Social Justice at the University of Southern California." In *Critical Theories, Radical Pedagogies, and Global Conflicts*, edited by Gustavo Fischman, Peter McLaren, Heinz Sünker, and Colin Lankshear, 317–42. Lanham, MD: Rowman and Littlefield.

Ho, Wan-Li. 2003. "Environmental Protection as Religious Action: The Case of Taiwanese Buddhist Women." In *Ecofeminism and Globalization: Exploring Culture, Context, and Religion*, edited by Heather Eaton and Lois Ann Lorentzen, 123–46. New York: Rowman and Littlefield.

Ibarra, Cristina. 2003. "*Señorita Extraviada*." *Criticas* 31 (January–February): 64.

Isasi-Díaz, Ada María. 1996. *Mujerista Theology: A Theology for the Twenty-First Century*. Maryknoll, NY: Orbis Books.

Johnson, Melissa, and Emily Niemeyer. 2008. "Ambivalent Landscapes: Environmental Justice in the US-Mexico Borderlands." *Human Ecology* 36 (3): 371–82.

Keating, AnaLouise. 2013. *Transformation Now! Toward a Post-Oppositional Politics of Change*. Urbana: University of Illinois Press.

King, Ynestra. 1983. "The Eco-Feminist Imperative." In *Reclaim the Earth: Women, Speak Out for Life on Earth*, edited by Leonie Caldecott and Stephanie Leland, 12–16. London: Woman's Press.

———. 1989. "Healing the Wounds: Feminism, Ecology, and Nature/Culture Dualism." In *Gender/Body/Knowledge: Feminist Reconstructions of Being and Knowing*, edited by Alison Jaggar and Susan Bordo, 115–41. New Brunswick, NJ: Rutgers University Press.

———. 1995. "The Ecology of Feminism and the Feminism of Ecology." In *Readings in Ecology and Feminist Theology*, edited by Mary Heather MacKinnon and Moni McIntyre, 150–60. Kansas City, MO: Sheed and Ward.

Kirk, Gwyn. 1998. "Ecofeminism and Chicano Environmental Struggles: Bridges across Gender and Race." In *Chicano Culture, Ecology, Politics: Subversive Kin*, edited by Devon Peña, 177–200. Tucson: University of Arizona Press.

Klahn, Norma. 2003. "Literary (Re)Mappings: Autobiographical (Dis)placements by Chicana Writers." In *Chicana Feminisms: A Critical Reader*, edited by Gabriella F. Arredondo, Aída Hurtado, Norma Klahn, Olga Nájera-Ramírez, and Patricia Zavella, 114–45. Durham, NC: Duke University Press.

Latorre, Guisela. 2007. "Chicana Art and Scholarship: On the Interstices of Our Disciplines." *Chicana/Latina Studies: The Journal of Mujeres Activas en Letras y Cambio Social* 6 (2): 10–21.

———. 2008. *Walls of Empowerment: Chicana/o Indigenist Murals of California*. Austin: University of Texas Press.

León, Luis D. 2004. *La Llorona's Children: Religion, Life, and Death in the U.S.-Mexican Borderlands*. Berkeley: University of California Press.

León-Portilla, Miguel. 1963. *Aztec Thought and Culture: A Study of the Ancient Nahuatl Mind*. Norman: University of Oklahoma Press.

———. 1990. *Endangered Cultures*. Dallas: Southern Methodist University Press.

López, Alma. 2002. "Tattoo, Santa Niña de Mochis, California Fashion Slaves, and Our Lady." *Frontiers: A Journal of Women Studies* 23 (1): 90–95.

Low, Alaine, and Soraya Tremayne, eds. 2001. *Women as Sacred Custodians of the Earth? Women, Spirituality and the Environment*. New York: Berghahn Books/Mackie.

Lowerison, Jean. 2003. "'*Señorita Extraviada* (Young Woman Missing)': The Politics of Murder Investigation." *San Diego Metropolitan*, February. Accessed May 15, 2013. http://sandiegometro.com/reel/index.php?reelID=510.

Maffie, James. 2013. *Aztec Philosophy: Understanding a World in Motion*. Boulder: University Press of Colorado.

Mancillas, Aida, Ruth Wallen, and Marguerite Waller. 1999. "Making Art, Making Citizens: Las Comadres and Postnational Aesthetics." In *With Other Eyes: Looking at Race and Gender in Visual Culture*, edited by Lisa Bloom, 107–32. Minneapolis: University of Minnesota Press.

"Maquilapolis Community Outreach Campaign." 2016. Accessed January 27. http://www.maquilapolis.com/outreach_eng.html.

Marks, Laura. 2000. "Signs of the Time: Deleuze, Peirce, and the Documentary Image." In *The Brain Is the Screen: Deleuze and the Philosophy of Cinema*, edited by Gregory Flaxman, 193–213. Minneapolis: University of Minnesota Press.

Martín-Junquera, Imelda, ed. 2013. *Landscapes of Writing in Chicano Literature*. New York: Palgrave Macmillan.

———. 2014. "Healing Family History/(Her) Story: Writing and Gardening in Pat Mora's *House of Houses*." In *International Perspectives of Chicana/o Studies: "This World Is My Place,"* edited by Catherine Leen and Niamh Thornton, 24–34. New York: Routledge.

McDuffie, Helen H. 1994. "Women at Work: Agriculture and Pesticides." *Journal of Occupational and Environmental Medicine* 36 (11): 1240–46.

Medina, Brenda. 2016. "Public Health in Anthony Community." Women's Intercultural Center. Accessed on January 27. http://womensinterculturalcenter.org/latest-news/459-public-health-in-anthony-community.

Medina, Enrique. 1996. "Overview of Transboundary Pollution Issues along the Mexico-US Border." In *Environmental Toxicology and Risk Assessment: Fourth Volume*, edited by Thomas W. La Point, Fred T. Price, and Edward E. Little, 1–17. Fredericksburg, VA: American Society for Testing and Materials.

Mellor, Mary. 1992. *Breaking the Boundaries: Towards a Feminist Green Socialism*. London: Virago Press.

Merchant, Carolyn. (1980) 1990. *The Death of Nature: Women, Ecology, and the Scientific Revolution*. Repr., with a new preface, New York: HarperOne.

Mesa-Bains, Amalia. 2001a. "Art and Spirit across the Landscape." *Women Environmental Artists Directory* 3. Accessed March 12, 2106. http://weadartists.org/art-and-spirit -across-the-landscape.

———. 2001b. "Spiritual Geographies." In *The Road to Aztlan: Art from a Mythic Homeland*, edited by Virginia M. Fields and Victor Zamudio-Taylor, 332–41. Los Angeles: Los Angeles County Museum of Art.

———. 2003. "*Domesticana*: The Sensibility of Chicana *Rasquachismo*." In *Chicana Feminisms: A Critical Reader*, edited by Gabriela F. Arredondo, Aída Hurtado, Norma Klahn, Olga Nájera-Ramírez, and Patricia Zavella, 298–315. Durham, NC: Duke University Press.

———. 2011. "Nature and Spirit." In *Amalia Mesa-Bains: Geography of Memory*, edited by Laura Meyer, 43–47. Fresno: Fresno Art Museum/Press at California State University, Fresno.

———. 2013. "A Latino Cabinet of Curiosities: A Postcolonial Reopening." *Museum and Curatorial Studies Review* 1 (1): 27–52.

Mies, Maria, and Vandana Shiva. 1993. *Ecofeminism*. Halifax, NS: Fernwood.

"Mission." 2016. Women's Intercultural Center. Accessed January 27. www.womensinter culturalcenter.org/mission.

Mohanty, Chandra Talpade. 2003. "'Under Western Eyes' Revisited: Feminist Solidarity through Anticapitalist Struggles." *Signs* 28 (2): 499–535.

Montoya, Delilah. 2016. "Artist Statement." Women Artists of the American West. Accessed January 27. https://www.cla.purdue.edu/waaw/ressler/artists/montoyastat.html.

Moore, Niamh. 2008a. "Debating Eco/Feminist Natures." *International Feminist Journal of Politics* 10 (3): 314–21.

———. 2008b. "Eco/Feminism, Non-Violence and the Future of Feminism." *International Feminist Journal of Politics* 10 (3): 282–98.

———. 2015. *The Changing Nature of Eco/Feminism: Telling Stories from Clayoquot Sound*. Vancouver: University of British Columbia Press.

Moraga, Cherríe. 1993. "Queer Aztlán: The Re-Formation of Chicano Tribe." In *The Last Generation: Prose and Poetry*, 145–74. Boston: South End Press.

Moraga, Cherríe, and Gloria Anzaldúa, eds. 1983. *This Bridge Called My Back: Writings by Radical Women of Color*, 2nd ed. New York: Kitchen Table/Women of Color Press.

Mora, Pat. 1995. *Agua Santa: Holy Water*. Boston: Beacon Press.

———. 1997. *House of Houses*. Boston: Beacon Press.

Morris, Marla. 2002. "Ecological Consciousness and Curriculum." *Journal of Curriculum Studies* 34 (5): 571–87.

Moya, Paula. 1997. "Postmodernism, 'Realism,' and the Politics of Identity: Cherríe Moraga and Chicana Feminism." In *Feminist Genealogies, Colonial Legacies, and Democratic Futures*, edited by M. Jacqui Alexander and Chandra Talpade Mohanty, 125–50. New York: Routledge.

Murphy, Patrick. 2013. "The Ecofeminist Subsistence Perspective Revisited in an Age of Land Grabs and Its Representations in Contemporary Literature." *Feminismo/s* 22:205–24.

Nanda, Meera. 1997. "'History Is What Hurts': A Materialist Feminist Perspective on the Green Revolution and Its Ecofeminist Critics." In *Materialist Feminism: A Reader in Class, Difference, and Women's Lives*, edited by Rosemary Hennessy and Chrys Ingraham, 364–94. New York: Routledge.

Narayan, Uma. 1997. *Dislocating Cultures: Identities, Traditions, and Third World Feminism*. New York: Routledge.

National Resources Defense Council. 2016. Accessed January 28. www.nrdc.org/ej /history/hej2. asp.

Navarro, Mireya. 2002. "A Filmmaker Seeks Answers about Killings in Mexico." *New York Times*, August 19. Accessed January 28, 2016. http://www.nytimes.com/2002/08/19 /arts/television/19JUAR.html.

New Mexico Acequia Association. 2016. Accessed January 28. http://www.lasacequias.org/.

Nichols, Bill. 1994. *Blurred Boundaries: Questions of Meaning in Contemporary Culture*. Bloomington: Indiana University Press.

———. 2001. *Introduction to Documentary*. Bloomington: Indiana University Press.

"No Echo: Juárez Murdered Women's Group Disbands." 2016. Women on the Border. Accessed January 28. http://www.womenontheborder.org/Articles/no%20echo.htm.

Nurminen, Tuula. 1995. "Maternal Pesticide Exposure and Pregnancy Outcome." *Journal of Occupational and Environmental Medicine* 37 (8): 935–40.

Oliver-Rotger, Maria Antònia. 2003. *Battlegrounds and Crossroads: Social and Imaginary Space in Writings by Chicanas*. New York: Rodopi.

O'Loughlin, Ellen. 1993. "Questioning Sour Grapes: Ecofeminism and the United Farm Workers Grape Boycott." In *Ecofeminism: Women, Animals, Nature*, edited by Greta Gaard, 146–66. Philadelphia: Temple University Press.

"On Art, Activism, and Social Justice: An Interview with Juana Alicia." 2016. *Apuntes: A Latino Journal*. Accessed January 28. http://apunteslj.com/on-art-activism-and -social-justice/.

Ortner, Sherry. 1974. "Is Female to Male as Nature Is to Culture?" In *Woman, Culture, and Society*, edited by Michelle Zimbalist Rosaldo and Louise Lamphere, 68–87. Stanford, CA: Stanford University Press.

O'Sullivan, Edmund, and Marilyn Taylor. 2004. *Learning toward an Ecological Consciousness*. New York: Palgrave Macmillan.

Page, Janice. 2003. "Flawed but Powerful 'Senorita' Evokes Outrage." *Boston Globe*, June 20, 9, Arts, third ed.

Pardo, Mary. 1990. "Mexican-American Women Grassroots Community Activists: 'Mothers of East Los Angeles.'" *Frontiers: A Journal of Women's Studies* 11 (1): 1–7.

Parra, Andrea. 1999. "Letter." *PMLA* 114 (5) (October): 1099–1100.

Peña, Devon, ed. 1998a. *Chicano Culture, Ecology, Politics: Subversive Kin*. Tucson: University of Arizona Press.

———. 1998b. "Los Animalitos: Culture, Ecology, and the Politics of Place in the Upper Rio Grande." In *Chicano Culture, Ecology, Politics: Subversive Kin*, edited by Devon Peña, 25–57. Tucson: University of Arizona Press.

———. 2002. "Endangered Landscapes and Disappearing Peoples? Identity, Place, and Community in Ecological Politics." In *The Environmental Justice Reader: Politics, Poetics, and Pedagogy*, edited by Joni Adamson, Mei Mei Evans, and Rachel Stein, 58–81. Tucson: University of Arizona Press.

———. 2005. *Mexican Americans and the Environment: Tierra y Vida*. Tucson: University of Arizona Press.

———. 2012. "Women of the Río Arriba Acequias." Environmental and Food Justice. May 15. Accessed January 28, 2016. http://ejfood.blogspot.com.au/2012/05/challenges-of-acequia-farming.html.

Perez, Daniel. 2013. "Chicana Aesthetics: A View of Unconcealed Alterities and Affirmations of Chicana Identity through Laura Aguilar's Photographic Images." *LUX: A Journal of Transdisciplinary Writing and Research from Claremont Graduate University* 2 (1): 1–8.

Perez, Domino Renee. 2008. *There Was a Woman: La Llorona from Folklore to Popular Culture*. Austin: University of Texas Press.

Pérez, Emma. 1999. *The Decolonial Imaginary: Writing Chicanas into History*. Bloomington: Indiana University Press.

Pérez, Laura. 1998. "Spirit Glyphs: Reimagining Art and Artist in the Work of Chicana Tlamatinime." *Modern Fiction Studies* 44 (1): 36–76.

———. 1999. "*El desorden*, Nationalism, and Chicana/o Aesthetics." In *Between Woman and Nation: Nationalisms, Transnational Feminisms, and the State*, edited by Caren Kaplan, Norma Alarcón, and Minoo Moallem, 19–46. Durham, NC: Duke University Press.

———. 2007. *Chicana Art: The Politics of Spiritual and Aesthetic Altarities*. Durham, NC: Duke University Press.

Plant, Judith. 1991. "Ecofeminism." In *The Green Reader: Essays toward a Sustainable Society*, edited by Andrew Dobson, 100–103. San Francisco: Mercury House.

———. 1994. *Feminism and the Mastery of Nature*. New York: Routledge.

———. 1997. "Learning to Live with Differences: The Challenge of the Ecofeminist Community." In *Ecofeminism: Woman, Culture, Nature*, edited by Karen Warren, 120–39. Bloomington: Indiana University Press.

Platt, Kamala. 1998. "Ecocritical Chicana Literature: Ana Castillo's 'Virtual Realism.'" In *Ecofeminist Literary Criticism: Theory, Interpretation, Pedagogy*, edited by Greta Gaard and Patrick Murphy, 139–57. Urbana: University of Illinois Press.

Plumwood, Val. 1986. "Ecofeminism: An Overview and Discussion of Positions and Arguments." *Australasian Journal of Philosophy* 64:120–38.

———. 1993. *Feminism and the Mastery of Nature*. New York: Routledge.

———. 2002. *Environmental Culture: The Ecological Crisis of Reason*. New York: Routledge.

Portilla, Elizabeth de la. 2009. *They All Want Magic: Curanderas and Folk Healing*. College Station: Texas A&M Press.

Portillo, Lourdes, dir. 2001. *Señorita Extraviada*. VHS. Distributed by Women Make Movies.

————. 2003. "Filming *Señorita Extraviada*." *Aztlán* 28 (2): 229–35.

Powell, Anna. 2005. *Deleuze and Horror Film*. Edinburgh: Edinburgh University Press.

"Principles of Environmental Justice." 1991. October. Accessed January 28, 2016. http:// www.ejnet.org/ej/principles.html.

Prindeville, Diane-Michele. 2003. "For the People: American Indian and Hispanic Women in New Mexico's Environmental Justice Movement." In *Our Backyard: A Quest for Environmental Justice*, edited by Gerald Visgilio and Diana Whitelaw, 139–57. Lanham, MD: Rowman and Littlefield.

Probyn, Elspeth. 1996. *Outside Belongings*. New York: Routledge.

Puar, Jasbir. 2012. "'I would rather be a cyborg than a goddess': Becoming Intersectional in Assemblage Theory." *philoSOPHIA* 2:49–66.

Pulido, Laura. 1998a. "Environmental History and Ecological Politics, Ecological Legitimacy and Cultural Essentialism: Hispano Grazing in Northern New Mexico." In *Chicano Culture, Ecology, Politics: Subversive Kin*, edited by Devon Peña, 121–40. Tucson: University of Arizona Press.

————. 1998b. "The Sacredness of 'Mother Earth': Spirituality, Activism and Social Justice." Book review of *Justice, Nature and the Geography of Difference*, by David Harvey. *Annals of the Association of American Geographers* 88 (4): 719–23.

————. 2009. "Restructuring and the Contraction and Expansion of Environmental Rights in the United States." In *Geographic Thought: A Praxis Perspective*, edited by George Henderson and Marvin Waterstone, 274–92. New York: Routledge.

Pulido, Laura, and Devon Peña. 1998. "Environmentalism and Positionality: The Early Pesticide Campaign of the United Farm Workers' Organizing Committee, 1965–71." *Race, Gender, and Class* 6 (1): 33–50.

"Raices." 2016. La Semilla Food Center. Accessed March 15. http://lasemillafoodcenter .org/index.php/what-we-do/community-farm-our-farm/raices#!ancestral_wellness _1__2_.

Ramirez, Sarah. 2003. "Borders, Feminism, and Spirituality: Movements in Chicana Aesthetic Revisioning." In *Decolonial Voices: Chicana and Chicano Cultural Studies in the 21st Century*, edited by Arturo Aldama and Naomi Quiñonez, 223–42. Bloomington: Indiana University Press.

Rebolledo, Tey Diana. 2013. "Landscaping a Poetics of Belonging: Maps of the Imagination in Chicana/o Literature." In *Landscapes of Writing in Chicano Literature*, edited by Imelda Martín-Junquera, 131–36. New York: Palgrave Macmillan.

Rechtshaffen, Michael. 2002. "Review from the Los Angeles Latino International Film Festival." *Hollywood Reporter*, August 5. Accessed May 5, 2013. http://www.allbusiness .com/services/motion-pictures/4786581-1.html.

"Reel Review: *Señorita Extraviada*." 2002. *La Prensa* 10 (43) (August 21): 8.

Rocheleau, Dianne, Barbara Thomas-Slayter, and Esther Wangari. 1999. "Gender and the Environment: A Feminist Political Economy Perspective." In *Feminist Political Ecology: Global Issues and Local Experience*, edited by Dianne Rocheleau, Barbara Thomas-Slayter, and Esther Wangari, 3–23. London: Routledge.

Román-Odio, Clara. 2013. *Sacred Iconographies in Chicana Cultural Productions.* New York: Palgrave Macmillan.

Rosaldo, Renato. 2003. "Translating Herstory: A Reading of and Responses to Elba Rosario Sánchez." In *Chicana Feminisms: A Critical Reader,* edited by Gabriella F. Arredondo, Aída Hurtado, Norma Klahn, Olga Nájera-Ramírez, and Patricia Zavella, 52–58. Durham, NC: Duke University Press.

Rosales, Francisco Arturo. 1997. *Chicano! The History of the Mexican-American Civil Rights Movement.* Houston: Arte Público Press.

Rowe, Aimee Carrillo. 2005. "Be Longing: Toward a Feminist Politics of Relation." *NWSA Journal* 17 (2) (Summer): 15–46.

Ruether, Rosemary Radford. 2005. *Integrating Ecofeminism, Globalization, and World Religions.* Lanham, MD: Rowman and Littlefield.

Saldaña-Portillo, Josefina. 2001. "Who's the Indian in Aztlán? Re-Writing Mestizaje, Indianism, and Chicanismo from the Lacandón." In *The Latin American Subaltern Studies Reader,* edited by Ileana Rodriguez and María Milagros López, 402–23. Durham, NC: Duke University Press.

Saldívar-Hull, Sonia. 2000. *Feminism on the Border: Chicana Gender Politics and Literature.* Berkeley: University of California Press.

Salleh, Ariel. 1997. *Ecofeminism as Politics: Nature, Marx and the Postmodern.* New York: Zed Books.

Salzinger, Leslie. 2000. "Manufacturing Sexual Subjects: 'Harassment,' Desire and Discipline on a Maquiladora Shopfloor." *Ethnography* 1:67–92.

Sánchez, Elba Rosario. 2003. *"Cartohistografía: Continente de una voz*/Cartohistography: One Voice's Continent." In *Chicana Feminisms: A Critical Reader,* edited by Gabriella F. Arredondo, Aída Hurtado, Norma Klahn, Olga Nájera-Ramírez, and Patricia Zavella, 19–51. Durham, NC: Duke University Press.

Sandilands, Catriona. 1997. "Mother Earth, the Cyborg, and the Queer: Ecofeminism and (More) Questions of Identity." *NWSA Journal* 9 (3): 18–40.

———. 1999. *The Good-Natured Feminist: Ecofeminism and the Quest for Democracy.* Minneapolis: University of Minnesota Press.

Sandoval, Chela. 2000. *Methodology of the Oppressed.* Minneapolis: University of Minnesota Press.

Saxena, M. C., M. K. Siddiqui, T. D. Seth, and C. R. Krishna Murti, A. K. Bhargava, and D. Kutty. 1981. "Organochlorine Pesticides in Specimens from Women Undergoing Spontaneous Abortion, Premature or Full-Term Delivery." *Journal of Analytical Toxicology* 5 (1): 6–9.

Seager, Richard, Mingfang Ting, Isaac Held, Yochanan Kushnir, Jian Lu, Gabriel Vecchi, Huei-Ping Huang, et al. 2007. "Model Projections of an Imminent Transition to a More Arid Climate in Southwestern North America." *Science* 316 (5828): 1181–84.

Shiva, Vandana. 1997. "Women in Nature." In *The Women, Gender and Development Reader,* edited by Nalini Visvanathan, Lynn Duggan, Laurie Nisonoff, and Nan Wiegersma, 62–67. London: Zed Books.

Smith, Sidonie, and Julia Watson, eds. 1996. *Getting a Life: Everyday Uses of Autobiography.* Minneapolis: University of Minnesota Press.

———. 2010. *Reading Autobiography: A Guide for Interpreting Life Narratives,* 2nd ed. Minneapolis: University of Minnesota Press.

Sobek, María Herrera. 1998. "The Nature of Chicana Literature: Feminist Ecological Literary Criticism and Chicana Writers." *Revista Canaria de Estudios Ingleses* 37:89–100.

Southwest Network for Environmental and Economic Justice (SNEEJ). 2016. "About." Facebook. Accessed January 28. https://www.facebook.com/pages/Southwest-Network-for-Environmental-and-Economic-Justice/107345243883.

Starhawk. 1997. "Marija Gimbutas' Work and the Question of the Sacred." In *From the Realm of the Ancestors: An Anthology in Honor of Marija Gimbutas,* edited by Joan Marler, 519–23. Manchester, CT: Knowledge, Ideas and Trends.

———. 1999. *The Spiral Dance: A Rebirth of the Ancient Religion of the Great Goddess,* 20th anniversary ed. San Francisco: Harper San Francisco.

———. 2002. *Webs of Power: Notes from the Global Uprising.* Gabriola Island, BC: New Society.

Steady, Filomina Chioma. 1998. "Gender Equality and Ecosystem Balance: Women and Sustainable Development in Developing Countries." *Race, Gender and Class* 6 (1): 13–25.

Steele, Allison. 2008. "Touching the Earth: Gloria Anzaldúa and the Tenets of Ecofeminism." In *Women Writing Nature,* edited by Barbara Cook, 95–108. Lanham, MD: Lexington Books.

Steinbaum Krauss Gallery. 1997. *Amalia Mesa-Bains: Cihuatlampa, the Place of the Giant Women.* Video recording of opening reception and installation. New York.

Stivale, Charles J., ed. 2005. *Gilles Deleuze: Key Concepts.* Montreal: McGill–Queen's University Press.

"The Story of Cesar Chavez." 2016. United Farm Workers. Accessed March 12. http://www.ufw.org/_page.php?menu=research&inc=history/07.html.

Stratton, Susan. 2001. "Intersubjectivity and Difference in Feminist Ecotopias." *Femspec* 3 (1): 33–43.

Sturgeon, Noël. 1997. *Ecofeminist Natures: Race, Gender, Feminist Theory and Political Action.* New York: Routledge.

———. 2003. "Ecofeminist Natures and Transnational Environmental Politics." In *Ecofeminism and Globalization: Exploring Culture, Context, and Religion,* edited by Heather Eaton and Lois Ann Lorentzen, 91–122. New York: Rowman and Littlefield.

———. 2009. *Environmentalism in Popular Culture: Gender, Race, Sexuality, and the Politics of the Natural.* Tucson: University of Arizona Press.

Sullivan, Kevin. 2006. "A Toxic Legacy on the Mexican Border." In *The Line between Us: Teaching about the Border and Mexican Immigration,* edited by Bill Bigelow, 102–4. Milwaukee: Rethinking Schools.

Sze, Julie. 2002. "From Environmental Justice Literature to the Literature of Environmental Justice." In *The Environmental Justice Reader: Politics, Poetics, and Pedagogy,* edited by Joni Adamson, Mei Mei Evans, and Rachel Stein, 163–80. Tucson: University of Arizona Press.

Tafolla, Carmen. (1974) 1993. "La Malinche." In *Infinite Divisions: An Anthology of Chicana Literature*, edited by Tey Diana Rebolledo and Eliana Rivero, 198–99. Tucson: University of Arizona Press.

Taylor, Dorceta. 1989. "Blacks and the Environment: Toward an Explanation of the Concern and Action Gap between Blacks and Whites." *Environment and Behavior* 21:175–205.

————. 2009. *The Environment and the People in American Cities, 1600s–1900s: Disorder, Inequality, and Social Change*. Durham, NC: Duke University Press.

Thayer, Robert. 2003. *Life Place: Bioregional Thought and Practice*. Berkeley: University of California Press.

Thien, Deborah. 2005. "After or Beyond Feeling? A Consideration of Affect and Emotion in Geography." *Area* 37:450–56.

Thomas, Kevin. 2003. "Sad Look at Serial Killings in Mexico." *Los Angeles Times*, February 21. Accessed March 27, 2016. http://articles.latimes.com/2003/feb/21/entertainment/et-kevin21.

Thomas-Slayter, Barbara, Esther Wangari, and Dianne Rocheleau. 1999. "Feminist Political Ecology: Crosscutting Themes, Theoretical Insights, Policy Implications." In *Feminist Political Ecology: Global Issues and Local Experience*, edited by Dianne Rocheleau, Barbara Thomas-Slayter, and Esther Wangari, 287–307. London: Routledge.

Thompson, Charis. 2006. "Back to Nature? Resurrecting Ecofeminism after Poststructuralist and Third Wave Feminisms." *Isis* 97:505–12.

Thrift, Nigel. 1999. "Steps to an Ecology of Place." In *Human Geography Today*, edited by Doreen Massey, John Allen, and Philip Sarre, 295–322. Cambridge: Polity Press.

Tiano, Susan. 1985. "Maquiladoras, Women's Work, and Unemployment in Northern Mexico." *Aztlán: A Journal of Chicano Studies* 15 (2): 341–78.

Tolia-Kelly, Divya. 2006. "Affect—An Ethnocentric Encounter? Exploring the 'Universalist' Imperative of Emotional/Affectual Geographies." *Area* 38 (2): 213–17.

Tong, Rosemarie. 1998. *Feminist Thought: A More Comprehensive Introduction*. Boulder, CO: Westview Press.

Turner, Kay. 2008. "*Voces de Fe*: Mexican American *Altaristas* in Texas." In *Mexican American Religions: Spirituality, Activism, and Culture*, edited by Gastón Espinosa and Mario T. García, 180–205. Durham, NC: Duke University Press.

Turner, Victor. 1995. *The Ritual Process: Structure and Anti-Structure*. Chicago: Aldine Transaction.

Tweit, Susan. 1995. *Barren, Wild, and Worthless: Living in the Chihuahuan Desert*. Albuquerque: University of New Mexico Press.

"UFW Chronology." 2016. United Farm Workers. Accessed January 28. http://ufw.org/_page.php?menu=research&inc=_page.php?menu=research&inc=history/01.html.

U.S. Department of Agriculture Economic Research Service/Alisha Coleman-Jenson, Christian Gregory, and Anita Singh. 2014. "Household Food Security in the United States in 2013." Economic research report no. 173 (September). Accessed January 30, 2016. http://www.ers.usda.gov/media/1565415/err173.pdf.

U.S. Department of Labor, Office of the Assistant Secretary for Policy and Office of Programmatic Policy. 2005. "Findings from the National Agricultural Workers Survey

(NAWS) 2001–2002: A Demographic and Employment Profile of United States Farm Workers." Research report no. 9 (March). Accessed January 30, 2016. http://www .doleta.gov/agworker/report9/naws_rpt9.pdf.

Vance, Linda. 1997. "Ecofeminism and Wilderness." *NWSA Journal* 9 (3): 60–76.

Vásquez, Francisco H., and Rodolfo D. Torres, eds. 2003. *Latino/a Thought: Culture, Politics, and Society*. Boulder, CO: Rowman and Littlefield.

Villaseñor Black, Charlene. 1999. "Sacred Cults, Subversive Icons: Chicanas and the Pictorial Language of Catholicism." In *Speaking Chicana: Voice, Power, and Identity*, edited by Delma Letticia Galindo and María Dolores Gonzales, 134–74. Tucson: University of Arizona Press.

Viramontes, Helena María. 1996. *Under the Feet of Jesus*. New York: Plume.

Visgilio, Gerald, and Diana Whitelaw, eds. 2003. *Our Backyard: A Quest for Environmental Justice*. Lanham, MD: Rowman and Littlefield.

Visvanathan, Nalini, Lynn Duggan, Laurie Nisonoff, and Nan Wiegersma, eds. 1997. *The Women, Gender and Development Reader*. London: Zed Books.

Volk, Stephen, and Marian Schlotterbeck. 2010. "Gender, Order, and Femicide: Reading the Popular Culture of Murder in Ciudad Juárez." In *Making a Killing: Femicide, Free Trade, and La Frontera*, edited by Alicia Gaspar de Alba with Georgina Guzmán, 121–54. Austin: Texas University Press.

Warren, Karen. 1990. "The Power and the Promise of Ecological Feminism." *Environmental Ethics* 12 (2): 123–44.

———, ed. 1997. *Ecofeminism: Women, Culture, Nature*. Bloomington: Indiana University Press.

———. 2000. *Ecofeminist Philosophy: A Western Perspective on What It Is and Why It Matters*. Lanham, MD: Rowman and Littlefield.

Wells, Ron. 2002. "*Señorita Extraviada*." *Film Threat*, January 28. Accessed April 19, 2013. http://www.filmthreat.com/reviews/2665/.

Whatmore, Sarah. 2008. "Dissecting the Autonomous Self: Hybrid Cartographies for a Relational Ethics." In *Geographic Thought: A Praxis Perspective*, edited by George Henderson and Marvin Waterstone, 109–22. London: Routledge.

"Where It Starts: Building Hope for Women in Anthony, New Mexico." 2016. Produced by W. K. Kellogg Foundation. YouTube. Accessed January 30. http://www.youtube .com/watch?v=9nAPUDbICVM.

Whitney, Kimberly. 2003. "Greening by Place: Sustaining Cultures, Ecologies, Communities." *Journal of Women and Religion* 19/20:11–25.

Wilson, Calvin. 2003. "*Señorita Extraviada*." *St. Louis Post-Dispatch*, September 12, E5, Everyday Magazine, Five Star Late Lift.

Wolfteich, Claire. 2005. "Devotion and the Struggle for Justice in the Farm Worker Movement: A Practical Theological Approach to Research and Teaching in Spirituality." *Spiritus* 5:158–75.

Wright, John B. 1994. "Hispano Forestry, Land Grants and the U.S. Forest Service in Northern New Mexico." *Focus on Geography* 44, no. 1 (Spring): 10–14.

Wright, Melissa. 2003. "The Politics of Relocation: Gender, Nationality, and Value in a Mexican Maquiladora." In *Ethnography at the Border*, edited by Pablo Vila, 23–45. Minneapolis: University of Minnesota Press.

Ybarra-Frausto, Tomás. 1991. "Rasquachismo: A Chicano Sensibility." In *Chicano Art: Resistance and Affirmation, 1965–1985*, edited by Richard Griswold del Castillo, Teresa McKenna, and Yvonne Yarbro-Bejarano, 155–62. Los Angeles: Wight Art Gallery/ University of California Press.

Ybarra, Priscilla Solis. 2004. "'Lo que quiero es tierra': Longing and Belonging in Cherríe Moraga's Ecological Vision." In *New Perspectives on Environmental Justice: Gender, Sexuality, and Activism*, edited by Rachel Stein, 240–48. New Brunswick, NJ: Rutgers University Press.

———. 2007. "Walden Pond in Aztlan? A Literary History of Chicana/o Environmental Writing since 1848." PhD diss., Rice University, Houston, Texas. http://hdl.handle.net /1911/20671.

———. 2009. "Borderlands as Bioregion: Jovita González, Gloria Anzaldúa, and the Twentieth Century Ecological Revolution in South Texas." *MELUS: Multi-Ethnic Literatures of the United States* 34 (2): 175–89.

Yuval-Davis, Nira. 1999. "What Is 'Transversal Politics?'" *Soundings* 12:94–98.

Zahm, S. H., and M. H. Ward. 1998. "Pesticides and Childhood Cancer." *Environmental Health Perspectives* 106 (3): 893–908.

Zamudio-Taylor, Victor. 2001. "Inventing Tradition, Negotiating Modernism: Chicano/a Art and the Pre-Columbian Past." In *The Road to Aztlan: Art from a Mythic Homeland*, edited by Virginia M. Fields and Victor Zamudio-Taylor, 342–57. Los Angeles: Los Angeles County Museum of Art.

Zehle, Soenke. 2002. "Notes on Cross-Border Environmental Justice Education." In *The Environmental Justice Reader: Politics, Poetics, and Pedagogy*, edited by Joni Adamson, Mei Mei Evans, and Rachel Stein, 331–49. Tucson: University of Arizona Press.

Zweifel, Helen. 1997. "The Gendered Nature of Biodiversity Conservation." *NWSA Journal* 9 (3): 107–22.

# Index

CHRISTINA HOLMES is an assistant professor of women's, gender, and sexuality studies at DePauw University.

National Women's Studies Association /
University of Illinois First Book Prize

Sex Tourism in Bahia: Ambiguous Entanglements    *Erica Lorraine Williams*
Ecological Borderlands: Body, Nature, and Spirit in Chicana Feminism    *Christina Holmes*

The University of Illinois Press
is a founding member of the
Association of American University Presses.

———————————————————————

Composed in 10.75/13 Arno Pro
by Kirsten Dennison
at the University of Illinois Press
Manufactured by Sheridan Books, Inc.

University of Illinois Press
1325 South Oak Street
Champaign, IL 61820-6903
www.press.uillinois.edu